Christopher Gist's Journals

with

Historical, Geographical and Ethnological Notes

and

Biographies of His Contemporaries

William M. Darlington

HERITAGE BOOKS
2006

HERITAGE BOOKS
AN IMPRINT OF HERITAGE BOOKS, INC.

Books, CDs, and more—Worldwide

For our listing of thousands of titles see our website
at
www.HeritageBooks.com

A Facsimile Reprint
Published 2006 by
HERITAGE BOOKS, INC.
Publishing Division
65 East Main Street
Westminster, Maryland 21157-5026

Originally published 1893

— Publisher's Notice —
In reprints such as this, it is often not possible to remove blemishes from the original. We feel the contents of this book warrant its reissue despite these blemishes and hope you will agree and read it with pleasure.

International Standard Book Number: 978-0-7884-2277-4

CONTENTS

Introductory Memoir 9
Gist's Three Journals 31
Christopher Gist 88
Notes to Christopher Gist's First Journal of 1750-51 90
Notes to Gist's Second Journal, 1751-52 137
Notes to Christopher Gist's Third Journal, 1753 147
A Journal Descriptive of Some of the French Forts 148
The Montours 152
Andrew Montour 159
George Croghan 176
Thomas Cresap 202
General James Grant 207
Guyasuta 210
Treaty of Lancaster 217
Ohio Company 220
Walpole Grant 241
Wm. Trent & Co. 245
Captain Trent 249
John Peter Salley 253
Scheme for a New Settlement 261
Robert Orme 267
Extracts from Analysis of Map 271
Pownall's Account of Lead Plate 273
Ensign Ward's Deposition 275
Letters and Speeches to Indians 279

Index 289

INTRODUCTORY MEMOIR.

THE riches realized by Spain and Portugal in the sixteenth century from their newly acquired possessions in America excited amongst enterprising Englishmen a determination to establish colonies in that part of the Northern Continent extending from Canada to Florida, claimed for England in right of its discovery by the Cabots; also, to seek new discoveries, and especially a short passage through the interior of the country to the South Sea.

In April, 1585, colonists were sent out by Sir Walter Raleigh, and in the following month of August they landed on the island of Roanoke, on the eastern border of the present State of North Carolina, and there commenced the first English settlement in America. After exploring the neighboring rivers and sounds, they were induced by the relation of the Indians respecting the river Meratue (Roanoke) to attempt its exploration and endeavor to reach the head thereof, which the natives told them sprang from a huge rock near the sea, thirty or forty days' voyage westward, and "in that abundance that it forthwith maketh a most violent stream."

In March, 1586, Governor Ralph Lane, with two boats and forty men, ascended the river about one hundred miles (near to the present town of Halifax), hoping, as he afterwards wrote, for the discovery of a gold mine or a passage to the South Sea; but they were assailed by hostile Indians and so nearly starved that "they ate their two mastiff dogs boiled with Sassafras leaves, and were compelled to return."[1] Their voyage is memorable for being the earliest attempt by the English to explore the interior of America from the Atlantic westward. The relation of the Indians to the colonists has been stigmatized by historians as "extravagant tales, which nothing but cupidity could have credited."[2] Now as the Roanoke, by its meanderings, is four hundred miles in length, thirty to forty days would be required to ascend to its source. Its various head springs, on the main ridge of the Alleghenies, in Montgomery County, Virginia, are scarce a mile from the waters of the Kanawha, or New River, and but eight miles from its main channel. The relation of the Indians was, in this respect at least, true, for the Roanoke does "forthwith make a most violent stream;" issuing by numerous creeks from this elevated tract and uniting into one body, it soon becomes the "rapid Roanoke," and on reaching Salem, in Roanoke County, "has fallen one thousand feet in little more than twenty miles."[3]

The natives, probably, meant, if their "tales" were rightly interpreted, that the head of the Roanoke was near another stream whose waters flowed to another and distant sea. The city, rich with gold and pearls, they called Chaunis Temocatan, was Mexico or Tetuan, its ancient name.

Discouraged by the prospect, the colonists abandoned their settlement and returned to England, with the fleet of Sir Francis Drake, in the following month of June. Subsequent attempts by Raleigh and some of his associates to re-establish the colony at Roanoke failed disastrously, almost ruining the fortune of the illustrious author of the project.

---

[1] Hakluyt's "Voyages," Vol. III. Lane and Harriot's Relation.

[2] Bancroft's "History of the United States," Vol. I, p. 99. Burke's "History of Virginia," Vol. I, p. 56.

[3] Martin's "Geographical Gazetteer of Virginia," p. 53.

Twenty years later, on May 14, 1606, the first permanent settlement by the English in America commenced at Jamestown, on the Powhatan or James River, and a week thereafter Captain Christopher Newport, with Captain John Smith and a company of twenty-three persons, sailed in a shallop from "James Fort" up the river, "with a perfect resolution not to return, but either to finde the heade of this ryver, the lake mentioned by others heretofore, the Sea againe, the mountaynes Apalatsi or some issue."[1]

They reached the Falls, at the site of the present city of Richmond, and on an islet in the river erected a wooden cross and proclaimed King James "with a greate showte."[2] The Governing Council in England had instructed them that the "Discovery of the South Sea (Pacific) as the certain and infallible way to immense riches was an object of which they were ever solicitous and intent."[3]

The successful establishment of the colony was of much less importance than searching for mines of gold or explorations westward by means of navigable rivers. In the summer of the following year Captain John Smith explored the Chesapeake Bay to the Susquehanna, entering into all the rivers and inlets as far as he could sail, of all of which he constructed an admirable map. In the fall of the same year Captain Newport returned from a visit to England with a private commission "Not to return without a lump of gold, a certainty of the South Sea, or one of the lost colony of Sir Walter Raleigh." He also had a large barge built, in five pieces, for convenience of carriage beyond the Falls, to convey them to the South Sea. With a number of boats and one hundred

---

[1] Captain Newport's "Discoveries," 1607. British State Paper Office. "Transactions of the American Antiquarian Society," Vol. IV, p. 40.

[2] Id., p. 47. Smith's "Virginia," Vol. I, p. 151.

[3] Smith's "Virginia," p. 43.

and twenty men he ascended the river to the Falls, and thence explored by land about forty miles farther on the south side of the stream to two towns of the Monacan Indians, returning, wearied and disappointed, by the same path after an ineffectual search for rich mines. The "quartered boat" was too cumbrous to be carried around the Falls, as Smith states, by even five hundred men, sarcastically adding "that if burned to ashes one might have carried her in a bag."[1] The desire for further exploration seems to have subsided for many years; wars with the natives, their own dissensions, a constant struggle for the means of subsistence, and the cultivation of tobacco occupied the attention of the colonists. In 1624 the petition of the Virginia Company to the House of Commons enumerates among other advantages accruing to England in their view and expectation, by the success of the colony, is the "no small hopes of an early and short passage to the South Sea, either by Sea or Land."

The prevailing illusion respecting the short distance across the continent was not entirely dispelled until near the close of the century and after the discovery and exploration of the Mississippi by the French became generally known.

Sir William Berkeley, Governor of Virginia, was informed by the Indians, in 1648, "that within five dayes journey to the Westward and by South there is a great high mountaine, and at foot thereof great Rivers that run into a great Sea; and that there are men that come hither in ships, (but not the same that ours be) they wear apparell and have reed caps on their heads, and ride on Beasts like our horses, but have much longer ears, and other circumstances they declare for the certainty of these things."[2] These rivers, doubtless, were those

[1] Smith's "History," Vol. I, p. 201.
[2] "A Perfect Description of Virginia," 1649, Vol. III, of Tracts, p. 13. Also in Massachusetts Historical Society Collection, Vol. IX, Second Series, p. 105.

now known as the Kanawha, Kentucky, Cumberland and Tennessee, whose waters flow from the western slope of the Allegheny Mountains to the Ohio and Mississippi and into the Gulf of Mexico, long before frequented by Spaniards. Governor Berkeley made preparations for discovery in person, with a company of fifty horse and fifty footmen, but abandoned the enterprise, probably in consequence of the disastrous results to the king in his contest with the Parliament engaging his attention—Berkeley being a firm Royalist.

The author of a tract—entitled "A Perfect Description of Virginia, etc.,"[1] published in London in 1649, wrote, that "for their better knowledge of the Land they dwell in, the Planters resolve to make a further Discovery into the Country, West and by South up above the Fall, and we are confident upon what they have learned from the Indians to find a way to a West or South Sea by Land or rivers, and to discover a way to China and East Indies, or unto some other Sea that shall carry them thither;" and that "Sir Francis Drake was on the back of Virginia in his voyage about the World in 37 degrees just opposite to Virginia, and called Nova Albion. And now all the question is only how broad the Land may be to that place from the head of James River above the Falls, but all men conclude if it be not narrow, yet that there is and will be found the like rivers issuing into a South Sea or West Sea on the other side of those Hills, as there is on this side, when they run from the West into an East Sea, after a course of 150 miles."

Prior to Governor Berkeley's administration, Walter Austin and others obtained from the Assembly, in 1642, the passage of an Act, authorizing them "to undertake the discovery of a new river or unknown land, bearing west, southerly from Appo-

---

[1] "Force's Tracts," Vol. II. Massachusetts Historical Collection, Vol. IX, Second Series, p. 105.

matake River."[1] It does not appear, however, that any attempt at exploration was made until the year 1650, when Edward Bland having petitioned the Assembly and obtained like authority in August and September of that year, in company with Edward Pennant, Abrahame Wood and Sackford Brewster, two Indian chiefs as guides, and two servants, explored southwest from Appomattox (now Petersburgh) to the Falls of Roanoke, or as they named the rapids, Blandina, above and near the present city of Halifax, North Carolina, and not far above the point on that river reached by Raleigh's colonists, sixty-five years before. This discovery was deemed of such importance as to occasion, in the year following, the publication in London of a narrative of the journey. In 1652 Colonel William Clayborne, Captain Henry Fleet, and their associates, were authorized by the Assembly to make discoveries, "and take up lands by pattents and enjoy benefits and trades as they shall find out in places where no English have ever been and discovered." The same day "the like order is granted to Major Abra Wood and his associates."

In the following year, the Assembly authorized any persons "to discover the Mountains, Provided they go with a considerable partie and strength, both of men and ammunition."[2] No farther attempt at exploration seems to have been made until the year 1669, when John Lederer, a German Surgeon, commissioned by Governor Berkeley to make discoveries, on March 9th, with three Indians, left the Falls of Pemencock (Pamunky) on York River, from an Indian village called Schickehanini—probably the old Indian town near the now noted "White House."[3] The next day he passed through the marshy grounds between the Pamunky and head-waters of

[1] "Laws of Virginia," p. 267.
[2] "Oldmixon's British Empire in America," Vol. I, p. 382.
[3] Jefferson, 1751.

the Matenenenhah (Mattepony), in the present King William
County, and crossed the Pamunky at its head,[1] formed by the
onfluence of the North and South Anna Rivers, in Hanover
County.[2] Continuing along the South Anna River, on the
13th he reached the first spring of the Pamunky,[3] a head of
the South Anna, near the present Gordonsville. On the 14th
he discovered from a high hill,[4] the "Apelatean" Mountains[5]
to the west. Next day, the 15th, they passed over the South
Branch of the Rappahannock, or Rapid Anne River,[6] and on
the 17th reached the Blue Ridge, in the present county of
Madison. He ascended to the top of the mountain and found
it very cold, with much snow; noticed the high mountain ranges
westward and the Atlantic Ocean southeastward; descended
and returned by the course he went out.

On the 20th of May, 1670, Lederer began his second expedition, in company with one Major Harris,[7] twenty Christian horsemen and five Indians. They marched from the Falls of James River to the Monakin[8] village, probably the same as marked on Fry and Jefferson's Map of 1751, on James River, in the present county of Cumberland, and continued westward one hundred miles farther to what he calls "the south branch of James River," and which "Major Harris vainly supposed to be an arm of the Lake of Canada," as he observed it ran

[1] In 1656.
[2] The peninsula between these two rivers he mentions bears the name of Tottopottemen, a great Indian king, slain in battle for the whites against their Indian enemies.
[3] A small creek that still bears this name.
[4] Southwest mountain in Orange County.
[5] Blue Ridge.
[6] In Orange County.
[7] Major William Harris of the Regiment of Charles City and Henrico Counties.
[8] Tuscarora,

northward, "and was inclined to erect a pillar in memory of the Discovery." It seems evident from the description, distance given and his map, that they had reached the James River, at its bend to the north, a few miles east from the the present city of Lynchburg, in Campbell County. Here he parted from his company, excepting one Susquehanna Indian, and then went south to the Roanoke, to the Island and town of Akenatzi[1] where he was well received. Here he met four strange Indians, survivors of fifty who had come, Lederer says, "from some land by the Sea to the northwest," (probably the great Lakes.) He calls them Rickahickans and states that "they were treacherously killed in the night by the Indians of Akenatzi." He conjectured that these strange Indians came from an arm or bay of the Sea of California, which he supposed stretched up into the continent. From Akenatzi he journeyed southward into Carolina and thence returned to Akamatuch.

These strange Indians, or Rickahickans, doubtless were fugitives of the tribe known as Eries, or the Nation of the Cat, whose country was on the south shore of Lake Erie. They were conquered and destroyed as a nation by the Iroquois in 1654–5.

The Fathers call the tribe Riguehronnous, or those of the Cat Nation.[2] The considerable number of the defeated Eries or Rickahickans appear to have reached Virginia in 1655, about which time the Iroquois completed their conquest.[3] A

---

[1] On "Fry and Jefferson's" Map the Occoneachy is laid down at the junction of the Staunton (Roanoke) and Dan Rivers, in the present Mecklenburg County. See also "Byrd's Journey to the Land of Eden." Richmond, 1866, p. 5.

[2] "Jesuit Relations," 1660, p. 7, Vol. III. Id., 1661, p. 29.

[3] See Charlevoix's "History of New France," Vol. II, p. 266 and not Parkman's "Jesuits in America," pp. 438-441.

special law was passed to remove by force "the new-come western and inland Indians drawn from the Mountaines and lately sett downe near the falls of James River to the number of six or seven hundred."[1]

Captain Edward Hill, at the head of 100 men, assisted by Tottopottemen, King of the Pomukies, with 100 warriors, attacked the Rickahickans. The allies were defeated, Tottopottemen slain. Captain Hill was cashiered for his conduct and his estate charged with the cost of procuring a peace with the Rickahickans. It is probable that with the fugitive Eries were some of the Neutres and Hurons, kindred tribes, and also routed by the Iroquois.[2]

On August 30th of the same year, Lederer again set out, in company with Captain Collet, nine Englishmen and five Indians. They first went to the Falls of Rappahannock, near the present Fredericksburg; next day they passed the junction of the Rapid Anna, in Culpepper County, and keeping along the north side of the Rappahannock, on the 26th reached the Blue Ridge, in the present county of Rappahannock; there they ascended the summit of the mountain, observed and noted the great mountain range east and west. The cold prevented them from proceeding any farther, and they returned, having penetrated much farther northwestward than any one previously. Inconsiderable as the distance may now seem, Lederer was convinced those persons were in error who supposed it but eight or ten days' journey from the Atlantic to the Indian Ocean, and that an arm or bay of the Sea of California extended up into the country. Nor were there to be found on the west of the mountains large rivers, like

---

[1] Hening, p. 402.
[2] Hening, p. 423, Burke's "History of Virginia," Vol. II, pp. 104-107. See also Galletin, in "Transactions of the American Antiquarian Society,' Vol. II, p. 73. Evan's "Analysis," 1755, p. 13.

those on the east. His opinions evidently were changed by the information obtained from the unfortunate stranger or Erie Indians.

In the year 1671, under authority of Governor Berkeley, a commission was granted by Major-General Abrahame Wood, "for ye finding out of the ebbing and flowing of ye water behind the mountains in order to the Discovery of the South Sea." Accordingly, Thomas Batts, Thomas Woods and Robert Fallam, with Jack Nesan, servant, and Perecute, chief of the Appomattox Indians, as guide, left the town of Appomattox, near where Petersburgh now stands, on the first day of September, 1671, and travelling westward, on the 4th arrived at the "Sapong Town," in the present county of Charlotte, near the little Roanoke River; there they were joined by seven Appomattox Indians and a Sapon also, as a guide, and by nightfall of the day following, the 5th, they reached the "Hanohaski"[1] Indian town, on an island in the Sapon River, (evidently the Long Island in the Roanoke, opposite the mouth of Seneca Creek, in Campbell County). On the next day they recommenced their journey, leaving Thomas Woods at the Indian town "dangerously sick."

On the 7th they came in sight of the mountains (the Blue Ridge, in Bedford County); on the 8th and 9th they passed along the Roanoke River and over the Blue Ridge. Arriving at a town of the Totero Indians "encircled about with mountains" (probably near the site of Salem in Roanoke County), they remained three days, resting. On the 12th they "set forward afoot leaving their horses at the Totero town," and travelling south and north, as the path went, over several high mountains and deep, descending valleys. Several times crossing the Roanoke River, by four o'clock in the afternoon, Perecute's ague and their own weariness made them encamp

[1] Akenatzi?

"by the side of the Roanoke, very near the head thereof, at the foot of a very high peat mountain."[1]

On the 13th they ascended a very high and steep mountain (probably Craig's Creek Mountain, in Craig County) and continuing a northwest course over mountains (evidently Potts' and Peters' Mountains) and "many small streams and rich meadows with grass above a man's hight," they came to a very steep descent, where they found a great current that emptied itself, as they supposed, into the great river "Nuthuardly;" they encamped in the evening by the side of this "great current" (probably the Greenbrier River). On the 14th, their path continued north by west (in the present County of Greenbrier); they saw "to the southwest a curious prospect of hills like waves," and "Mr. Batts supposed he saw houses, but Mr. Fallam rather took them to be white cliffs," as doubtless they were the limestone cliffs on New River; "they marched about twenty miles this day."

On the 15th "they came to a large current, it emptied itself W. and by N. as they supposed into a great river," (probably the Meadow or main fork of the Gauley River, between the counties of Nicholas and Fayette). On the 16th they travelled ten miles, when "they had sight of a curious river like the Thames at Chelsea, but had a fall that made a great noise; its course was North and they supposed ran west about certain pleasant mountains which they saw to the westward." Here they found Indian fields with cornstalks in them and understood afterward three Mohetans (Monakens or Tuscaroras) had lived there not long before. They found the river broad as the Thames at Wapping. They supposed by the marks that it flowed there about three feet, but ebbed very slowly.[2]

[1] Probably the North Mountain, in the county of Montgomery.
[2] Clayton, 1688. Force's Tracts, Vol. III, p. 20.

On the 17th they proclaimed the King in these words: "Long live King Charles ye 2d King of England Scotland France Ireland and Virginia and all the teritory thereunto belonging; deffender of ye faith." Guns were fired and with a pair of marking irons they marked trees " 1st C R " for his Sacred Majesty; " 2d W B " for the governor; " 3d A W " for the Major-General, Abrahame Wood; another for Perecute, and also for the rest of the company.

They had reached the Kanawha at the Great Falls, eighty miles from the Ohio River. On their return to the town of the Toteros they found a Mohetan (Tuscarora) Indian, who was sent to inquire the object of their journey; satisfying him with a little powder, he informed them they had been from the mountains half way to that town, and at the next town beyond there was a level plain with abundance of salt. (This description applies correctly to the locality, as the Falls are about half way by the road from Sewall's mountain to the Salines, above Charleston, where there are wide river bottoms.)

They left the Toteros on the 21st and on the 24th reached the Hanahaskis (Long Island) where they found Mr. Woods was dead and buried. Continuing homeward by the Sapong town and the Appomattox town they arrived safe at Fort Henry on the 1st of October. This journey is remarkable for being the very earliest exploration, by the English, to the waters of the Ohio, and about the same time of the discovery of that stream claimed by La Salle at the Falls of the Ohio.

It has been incorrectly noticed by various authors: Beverley's "History of Virginia, 1722," p. 62. Burke's ditto, as in Beverley. In Coxe's "Carolina, Florida and the River Mississippi," published in 1722, it is stated, p. 120, that Colonel Wood, inhabiting at the Falls of James River from the year 1654 to 1664, discovered at several times several branches of the great rivers Ohio and Meschacehe, "and further that he was possessed, about twenty years ago, of the Journal of Mr. Needham, employed by the aforesaid Colonel." Campbell's "Virginia," pp. 268, 9. See also "State of the British Colonies in North America, 1755," p. 118.

The Kanawha was first known to the whites as "Wood's River," so called for Colonel Abrahame Wood, the originator of the expedition which discovered it. ("Contest in America, by an impartial hand," London, 1757, p. 176.) On Fry and Jefferson's Map of Virginia of 1751 it is marked "Great Kenhaway," called also "Wood's River" and "New River," *North American Review*, January, 1839. Parkman's "Discovery of the Great West." Introduction, p. 20, "The Journal and Relation of a New Discovery made behind the Apuleian Mountains, to the West of Virginia Plantations." General Papers, State Paper Office, 1, 21. "New York Colonial History," Vol. III, p. 193.

No further attempt at discovery or exploration westward was made for many years, although away at the north, in 1677, Wentworth Greenhalgh journeyed westward from Albany to the Seneca villages, near the Genesee River. Narrated in the "New York Colonial History," Vol. III, p. 250. In 1709, and for several years subsequent, it was not known that the Potomac River flowed through the Blue Ridge.[1]

In August, 1716, Governor Spotswood, of Virginia, with a company of about fifty persons, gentlemen, rangers, Indians and servants, made his famous transmontane expedition of discovery.

Proceeding from Williamsburgh to Germantown, ten miles below the Falls of Rappahannock (the present Fredericksburgh), and thence by easy stages, with much feasting and parade, on the thirty-sixth day the party reached the summit

[1] Byrd MSS., Vol. II, p. 125. Richmond, 1866.

of the Appalachian Mountains (Blue Ridge), at the pass now known as the "Swift's Run Gap," in the counties of Madison and Rockingham; thence they descended to the Shenandoah River, which they named the "Euphrates;" crossed it, returned, and encamped on the right bank, at "Spotswood Camp," named for the Governor. Returning, they arrived at home on the 17th of September, after an absence of sixteen weeks, Four years afterwards the new county of Spotsylvania was formed, with the Shenandoah for its western boundary.[1]

Colonel William Byrd, one of the most intelligent and accomplished men in Virginia, wrote in 1729 that "we hardly know anything of the Apalatean mountains that are no where above two hundred and fifty miles from the sea," [2] and farther "that the Sources of the Potomac, Roanoke and even of the Shenandoah are unknown to the Virginian authorities; although woodsmen tell them they head in the same mountains with a branch of Mississippi." Colonel Byrd calls this "conjectured Geography." [3]

In 1728 Colonel Wm. Byrd and the Commissioners of Virginia and North Carolina surveyed the dividing line between these two provinces from Currituck Inlet, on the Atlantic, westward in a straight line two hundred and forty-one miles to Peter's Creek, in the present county of Patrick. Twenty-one years later, in 1749, Joshua Fry and Peter Jefferson, with the Commissioners of North Carolina, surveyed the line ninety miles further, to "Steep Rock Creek," the White Top or Laurel Fork, of Holston River, in the present county of Grayson, and in 1779 Dr. Thomas Walker and Daniel Smith

[1] Journal of John Fontaine, in the "Memoirs of a Huguenot Family," New York, 1872. Jones' "Present State of Virginia," 1724, p. 14. Campbell's "History of Virginia," 1860, p. 387. Hening's "Statutes of Virginia," Vol. IV, p. 77.
[2] Burke's "History of Virginia," Vol. III, p. 114.
[3] Byrd's "Virginia," Vol. I, p. 137. Richmond, 1866.

continued the survey of the line from Steep Rock Creek to the Tennessee River. The boundary-line between the States of Kentucky and Tennessee, from the Tennessee River to the Mississippi, was run in 1819.[1]

In the report made in August, 1737, of the "Proceedings of the Commissioners to Lay out the Bounds of the Northern Neck"[2] of Virginia, or Lord Fairfax's Grant, it appears that they employed Colonel Wm. Mayo, who, at the head of a party of surveyors, in 1736, explored and surveyed the Cohongoronta, or Potomac, up to its head spring, in a ridge of the Alleghenies, at the southwest point of the boundary between Virginia and Maryland. Near it they found waters flowing northward into the Monongahela River, the southern fork of the upper Ohio. At that point, "the spring head of the Potomac, the Fairfax Stone was placed by the Commissioners at a subsequent survey in 1746."[3]

The first of our American race who seem to have penetrated the canebrakes of what has since been termed Kentucky, were Dr. Walker and Christopher Gist, both of Virginia, and James Smith, of Pennsylvania. Thomas Walker was born in King and Queen County, Virginia, in 1710. He studied medicine and became a skilful physician. His home was at Castle Hill, Albemarle County. He was an extensive land speculator. In 1748 he went on a tour of discovery down the Holston. In the month of March, 1750, in company with five others, he started upon a trip to explore the country west of the back settlements of Virginia. Before his return he penetrated far into the present State of

---

[1] "History of the Dividing Line," in Byrd, Vol. I.

[2] Fry and Jefferson's Map of Virginia. "Report of Survey." Hening's "Statutes," Vol. IX, p. 562.

[3] Byrd, Vol. II. Mayo's Map, 173. Faulkner's Report, in Kercheral's "History of the Valley of Virginia."

Kentucky. His party in April erected a small cabin in what is now Knox County, the first one probably ever built by an American within the limits of that State. "Walker's Settlement" is noted on some of the old maps. He died at Castle Hill, in 1794. He ranked high in Virginia, as is proved by his frequent appointments under that colony. He was with the Virginia troops at the defeat of Braddock, in 1755, of which he gave a graphic description to Judge Yeates, in August, 1776, on the battle-field. He was a member of the Virginia Assembly in 1758. In 1768, Commissioner from Virginia at the Treaty held at Fort Stanwix with the Indians of the Six Nations. In 1769 he was appointed, with Colonel Andrew Lewis, Commissioner, relative to settling a boundary-line with the Cherokees. He was at the head of the Committee of Louisa County, May 8, 1775; also member of the Virginia Committee of Safety, and Delegate to the Convention of Virginia, 1775-76, and to the House of Burgesses, in 1775.

To reconcile the conflicting statements relative to the precise year of the first visit of Dr. Thomas Walker to the eastern part of Kentucky is a difficult but not hopeless task. It appears that in 1747 Dr. Walker, with a small party, Colonel James Wood, Colonel James Pattin, Captain Charles Campbell, and others, having large grants of land to the west of the mountains, explored as far as Powell's Valley, in the present Lee County, southwestern Virginia, near the great Laurel Ridge of the Alleghenies, which he named the Cumberland.

Misled by information as to the distance of the Ohio River and the correct course to be taken to reach it expeditiously, they turned northeastwardly and came to the heads of the Totery or Big Sandy River, in Buchanan County, which they named Frederick's River, after the Prince of Wales, (now Russell's

Fork). Continuing the same course, they struck on the next Fork, which they named Louisa, a designation it still retains; (on Evans' Map of 1755 it is made to flow to the Kanawha) passing thence eastward, after a toilsome journey along the foot of the mountain range and stream, in Giles and Bland Counties, called Walker's, to the New River, and thence to Albemarle County.

Lewis Evans, in his "Analysis of a Map of the Middle Colonies of 1755," says: "As for the branches of the Ohio, which head in the New Virginia, I am particularly obliged to Mr. Thomas Walker for the intelligence of what names they bear and what rivers they fall into northward and westward;" and at page 29 he mentions Louisa as a branch of the Kanawha, and so places it on the accompanying map.

The Valley of the Ohio remained unexplored and almost unknown for near two centuries after the discovery of America in 1492.[1]

The Spaniard, Hernando De Soto, reached the Mississippi in 1541, pausing with his forces on the eastern bank of the mighty stream but a few days, to build boats to cross it and continue westward in his fruitless search for a land abounding in gold and silver.[2] Jean Nicollet was the first to reach the waters of the upper Mississippi. In 1639 he ascended the Ottawa from the St. Lawrence,[3] thence across Lake Huron and through the Straits of Mackinaw to Green Bay, and up the Fox River to the portage across the Wisconsin River, but no further. The route by the Ottawa was usually taken by the French missionaries and fur traders, until 1669–70, when they first traversed Lake Erie by its northern shore and thence by the Detroit River to Lake Huron.

[1] "Jesuit Relations," 1640.
[2] "Histoire de la Colonie Française," 1866.
[3] Charlevoix.

The Ohio, the "Beautiful River" of the Iroquois, was discovered by Robert Cavalier—the Sieur de la Salle—in 1670-71. He was a native of Rouen, France; came to Canada and engaged in the fur trade. Being an ardent and indefatigable explorer and ambitious to discover new countries, he was authorized by Talon, the Intendant (Justice) of Canada, to explore southwest and south for the discovery of a passage to the South Sea. Among the Iroquois near Lake Ontario, in the present Western New York, he found a Shawnee prisoner who informed him of the Ohio.

Procuring a guide from the Onondagas, he proceeded to the Allegheny River and descended it and the Ohio as far as the Falls, at the site of the present city of Louisville, Kentucky.[1] Then, deserted by his men, he returned through the forests to Canada, subsisting on game and roots, and befriended by the Indians he met on his way.[2] Three years later (1673) Marquette and Joliet reached the Mississippi by way of the Fox and Wisconsin rivers.[3] They descended it as far as the mouth of the Arkansas and then returned.[4] They saw the Ohio at its junction with the great river and noted it on their map and in their journal as the Oubaskison (Wabash), coming from the country inhabited by the Chouonans (Shawnese) in great numbers.

In 1682 La Salle made his great voyage of discovery, descending the Mississippi from the Illinois to its mouth; on his way he remained a short time at the mouth of the Ohio, which was noted as being more than five hundred leagues in length, and the river by which the war parties of the Iroquois descended to make war against the Southern Nations.

[1] Gravier.
[2] Ferland.
[3] La Salle.
[4] Charlevoix.

On the shore of the Gulf of Mexico La Salle, with great ceremony, proclaimed possession taken for Louis XIV of all the country watered by the Mississippi, St. Louis, Ohio, Allegheny, and their tributaries. For more than fifty years after its discovery by La Salle, the Ohio above the Wabash was unavailable to the French as a route to the Mississippi, owing to the hostility of the Iroquois, in whose country it had its source.

Early in the eighteenth century emigrants from Canada came by way of the Lakes to the head of Lake Michigan, and thence to the Illinois and Mississippi, or by the Maumee and Wabash, forming settlements along these rivers and also at Detroit and its neighborhood, while the Ohio remained still in an unknown wilderness and of minor importance. As late as 1750 to 1756 it was considered by the French authorities as a tributary of the Wabash, and it is so mentioned in official documents and laid down on most of their maps.

In 1726, by consent of the Iroquois, the French reconstructed the fort at Niagara, which they had abandoned in 1688. By 1728-9 the Shawanese were settled along the Allegheny, to which region they were drawn chiefly by the measures adopted by the Marquis Vaudreuil in 1724.

The way being now open, in 1729 M. de Lery, Chief Engineer of Canada, with a detachment of troops, crossed from Lake Erie to the Chautauqua Lake and thence to the Conewango Creek and the Allegheny River, descending it and the Ohio. They made a careful topographical survey of the course of the rivers, with observations of the latitude, longitude and distances as far as the Great Miami.

The French, down to the surrender of Canada to the British, in 1763, derived their right against that of the Iroquois to the Ohio country, asserting it to be theirs by virtue of its discovery by La Salle, and of their resorting to it when no other

Indians occupied it but their allies, the Shawanese, with whom the Iroquois were at war. The latter tribe claimed it by reason of their conquest of the Shawanese, and the English claimed that it was ceded to them by the Six Nations at the Treaty of Lancaster, 1744. It is remarkable, however, that the French never made any attempts to form settlements on the Ohio; confining themselves to the Wabash, Illinois, Mississippi and Detroit.

In 1753 Forts Presque Isle (Erie, Pennsylvania) and Le Bœuf (now Waterford, Erie County, Pennsylvania) were erected.

In 1754 Forts Franklin (at Venango, now Franklin) and Du Quesne (now Pittsburgh) were built, and in 1756 the erection of Fort Massac (now in Massac County, Illinois) completed the chain of forts deemed essential by French policy for the connection of Canada and Louisiana and the maintenance of possession of the Valley of the Ohio.

The steady increase of the English settlements towards the Alleghenies, the great numbers of their traders throughout the country west of the mountains, and, above all, the immense land grants on the waters of the Ohio by the British King and the Council of Virginia, incited the French to vigorous measures. Accordingly, Captain Céleron de Bienville was dispatched by Governor de la Galissonnière, in 1749, to expel the English traders and take military possession of the Ohio country. With a detachment of two hundred soldiers and thirty Indians he proceeded, by way of Chautauqua Lake and the Conewango Creek, to its junction with the Allegheny or Ohio as he called it. There he buried a leaden plate, on the 29th of July, with a suitable inscription, as a monument of having retaken possession of the said river Ohio and branches and the lands thereon. This plate was stolen by the Seneca Indians, probably directly after its deposit, and sent to Colonel

William Johnson. (Governor Clinton's letter to Governor Hamilton.[1]) Letter of Governor Clinton to Board of Trade, and fac-simile of the plate, with its "devilish writing," as the Indian chief called it, who took it to Colonel Johnson.

Céleron, with his flotilla, proceeded down the river, depositing plates at different points, generally at the mouths of streams emptying into the main river. The inscriptions on the plates were all alike, except the name of the place and date of deposit. A number of them were found in after-years; one, at the confluence of the Allegheny, Monongahela and Ohio, at Pittsburgh, was dated, August 3, 1749, at the "Three Rivers." (MSS. copy of plate by Governor Pownall in my possession.) Another was found in 1798 near Marietta, at the mouth of the Muskingum. It bore date August 16, 1749, at the entrance of the river "Yenangue."[2] The last discovered was at the mouth of the Great Kanawha, near Point Pleasant, in April, 1846. It was dated August 18, 1749, at the entrance of the river Chinodahichatha. (See fac-simile and account of in the "History of Western Virginia," by de Hass, 1851, p. 50).[3] On his way down Céleron encamped for a few days at Logstown, eighteen miles below Pittsburgh, from which he expelled the English traders, by whom he sent letters to Governor Hamilton of Pennsylvania, dated the 6th and 10th of August, and explained the object of his mission.[4]

In 1750 and 1751 Christopher Gist, the Agent of the Ohio Company of Virginia, explored the greater portion of the region now included within the boundaries of the States of Ohio, Kentucky and West Virginia, and parts of Western Maryland and Southwestern Pennsylvania. These explora-

---

[1] "New York Colonial History," Vol. VI.
[2] Hildreth's "Pioneer."
[3] See "Fort Pitt" for complete history.
[4] "Colonial Records."

tions were the earliest made, so far west, for the single object of examining the country, as they are the first also of which a regular journal was kept. The result of Gist's journeys, however, was not made known generally, being in the interest of a great Land Company; but in 1776 the Journal of 1750 was published by Governor Pownall, in London, in the Appendix to his "Topographical Description of North America." At that time but few copies of that work could have found their way to America, and at the close of the Revolutionary War it seemed to have become comparatively scarce and is now but little known. The second Journal has never before been printed here or elsewhere. The third, 1753, was printed for James Mease, by the Historical Society of Pennsylvania.

FOR THE HONORABLE ROBERT DINWIDDIE ESQUIRE, GOVERNOR & COMMANDER OF VIRGINIA.

INSTRUCTIONS GIVEN Mr CHRISTOPHER GIST BY THE COMMITTEE OF THE OHIO COMPANY THE 11th DAY OF SEPTEMBER 1750.

You are to go out as soon as possible to the Westward of the great Mountains, and carry with you such a Number of Men, as You think necessary, in Order to search out and discover the Lands upon the River Ohio, & other adjoining Branches of the Mississippi down as low as the great Falls thereof: You are particularly to observe the Ways & Passes thro all the Mountains you cross, & take an exact Account of the Soil, Quality, & Product of the Land, and the Wideness and Deepness of the Rivers, & the several Falls belonging to them, together with the Courses & Bearings of the Rivers & Mountains as near as you conveniently can: You are also to observe what Nations of Indians inhabit there, their Strength & Numbers, who they trade with, & in what Comodities they deal.

When you find a large Quantity of good, level Land, such as you think will suit the Company, You are to measure the Breadth of it, in three or four different Places, & take the Courses of the River and Mountains on which it binds in Order to judge the Quantity: You are to fix the Beginning & Bounds in such a Manner that they may be easily found again by your Description; the nearer in the Land lies, the better, provided it be good & level, but we had rather go quite down the Mississippi than take mean broken Land. After finding a large Body of good level Land, you are not to stop, but proceed farther, as low as the Falls of the Ohio, that We may be informed of that Navigation; And You are to take an exact Account of all the large Bodies of good level Land, in the same Manner as above directed, that the Company may the better judge where it will be most convenient for them to take their Land.

You are to note all the Bodies of good Land as you go along, tho there is not a sufficient Quantity for the Company's Grant, but You need not be so particular in the Mensuration of that, as in the larger Bodies of Land.

You are to draw as good a Plan as you can of the Country You pass thro: You are to take an exact and particular Journal of all your Proceedings, and make a true Report thereof to the Ohio Company.

1750.—In Complyance with my Instructions from the Committee of the OHIO COMPANY bearing Date the 11th Day of September 1750

Wednesday Octr 31.—Set out from Col° Thomas Cresap's at the old Town on Potomack River in Maryland, and went along an old Indian Path N 30 E about 11 Miles.

Thursday Nov 1.—Then N 1 Mile N 30 E 3 M here I was taken sick and stayed all Night.

Friday 2.—N 30 E 6 M, here I was so bad that I was not able to proceed any farther that. Night, but grew better in the Morning.

Saturday 3.—N 8 M to Juniatta, a large Branch of Susquehannah, where I stayed all Night.

Sunday 4.—Crossed Juniatta and went up it S 55 W about 16 M.

Monday 5.—Continued the same Course S 55 W 6 M to

the Top of a large Mountain called the Allegany Mountain, here our Path turned, & we went N 45 W 6 M here we encamped.

Tuesday 6 Wednesday 7 and Thursday 8.—Had Snow and such bad Weather that We could not travel for three Days; but I killed a young Bear so that we had Provision enough.

Friday 9.—Set out N 70 W about 8 M here I crossed a Creek of Susquehannah and it raining hard, I went into an old Indian Cabbin where I stay'd all Night.

Saturday 10.—Rain and Snow all Day but cleared away in the Evening.

Sunday 11.—Set out late in the Morning N 70 W 6 M crossing two Forks of a Creek of Susquehannah, here the Way being bad, We encamped and I killed a Turkey.

Monday 12.—Set out N 45 W 8 M crossed a great Laurel Mountain.

Tuesday 13.—Rain and Snow.

Wednesday 14.—Set out N 45 W 6 M to Loylhannan an old Indian Town on a Creek of Ohio called Kiscominatis, then N 1 M NW 1 M to an Indian's Camp on the said Creek.

Thursday 15.—The Weather being bad and I unwell I stayed here all Day: The Indian to whom this Camp belonged spoke good English and directed Me the Way to his Town, which is called Shannopini Town: He said it was about 60 M and a pretty good Way.

Friday 16.—Set out S 70 W 10 M.

Saturday 17.—The same Course (S 70 W) 15 M to an old Indian's Camp.

Sunday 18.—I was very sick, and sweated myself according to the Indian Custom in a Sweat-House, which gave Me Ease, and my Fever abated.

Monday 19.—Set out early in the Morning the same Course (S 70 W) travelled very hard about 20 M to a small Indian

Town of the Delawares called Shannopin on the SE Side of the River Ohio, where We rested and got Corn for our Horses.

Tuesday 20 Wednesday 21 Thursday 22 and Friday 23.—I was unwell and stayed in this Town to recover myself; While I was here I took an Opportunity to set my Compass privately, & took the Distance across the River, for I understood it was dangerous to let a Compass be seen among these Indians: The River Ohio is 76 Poles wide at Shannopin Town: There are about twenty Families in this Town: The Land in general from Potomack to this Place is mean stony and broken, here and there good Spots upon the Creeks and Branches but no Body of it.

Saturday 24.—Set out from Shannopin's Town, and swam our Horses across the River Ohio, & went down the River S 75 W 4 M, N 75 W 7 M W 2 M, all the Land from Shannopin's Town is good along the River, but the Bottoms not broad; At a Distance from the River good Land for Farming, covered with small white and red Oaks and tolerable level; fine Runs for Mills &c.

Sunday Nov 25.—Down the River W 3˙M, NW 5 M to Loggs Town; the Lands these last 8 M very rich the Bottoms above a Mile wide, but on the SE side, scarce a Mile wide, the Hills high and steep. In the Loggs Town, I found scarce any Body but a Parcel of reprobate Indian Traders, the Chiefs of the Indians being out a hunting: here I was informed that George Croghan & Andrew Montour who were sent upon an Embassy from Pensylvania to the Indians, were passed about a Week before me. The People in this Town, began to enquire my Business, and because I did not readily inform them, they began to suspect me, and said, I was come to settle the Indian's Lands and they knew I should never go Home again safe;. I found this Discourse was like to be of ill Consequence to me, so I pretended to speak very slightingly of what they had said to me, and enquired for Croghan (who is a meer Idol among his Countrymen the Irish Traders) and Andrew Montour the Interpreter for Pensylvania, and told them I had a Message to deliver the Indians from the King, by Order of the President of Virginia, & for that Reason wanted to see M Montour: This made them all pretty easy (being afraid to interrupt the King's Message) and obtained me Quiet and Respect among them, otherwise I doubt not they woud have contrived some Evil against me— I imediately wrote to M Croghan, by one of the Trader's People.

Monday 26.—Tho I was unwell, I prefered the Woods to such Company & set out from the Loggs Town down the River NW 6 M to great Beaver Creek where I met one Barny Curran a Trader for the Ohio Company, and We continued together as far as Muskingum. The Bottoms upon the River below the Logg's Town very rich but narrow, the high Land pretty good but not very rich, the Land upon Beaver Creek the same kind; From this Place We left the River Ohio to the SE & travelled across the Country.

Tuesday 27.—Set out from E side of Beaver Creek NW 6 M, W 4 M; up these two last Courses very good high Land, not very broken, fit for farming.

Wednesday 28.—Rained, We could not travel.

Thursday 29.—W 6 M thro good Land, the same Course continued 6 M farther thro very broken Land; here I found myself pretty well recovered, & being in Want of Provision, I went out and killed a Deer.

Friday 30.—Set out S 45 W 12 M crossed the last Branch of Beaver Creek where one of Curran's Men & myself killed 12 Turkeys.

Saturday Dec' 1.—N 45 W 10 M the Land high and tolerable good.

NOTE; by Mr Gist's Plat he makes these 2 Courses N 45 W 10 M, & N 45 W 8 M, to be W 8 M and N 45 W 6 M.

Sunday 2.—N 45 W 8 M the same Sort of Land, but near the Creeks bushy and very full of Thorns

Monday 3.—Killed a Deer, and stayed in our Camp all Day.

Tuesday 4.—Set out late S 45 W about 4 M here I killed three fine fat Deer, so that tho we were eleven in Company, We had great Plenty of Provision.

Wednesday 5.—Set out down the Side of a Creek called Elk's Eye Creek S 70 W 6 M, good Land, but void of Timber, Meadows upon the Creek, fine Runs for Mills.

Thursday 6.—Rained all Day so that we were obliged to continue in our Camp.

Friday 7.—Set out SW 8 M crossing the said Elk's Eye Creek to a Town of the Ottaways, a Nation of French Indians; an old French Man (named Mark Coonce) who had married an Indian Woman of the six Nations lived here; the Indians were all out a hunting; the old Man was very civil to me, but after I was gone to my Camp, upon his understanding I came from Virginia, he called Me the Big Knife. There are not above six or eight Families belonging to this Town.

Saturday 8.—Stayed in the Town.

Sunday 9.—Set out down the said Elk's Eye Creek S 45 W 6 M to Margarets Creek a Branch of the said Elk's Eye Creek.

Monday Dec 10.—The same Course (S 45 W) 2 M to a large Creek.

Tuesday 11.—The same Course 12 M killed 2 Deer.

Wednesday 12.—The same Course 8 M encamped by the Side of Elk's Eye Creek.

Thursday 13.—Rained all Day.

Friday 14.—Set out W 5 M to Muskingum a Town of the Wyendotts. The Land upon Elk's Eye Creek is in general very broken, the Bottoms narrow. The Wyendotts or little Mingoes are divided between the French and English, one half of them adhere to the first, and the other half are firmly attached to the latter. The Town of Muskingum consists of about one hundred Families. When We came within Sight of the Town, We perceived English Colours hoisted on the King's House, and at George Croghan's; upon enquiring the Reason I was informed that the French had lately taken several English Traders, and that Mr Croghan had ordered all the White Men to come into this Town, and had sent Expresses to the Traders of the lower Towns, and among the Pickweylinees; and the Indians had sent to their People to come to Council about it.

Saturday 15 & Sunday 16.—Nothing remarkable happened.

Monday 17.—Came into Town two Traders belonging to M Croghan, and informed Us that two of his People were taken by 40 French Men, & twenty French Indians who had carried them with seven Horse Loads of Skins to a new Fort that the French were building on one of the Branches of Lake Erie.

Tuesday 18.—I acquainted Mr Croghan and Andrew Montour with my Business with the Indians, & talked much of a Regulation of Trade with which they were much pleased, and treated Me very kindly.

From Wednesday 19 to Monday 24.—Nothing remarkable.

Tuesday 25.—This being Christmass Day, I intended to read Prayers, but after inviting some of the White Men, they informed each other of my Intentions, and being of several different Persuasions, and few of them inclined to hear any Good, they refused to come. But one Thomas Burney a Black Smith who is settled there went about and talked to them, & then several of them came; and Andrew Montour invited several of the well disposed Indians, who came freely; by this Time the Morning was spent, and I had given over all Thoughts of them, but seeing Them come, to oblige All, and offend None, I stood up and said, Gentlemen, I have no Design or Intention to give Offence to any particular Sectary or Religion, but as our King indulges Us all in a Liberty of Conscience and hinders none of You in the Exercise of your religious Worship, so it would be unjust in You, to endeavour to stop the Propagation of His; The Doctrine of Salvation Faith, and good Works, is what I only propose to treat of, as I find it extracted from the Homilies of the Church of England, which I then read them in the best Manner I coud, and after I had done the Interpreter told the Indians what I had read, and that it was the true Faith which the great King and His Church recomended to his Children: the Indians seemed well pleased, and came up to Me and returned Me their Thanks; and then invited Me to live among Them, and gave Me a Name in their Language Annosanah: the Interpreter told Me this was a Name of a good Man that had formerly lived among them, and their King said that must be always my Name, for which I returned them Thanks; but as to living among them I excused myself by saying I did not know whether the Governor woud give Me Leave, and if he did the French woud come and carry me away as they had done the English Traders, to which they answered I might bring great Guns and make a Fort, that they had now left the French, and were very desirous of being instructed in the Principles of Christianity; that they liked Me very well and wanted Me to marry Them after the Christian Manner, and baptize their Children; and then they said they woud never desire to return to the French, or suffer Them or their Priests to come near them more, for they loved the English, but had seen little

Religion among Them: and some of their great Men came and wanted Me to baptize their Children; for as I had read to Them and appeared to talk about Religion they took Me to be a Minister of the Gospel; Upon which I desired Mr Montour (the Interpreter) to tell Them, that no Minister coud venture to baptize any Children, until those that were to be Sureties for Them, were well instructed in the Faith themselves, and that this was according to the great' King's Religion, in which He desired his Children shoud be instructed & We dare not do it in any other Way, than was by Law established, but I hoped if I coud not be admitted to live among them, that the great King woud send Them proper Ministers to exercise that Office among them, at which they seemed well pleased; and one of Them went and brought Me his Book (which was a Kind contrived for Them by the French in which the Days of the Week were so marked that by moving a Pin every Morning they kept a pretty exact Account of the Time) to shew Me that He understood Me, and that He and his Family always observed the Sabbath Day.

Wednesday Decr 26.—This Day a Woman, who had been a long Time a Prisoner, and had deserted, & been retaken, and brought into the Town on Christmass Eve, was put to Death in the following manner: They carried her without the Town, & let her loose, and when she attempted to run away, the Persons appointed for that Purpose pursued her, & struck Her on the Ear, on the right Side of her Head, which beat her flat on her Face on the Ground; they then stuck her several Times, thro the Back with a Dart, to the Heart, scalped Her, & threw the Scalp in the Air, and another cut off her Head: There the dismal Spectacle lay till the Evening, & then Barny Curran desired Leave to bury Her, which He, and his Men, and some of the Indians did just at Dark.

From Thursday Decr 27 to Thursday Jany 3 1751.—Nothing remarkable happened in the Town.

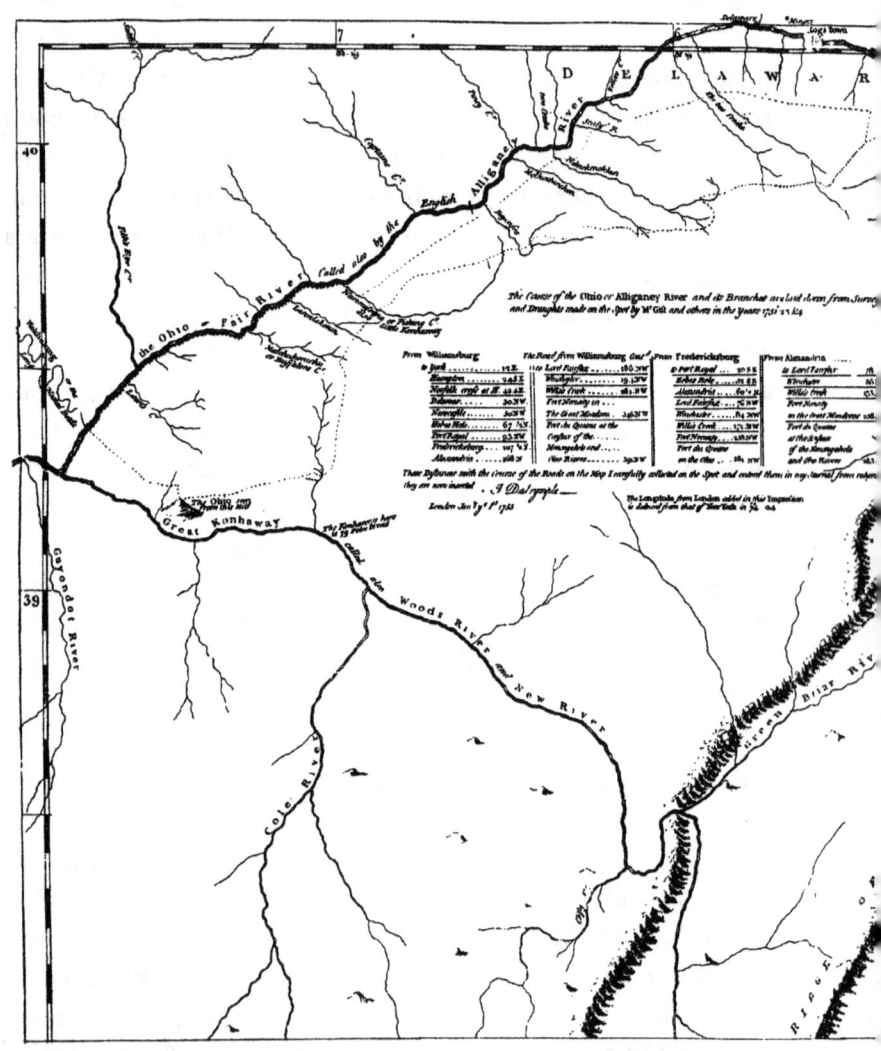

FRY AND JEFFERSON MAP, 1755.

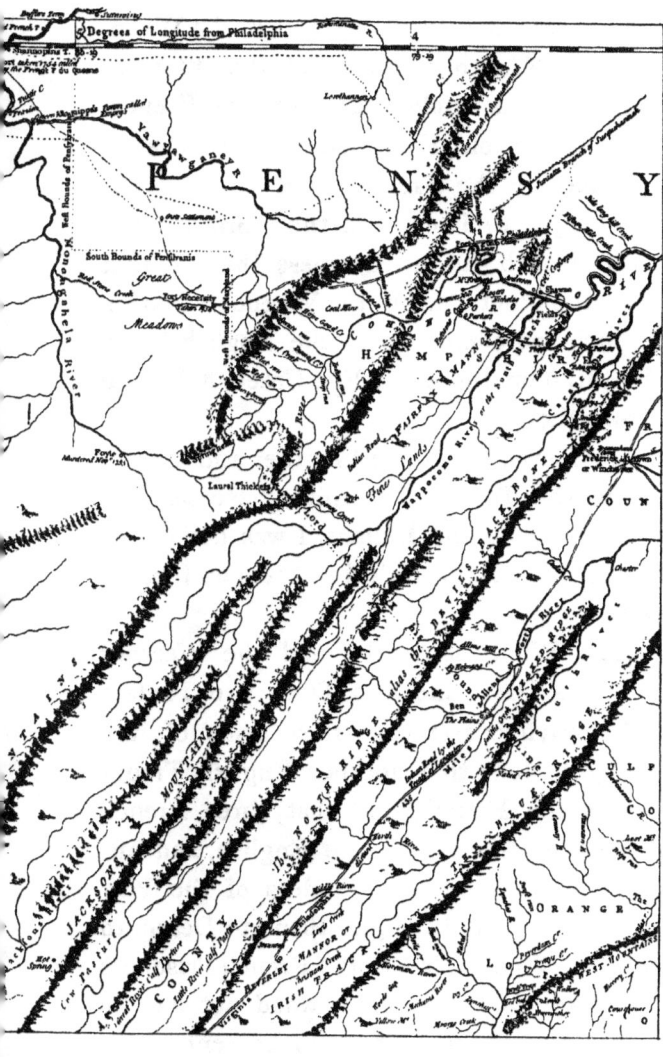

Friday Jan 4.—One Teafe (an Indian Trader) came to Town from near Lake Erie, & informed Us, that the Wyendott Indians had advised Him to keep clear of the Ottaways (these are a Nation of Indians firmly attached to the French, & inhabit near the Lakes) & told Him that the Branches of the Lakes are claimed by the French; but that all the Branches of Ohio belonged to Them, and their Brothers the English, and that the French had no Business there, & that it was expected that the other Part of the Wyendott Nation woud desert the French and come over to the English Interest, & join their Brethren on the Elk's Eye Creek, & build a strong Fort and Town there.

From Saturday 5 to Tuesday 8.—The Weather still continuing bad, I stayed in the Town to recruit my Horses, and tho Corn was very dear among the Indians, I was obliged to feed them well, or run the Risque of losing them as I had a great Way to travel.

Wednesday 9.—The Wind Southerly, and the Weather something warmer: this Day came into Town two Traders from among the Pickwaylinees (these are a Tribe of the Twigtwees) and brought News that another English Trader was taken prisoner by the French, and that three French Soldiers had deserted and come over to the English, and surrendered themselves to some of the Traders of the Pick Town, & that the Indians woud have put them to Death, to revenge their taking our Traders, but as the French Prisoners had surrendered themselves, the English woud not let the Indians hurt them, but had ordered them to be sent under the Care of three of our Traders and delivered at this Town, to George Croghan.

Thursday 10.—Wind still at South and warm.

Friday 11.—This Day came into Town an Indian from over the Lakes & confirmed the News we had heard.

Saturday 12.—We sent away our People towards the lower Town intending to follow them the next Morning, and this Evening We went into Council in the Wyendott's King's House—The Council had been put off a long Time expecting some of their great Men in, but few of them came, & this Evening some of the King's Council being a little disordered with Liquor, no Business coud be done, but We were desired to come next Day.

Sunday Jan^{ry} 13.—No Business done.

Monday 14.—This Day George Croghan, by the Assistance of Andrew Montour, acquainted the King and Council of this Nation (by presenting them four Strings of Wampum) that the great King over the Water, their Roggony [Father] had sent under the Care of the Governor of Virginia, their Brother, a large Present of Goods which was now landed safe in Virginia, & the Governor had sent Me to invite Them to come and see Him, & partake of their Father's Charity to all his Children on the Branches of Ohio. In Answer to which one of the Chiefs stood up and said, "That their King and "all of Them thanked their Brother the Governor of Virginia "for his Care, and Me for bringing them the News, but they "coud not give Me an Answer untill they had a full or gen- "eral Council of the several Nations of Indians which coud "not be till next Spring : & so the King and Council shaking "Hands with Us, We took our Leave.

Tuesday 15.—We left Muskingum, and went W 5 M, to the White Woman's Creek, on which is a small Town; this White Woman was taken away from New England, when she was not above ten Years old, by the French Indians; She is now upwards of fifty, and has an Indian Husband and several Children — Her name is Mary Harris, she still remembers they used to be very religious in New England, and wonders how the White Men can be so wicked as she has seen them in these Woods.

Wednesday 16.—Set out SW 25 M, to Licking Creek—The Land from Muskingum to this Place rich but broken—Upon the N Side of Licking Creek about 6 M from the Mouth, are several Salt Licks, or Ponds, formed by little Streams or Dreins of Water, clear but of a blueish Colour, & salt Taste the Traders and Indians boil their Meat in this Water, which (if proper Care be not taken) will sometimes make it too salt to eat.

Thursday 17.—Set out W 5 M, SW 15 M, to a great Swamp.

Friday 18.—Set out from the great Swamp SW 15 M.

Saturday 19.—W 15 M to Hockhockin a small Town with only four or five Delaware Families.

Sunday 20.—The Snow began to grow thin, and the Weather warmer; Set out from Hockhockin S 5 M, then W 5 M, then SW 5 M, to the Maguck a little Delaware Town of about ten Families by the N Side of a plain or clear Field about 5 M in Length NE & SW & 2 M broad, with a small Rising in the Middle, which gives a fine Prospect over the whole Plain, and a large Creek on the N Side of it called Sciodoe Creek. All the Way from Licking Creek to this Place is fine rich level Land, with large Meadows, fine Clover Bottoms & spacious Plains covered with wild Rye: the Wood chiefly large Walnuts and Hickories, here and there mixed with Poplars Cherry Trees and Sugar Trees.

From Monday 21 to Wednesday 23—Stayed in the Maguck Town.

Thursday 24.—Set out from the Maguck Town S about 15 M, thro fine rich level Land to a small Town called Harrickintoms consisting of about five or six Delaware Families, on the SW Sciodoe Creek.

Friday 25.—The Creek being very high and full of Ice, We coud not ford it, and were obliged to go down it on the SE Side SE 4 M to the Salt Lick Creek—about 1 M up this Creek on the S Side is a very large Salt Lick, the Streams which run into this Lick are very salt, & tho clear leave a blueish Sediment: The Indians and Traders make salt for their Horses of this Water, by boiling it; it has at first a blueish Colour, and somewhat bitter Taste, but upon being dissolved in fair Water and boiled a second Time, it becomes tolerable pure Salt.

Saturday 26.—Set out S 2 M, SW 14 M.

Sunday 27.—S 12 M to a small Delaware Town of about twenty Families on the SE Side of Sciodoe Creek—We lodged at the House of an Indian whose Name was Windaughalah, a great Man and Chief of this Town, & much in the English Interest. He entertained Us very kindly, and ordered a Negro Man that belonged to him to feed our Horses well; this Night it snowed, and in the Morning tho the Snow was six or seven Inches deep, the wild Rye appeared very green and flourishing thro it, and our Horses had fine Feeding.

Monday Jany 28.—We went into Council with the Indians of this Town, and after the Interpreter had informed them of his Instructions from the Governor of Pensylvania, and given them some Cautions in Regard to the French, they returned for Answer as follows. The Speaker with four Strings of Wampum in his Hand stood up, and addressing Himself as to the Governor of Pensylvania, said, "Brothers, "We the Delawares return You our hearty Thanks for the "News You have sent Us, and We assure You, We will not "hear the Voice of any other Nation for We are to be directed "by You our Brothers the English, & by none else: We shall "be glad to hear what our Brothers have to say to Us at the "Loggs Town in the Spring, and to assure You of our hearty "Good will & Love to our Brothers We present You with "these four Strings of Wampum This is the last Town of the Delawares to the Westward—The Delaware Indians by the best Accounts I coud gather consist of about 500 fighting Men all firmly attached to the English Interest, they are not properly a Part of the six Nations, but are scattered about among most of the Indians upon the Ohio, and some of them among the six Nations, from whom they have Leave to hunt upon their Lands.

Tuesday 29.—Set out SW 5 M, S 5 M, to the Mouth of Sciodoe Creek opposite to the Shannoah Town, here We fired our Guns to alarm the Traders, who soon answered, and came and ferryed Us over to the Town—The Land about the Mouth of Sciodoe Creek is rich but broken fine Bottoms upon the River & Creek—The Shannoah Town is situate upon both Sides the River Ohio, just below the Mouth of Sciodoe Creek, and contains about 300 Men, there are about 40 Houses on the S Side of the River and about 100 on the N Side, with a Kind of State-House of about 90 Feet long, with a light Cover of Bark in wch they hold their Councils—The Shanaws are not a Part of the six Nations, but were formerly at Variance with them, tho now reconciled: they are great Friends to the English who once protected them from the Fury of the six Nations, which they gratefully remember.

Wednesday 30.—We were conducted into Council, where George Croghan delivered sundry Speeches from the Government of Pensylvania to the Chiefs of this Nation, in which He informed them, "That two Prisoners who had been "taken by the French, and had made their Escape from the "French Officer at Lake Erie as he was carrying them towards "Canada brought News that the French offered a large Sum "of Money to any Person who would bring to them the said "Croghan and Andrew Montour the Interpreter alive, or if "dead their Scalps; and that the French also threatened "these Indians and the Wyendotts with War in the Spring" the same Persons farther said "that they had seen ten French

"Canoes loaded with Stores for a new Fort they designed on the S Side Lake Erie. Mr Croghan also informed them of several of our Traders having been taken, and advised them to keep their Warriors at Home, until they coud see what the French intended which he doubted not woud appear in the Spring—Then Andrew Montour informed this Nation as He had done the Wyendotts & Delawares "That the King of "Great Britain had sent Them a large Present of Goods, in "Company with the six Nations, which was under the Care "of the Governor of Virginia, who had sent Me out to invite "them to come and see Him, & partake of their Father's "Present next Summer" to which We received this Answer—Big Hannaona their Speaker taking in his Hand the several Strings of Wampum which had been given by the English, He said "These are the Speeches received by Us from your "great Men: From the Beginning of our Friendship, all that "our Brothers the English have told Us has been good and "true, for which We return our hearty Thanks" Then taking up four other Strings of Wampum in his Hand, He said "Brothers I now speak the Sentiments of all our People; "when first our Forefathers did meet the English our Bro- "thers, they found what our Brothers the English told them "to be true, and so have We—We are but a small People, & "it is not to Us only that You speak, but to all Nations—We "shall be glad to hear what our Brothers will say to Us at the "Loggs Town in the Spring, & We hope that the Friendship "now subsisting between Us & our Brothers, will last as long "as the Sun shines, or the Moon gives Light—We hope that "our Children will hear and believe what our Brothers say to "them, as We have always done, and to assure You of our "hearty Good-Will towards You our Brothers, We present "You with these four Strings of Wampum" After the Council was over they had much Talk about sending a Guard with Us to the Pickwaylinees Towns (these are a Tribe of Twigtwees) which was reckoned near 200 Miles, but after long Consultation (their King being sick) they came to no Determination about it.

From Thursday Jan 31 To Monday Feby 11.—Stayed in the Shannoah Town, while I was here the Indians had a very extraordinary Kind of a Festival, at which I was present and which I have exactly described at the End of my Journal— As I had particular Instructions from the President of Virginia to discover the Strength & Numbers of some Indian Nations to the Westward of Ohio who had lately revolted from the French, and had some Messages to deliver them from Him, I resolved to set out for the Twigtwee Town.

Tuesday 12.—Having left my Boy to take Care of my Horses in the Shannoah Town, & supplied myself with a fresh Horse to ride, I set out with my old Company viz George Croghan Andrew Montour, Robert Kallandar, and a Servant to carry our Provisions &c NW 10 M.

Wednesday 13.—The same Course (NW) about 35 M.

Thursday 14.—The same Course about 30 M.

Friday 15.—The same Course 15 M. We met with nine Shannoah Indians coming from one of the Pickwaylinees Towns, where they had been to Council, they told Us there were fifteen more of them behind at the Twigtwee Town, waiting for the Arrival of the Wawaughtanneys, who are a Tribe of the Twigtwees, and were to bring with them a Shannoah Woman and Child to deliver to their Men that were behind: this Woman they informed Us had been taken Prisoner last Fall, by some of the Wawaughtanney Warriors thro a Mistake, which had like to have engaged these Nations in a War.

Saturday 16.—Set out the same Course (NW) about 35 M, to the little Miamee River or Creek

Sunday 17.—Crossed the little Miamee River, and altering our Course We went SW 25 M, to the big Miamee River, opposite the Twigtwee Town. All the Way from the Shannoah Town to this Place (except the first 20 M which is broken) is 'fine, rich level Land, well timbered with large Walnut, Ash, Sugar Trees, Cherry Trees &c, it is well watered with a great Number of little Streams or Rivulets, and full of beautiful natural Meadows, covered with wild Rye, blue Grass and Clover, and abounds with Turkeys, Deer, Elks and most Sorts of Game particularly Buffaloes, thirty or forty of which are frequently seen feeding in one Meadow: In short it wants Nothing but Cultivation to make it a most delightfull Country —The Ohio and all the large Branches are said to be full of fine Fish of several Kinds, particularly a Sort of Cat Fish of a prodigious Size; but as I was not there at the proper Season, I had not an opportunity of seeing any of them—The Traders had always reckoned it 200 M, from the Shannoah Town to the Twigtwee Town, but by my Computation I could make it no more than 150—The Miamee River being high, We were obliged to make a Raft of old Loggs to transport our Goods and Saddles and swim our Horses over—After firing a few Guns and Pistols, & smoking in the Warriours Pipe, who came to invite Us to the Town (according to their Custom of inviting and welcoming Strangers and Great Men) We entered the Town with English Colours before Us, and were kindly received by their King, who invited Us into his own House, & set our Colours upon the Top of it—The Firing of Guns held about a Quarter of an Hour, and then all the white Men and Traders that were there, came and welcomed Us to the the Twigtwee Town—This Town is situate on the NW Side of the Big Miamee River about 150 M from the Mouth thereof; it consists of about 400 Families, & daily encreasing, it is accounted one of the strongest Indian Towns upon this Part of the Continent—The Twigtwees are a very numerous People consisting of many different Tribes under the same Form of Government. Each tribe has a particular Chief or King, one of which is chosen indifferently out of any Tribe to rule the whole Nation, and is vested with greater Authorities than any of the others—They are accounted the most powerful People to the Westward of the English Settlements, & much superior to the six Nations with whom they are now in Amity: their Strength and Numbers are not thoroughly known, as they have but lately traded with the English, and indeed have very little Trade among them: they deal in much the same Comodities with the Northern Indians. There are other Nations or Tribes still further to the Westward daily coming in to them, & 'tis thought their Power and Interest reaches to the Westward of the Mississippi, if not across the Continent; they are at present very well affected to the English, and seem fond of an Alliance with them—they formerly lived on the farther Side of the Obache, and were in the French Interest, who supplied them with some few Trifles at a most exorbitant Price—they were called by the French Miamees; but they have now revolted from them, and left their former Habitations for the Sake of trading with the English; and notwithstanding all the Artifices the French have used, they have not been able to recall them.

After We had been some Time in the King's House Mr Montour told Him that We wanted to speak with Him and the Chiefs of this Nation this Evening upon which We were invited into the long House, and having taken our Places Mr Montour began as follows—" Brothers the Twigtwees as
" We have been hindered by the high Waters and some other
" Business with our Indian Brothers, no Doubt our long Stay
" has caused some Trouble among our Brethren here, There-
" fore We now present you with two Strings of Wampum to

"remove all the Trouble of your Hearts, & clear your Eyes, "that You may see the Sun shine clear, for We have a great "Deal to say to You, & We woud have You send for one of "Your Friends that can speak the Mohickon or the Mingoe "Tongues well, that We may understand each other thoroughly, "for We have a great Deal of Business to do"—The Mohickons are a small Tribe who most of them speak English, and are also well acquainted with the Language of the Twigtwees, and they with theirs— Mr Montour then proceeded to deliver Them a Message from the Wyendotts and Delawares as follows " Brothers the Twigtwees, this comes by our Bro- "thers the English who are coming with good News to You : "We hope You will take Care of Them, and all our Brothers "the English who are trading among You : You made a Road "for our Brothers the English to come and trade among You, "but it is now very foul, great Loggs are fallen across it, and "We would have You be strong like Men, and have one "Heart with Us, and make the Road clear, that our Brothers "the English may have free Course and Recourse between "You and Us—In the Sincerity of our Hearts We send You "these four Strings of Wampum, to which they gave the usual Yo Ho—Then they said they wanted some Tobacco to smoak with Us, and that tomorrow they woud send for their Interpreter.

Monday Feby 18.—We walked about viewed the Fort which wanted some Repairs, & the Trader's Men helped Them to bring Loggs to line the Inside.

Tuesday 19.—We gave their Kings and great Men some Clothes, and Paint Shirts, and now they were busy dressing and preparing themselves for the Council—The Weather grew warm and the Creeks began to lower very fast.

Wednesday 20.—About 12 of the Clock We were informed that some of the foreign Tribes were coming, upon which proper Persons were ordered to meet them and conduct Them into the Town, and then We were invited into the long House; after We had been seated about a Quarter of an Hour four Indians, two from each Tribe (who had been sent before to bring the long Pipe, and to inform that the rest were coming) came in, & informed Us that their Friends had sent these Pipes that We might smoak the Calamut Pipe of Peace with Them and that they intended to do the same with Us.

Thursday Feby 21.—We were again invited into the long House where Mr Croghan made them(with the foreign Tribes) a Present to the Value of £100 Pensylvania Money, and delivered all our Speeches to Them, at which they seemed well pleased, and said, that they would take Time and consider well what We had said to Them.

Friday 22.—Nothing remarkable happened in the Town.

Saturday 23.—In the Afternoon there was an Alarm in the Town which caused a great Confusion and running about among the Indians, upon enquiring into the Reason of this Stir, they told Us that it was occasioned by six Indians that came to war against Them, from the Southward : three of them Cutaways, and three Shanaws (these were some of the Shanaws who had formerly deserted from the other Part of the Nation, and now live to the Southward) Towards Night there was a report spread in Town that four Indians, and four hundred French, were on their March and just by the Town : But soon after the Messenger who brought this News said, there were only four french Indians coming to Council, and that they bid him say so, only to see how the English woud behave themselves; but as they had behaved themselves like Men, He now told the Truth.

Sunday 24.—This Morning the four French Indians came into Town and were kindly received by the Town Indians; they marched in under French Colours, and were conducted into the long House, and after they had been in about a Quarter of an Hour, the Council sate, and We were sent for that We might hear what the French had to say to them— The Pyankeshee King (who was at that Time the principal Man, and Comander in Chief of the Twigtwees) said, He woud have the English Colours set up in this Council as well as the French, to which We answered he might do as he thought fit. After We were seated right opposite to the French Embassadors, One of Them said, He had a Present to make Them, so a Place was prepared (as they had before done for our Present) between Them and Us, and then their Speaker stood up, and layed His hands upon two small Caggs of Brandy that held about seven Quarts each, and a Roll of Tobacco of about ten Pounds Weight, then taking two strings of Wampum in his Hand, He said, "What he had to deliver Them was "from their Father (meaning the French King) "and he desired they woud hear what he was about to say to "Them;" then he layed them two Strings of Wampum down upon the Caggs, and taking up four other Strings of black and white Wampum, he said, "that their Father remembring "his Children, had sent them two Caggs of Milk, and some "Tobacco, and that he now had made a clear Road for them, "to come and see Him and his Officers; and pressed them "very much to come; then he took another String of Wampum in his Hand, and said, "their Father now woud forget all lit- "tle Differences that had been between Them, and desired "Them not to be of two Minds, but to let Him know their "Minds freely, for He woud send for Them no more"—To which the Pyankeshee King replyed, "it was true their "Father had sent for them several Times, and said the Road "was clear, but He understood it was made foul & bloody, "and by Them—We (said He) have cleared a Road for our "Brothers the English, and your Fathers have made it bad, "and have taken some of our Brothers Prisoners, Which We "look upon as done to Us, and he turned short about and "went out of Council"—After the French Embassador had delivered his Message He went into one of the private Houses and endeavoured much to prevail on some Indians, and was seen to cry and lament (as he said for the Loss of that Nation.

Monday Feby 25.—This Day We receieved a Speech from the Wawaughtanneys and Pyankeshees (two Tribes of the Twigtwees) One of the Chiefs of the former spoke "Broth-"ers, We have heard what You have said to Us by the Inter-"preter and We see You take Pity upon our poor Wives and "Children, and have taken Us by the Hand into the great "Chain of Friendship; therefore We present You with these "two Bundles of Skins to make Shoes for your People, and "this Pipe to smoak in, to assure You that our Hearts are "good and true towards You our Brothers; and We hope that "We shall all continue in true Love and Friendship with one "another, as People with one Head and one Heart ought to "do; You have pityed Us as You always did the rest of our "Indian Brothers, We hope that Pity You have always shewn, "will remain as long as the Sun gives Light, and on our Side "you may depend upon sincere and true Friendship towards "You as long as We have Strength"—This Person stood up and spoke with the Air and Gesture of an Orator.

Tuesday 26.—The Twigtwees delivered the following Answer to the four Indians sent by the French—The Captain of the Warriors stood up and taking some Strings of black and white Wampum in his Hand he spoke with a fierce Tone and very warlike Air—" Brothers the Ottaways, "You are always differing with the French Yourselves, and "yet You listen to what they say, but We will let You know by "these four Strings of Wampum, that We will not hear any

"Thing they say to Us, nor do any Thing they bid Us"—Then the same Speaker with six Strouds two Match-Coats, and a String of black Wampum (I understood the Goods were in Return for the Milk and Tobacco) and directing his Speech to the French said, "Fathers, you desire that We
" may speak our Minds from our Hearts, which I am going to
" do; You have often desired We shoud go Home to You,
" but I tell You it is not our Home, for We have made a Road
" as far as the Sea to the Sun-rising, and have been taken by
" the Hand by our Brothers the English, and the six Nations,
" and the Delawares Shannoahs and Wyendotts, and We as-
" sure You it is the Road We will go; and as You threaten
" Us with War in the Spring, We tell You if You are angry
" We are ready to receive You, and resolve to die here before
" We will go to You; And that You may know that this our
" Mind, We send You this String of black Wampum." After a short Pause the same Speaker spoke again thus—" Brothers
" the Ottaways, You hear what I say, tell that to your Fath-
" ers the French. for that is our Mind, and We speak it from
" our Hearts.

Wednesday 27.—This Day they took down their French Colours, and dismissed the four French Indians, so they took their Leave of the Town and set off for the French Fort.

Thursday 28.—The Crier of the Town came by the King's Order and invited Us to the long House to see the Warriors Feather Dance; it was performed by three Dancing-Masters, who were painted all over with various Colours, with long Sticks in their Hands, upon the Ends of which were fastened long Feathers of Swans, and other Birds, neatly woven in the Shape of a Fowls Wing: in this Disguise they performed many antick Tricks, waving their Sticks and Feathers about with great Skill to imitate the flying and fluttering of Birds, keeping exact Time with their Musick: while they are dancing some of the Warriors strikes a Post, upon which the Musick and Dancers cease, and the Warrior gives an Account of his Atchievements in War, and when he has done, throws down some Goods as a Recompence to the Performers and Musicians; after which they proceed in their Dance as before till another Warrior strikes ye Post, and so on as long as the Company think fit

Friday March 1.—We received the following Speech from the Twigtwees the Speaker stood up and addressing himself as to the Governor of Pensylvania with two Strings of Wampum in his Hand, He said—" Brothers our Hearts are "glad that You have taken Notice of Us, and surely Brothers "We hope that You will order a Smith to settle here to "mend our Guns and Hatchets, Your Kindness makes Us "so bold to ask this Request. You told Us our Friendship "should last as long, and be as the greatest Mountain, We "have considered well, and all our great Kings & Warriors "are come to a Resolution never to give Heed to what the "French say to Us, but always to hear & believe what You "our Brothers say to Us—Brothers We are obliged to You "for your kind Invitation to receive a Present at the Loggs "Town, but as our foreign Tribes are not yet come, We must "wait for them, but You may depend We will come as soon "as our Women have planted Corn to hear what our Brothers "will say to Us—Brothers We present You with this Bundle "of Skins, as We are but poor to be for Shoes for You on "the Road, and We return You our hearty Thanks for the "Clothes which You have put upon our Wives and Children" —We then took our Leave of the Kings and Chiefs, and they ordered that a small Party of Indians shoud go with Us as far as Hockhockin; but as I had left my Boy and Horses at the lower Shannoah Town, I was obliged to go by myself or to go sixty or seventy Miles out of my Way, which I did not care to do; so we all came over the Miamee River together this Evening, but Mr Croghan & Mr Montour went over again & lodged in the Town, but I stayed on this Side at one Robert Smith's (a Trader) where We had left our Horses—Before the French Indians had come into Town, We had drawn Articles of Peace and Alliance between the English and the Wawaughtanneys and Pyankeshees; the Indentures were signed sealed and delivered on both Sides, and as I drew them I took a Copy—The Land upon the great Miamee River is very rich level and well timbered, some of the finest Meadows that can be: The Indians and Traders assure Me that the Land holds as good and if possible better, to the Westward as far as the Obache which is accounted 100 Miles, and quite up to the Head of the Miamee River, which is 60 Miles above the Twigtwee Town, and down the said River quite to the Ohio which is reckoned 150 Miles—The Grass here grows to a great Height in the clear Fields, of which there are a great Number, & the Bottoms are full of white Clover, wild Rye, and blue Grass.

Saturday March 2.—George Croghan and the rest of our Company came over the River, We got our Horses, & set out about 35 M. to Mad Creek (this is a Place where some English Traders had been taken Prisoners by the French.)

Sunday 3.—This Morning We parted, They for Hockhockin, and I for the Shannoah Town, and as I was quite alone and knew that the French Indians had threatened Us, and woud probably pursue or lye in Wait for Us, I left the Path, and went to the South Westward down the little Miamee River or Creek, where I had fine traveling thro rich Land and beautiful Meadows, in which I coud sometimes see forty or fifty Buffaloes feeding at once—The little Miamee River or Creek continued to run thro the Middle of a fine Meadow, about a Mile wide very clear like an old Field, and not a Bush in it, I coud see the Buffaloes in it above two Miles off: I travelled this Day about 30 M.

Monday 4.—This Day I heard several Guns, but was afraid to examine who fired Them, lest they might be some of the French Indians, so I travelled thro the Woods about 30 M; just at Night I killed a fine barren Cow-Buffaloe and took out her Tongue, and a little of the best of her Meat: The Land still level rich and well timbered with Oak, Walnut, Ash, Locust, and Sugar Trees.

Tuesday 5.—I travelled about 30 M.

Wednesday 6.—I travelled about 30 M, and killed a fa: B. r.

Thursday 7.—Set out with my Horse Load of Bear and travelled about 30 M this Afternoon I met a young Man (a Trader) and We encamped together that Night; He happened to have some Bread with Him, and I had plenty of Meat, so We fared very well.

Friday 8.—Travelled about 30 M, and arrived at Night at the Shannoah Town—All the Indians, as well as the white Men came out to welcome my Return to their Town, being very glad that all Things were rightly settled in the Miamee Country, they fired upwards of 150 Guns in the Town, and made an Entertainment in Honour of the late Peace with the western Indians—In my Return from the Twigtwee to the Shannoah Town, I did not keep an exact Account of Course or Distance; for as the Land thereabouts was every where much the same, and the Situation of the Country was sufficiently described in my Journey to the Twigtwee Town, I thought it unnecessary, but have notwithstanding laid down my Tract pretty nearly in my Plat.

Saturday March 9.—In the Shannoah Town, I met with one of the Mingoe Chiefs, who had been down at the Falls of Ohio, so that We did not see Him as We went up; I informed Him of the King's Present, and the Invitation down to Virginia—He told that there was a Party of French Indians hunting at the Falls, and if I went there they would certainly kill Me or carry Me away Prisoner to the French; For it is certain they would not let Me pass: However as I had a great Inclination to see the Falls, and the Land on the E Side the Ohio, I resolved to venture as far as possible.

Sunday 10 & Monday 11.—Stayed in the Town, and prepared for my Departure.

Tuesday 12.— I got my Horses over the River and after Breakfast my Boy and I got ferryed over—The Ohio is near ¾ of a Mile wide at Shannoah Town, & is very deep and smooth.

Wednesday 13.—We set out S 45 W, down the said River on the SE Side 8 M, then S 10 M, here I met two Men belonging to Robert Smith at whose House I lodged on this Side the Miamee River, and one Hugh Crawford, the said Robert Smith had given Me an Order upon these Men, for two of the Teeth of a large Beast, which they were bringing from towards the Falls of Ohio, one of which I brought in and delivered to the Ohio Company—Robert Smith informed Me that about seven Years ago these Teeth and Bones of three large Beasts (one of which was somewhat smaller than the other two) were found in a salt Lick or Spring upon a small Creek which runs into the S Side of the Ohio, about 15 M, below the Mouth of the great Miamee River, and 20 above the Falls of Ohio—He assured Me that the Rib Bones of the largest of these Beasts were eleven Feet long, and the Skull Bone six feet wide, across the Forehead, & the other Bones in Proportion; and that there were several Teeth there, some of which he called Horns, and said they were upwards of five Feet long, and as much as a Man coud well carry: that he had hid one in a Branch at some Distance from the Place, lest the French Indians shoud carry it away

—The Tooth which I brought in for the Ohio Company, was a Jaw Tooth of better than four Pounds Weight; it appeared to be the furthest Tooth in the Jaw, and looked like fine Ivory when the outside was scraped off—I also met with four Shannoah Indians coming up the River in their Canoes, who informed me that there were about sixty French Indians encamped at the Falls.

Thursday 14.—I went down the River S 15 M, the Land upon this Side the Ohio chiefly broken, and the Bottoms but narrow.

Friday 15.—S 5 M, SW 10 M, to a Creek that was so high, that We coud not get over that Night.

Saturday 16.—S 45 W about 35 M.

Sunday 17.—The same Course 15 M, then N 45 W 5 M.

Monday 18.— N 45 W 5 M then SW 20 M, to the lower Salt Lick Creek, which Robert Smith and the Indians told Us was about 15 M above the Falls of Ohio; the Land still hilly, the Salt Lick here much the same with those before described—this Day We heard several Guns which made me imagine the French Indians were not moved, but were still hunting, and firing thereabouts: We also saw some Traps newly set, and the Footsteps of some Indians plain on the Ground as if they had been there the Day before—I was now much troubled that I could not comply with my Instructions, & was once resolved to leave the Boy and Horses, and to go privately on Foot to view the Falls; but the Boy being a poor Hunter, was afraid he woud starve if I was long from him, and there was also great Danger lest the French Indians shoud come upon our Horses Tracts, or hear their Bells, and as I had seen good Land enough, I thought perhaps I might be blamed for venturing so far, in such dangerous Times, so I concluded not to go to the Falls; but travell'd away to the Southward till We were over the little Cuttaway River—The Falls of Ohio by the best

Information I coud get are not very steep, on the SE Side there is a Bar of Land at some Distance from the Shore, the Water between the Bar and the Shore is not above 3 feet deep, and the Stream moderately strong, the Indians frequently pass safely in their Canoes thro this Passage, but are obliged to take great Care as they go down lest the Current which is much the strongest on the NW Side shoud draw them that Way; which woud be very dangerous as the Water on that Side runs with great Rapidity over several Ledges of Rocks; the Water below the Falls they say is about six Fathoms deep, and the River continues without any Obstructions till it empties itself into the Missisippi which is accounted upwards of 400 M—The Ohio near the Mouth is said to be very wide, and the Land upon both Sides very rich, and in general very level, all the Way from the Falls—After I had determined not to go to the Falls, We turned from Salt Lick Creek, to a Ridge of Mountains that made towards the Cuttaway River, & from the Top of the Mountain We saw a fine level Country SW as Far as our Eyes coud behold, and it was a very clear Day; We then went down the Mountain and set out S 20 W about 5 M, thro rich level Land covered with small Walnut Sugar Trees, Red-Buds, &c.

Tuesday March 19.—We set out S and crossed several Creeks all running to the SW, at about 12 M, came to the little Cuttaway River: We were obliged to go up it about 1 M to an Island, which was the shoalest Place We coud find to cross at, We then continued our Course in all about 30 M thro level rich Land except about 2 M which was broken and indifferent—This Level is about 35 M broad, and as We came up the Side of it along the Branches of the little Cuttaway We found it about 150 M long; and how far toward the SW We coud not tell, but imagined it held as far as the great Cuttaway River, which woud be upwards of 100 M more, and appeared much broader that Way than here, as I coud discern from the Tops of the Mountains

Wednesday 20.—We did not travel, I went up to the Top of a Mountain to view the Country, to the SE it looked very broken, and mountainous but to the Eastward and SW it appeared very level.

Thursday 21.—Set out S 45 E 15 M, S 5 M, here I found a Place where the Stones shined like high-coloured Brass, the Heat of the Sun drew out of them a Kind of Borax or Salt Petre only something sweeter; some of which I brought in to the Ohio Company, tho I believe it was Nothing but a Sort of Sulphur.

Friday 22.—SE 12 M, I killed a fat Bear, and was taken sick that Night.

Saturday 23.—I stayed here, and sweated after the Indian Fashion, which helped Me.

Sunday 24.—Set out E 2 M, NE 3 M, N 1 M, E 2 M, SE 5 M, E 2 M, N 2 M, SE 7 M to a small Creek, where We encamped in a Place where We had but poor Food for our Horses, & both We and They were very much wearied: the Reason of our making so many short Courses was, We were driven by a Branch of the little Cuttaway River (whose Banks were so exceeding steep that it was impossible to ford it) into a Ledge of rocky Laurel Mountains which were almost impassable.

Monday 25.—Set out SE 12 M, N 2 M, E 1 M, S 4 M, SE 2 M, We killed a Buck Elk here and took out his Tongue to carry with Us.

Tuesday 26.—Set out SE 10 M, SW 1 M, SE 1 M, SW 1 M SE 1 M, SW 1 M, SE 1 M SW 1 M SE 5 M killed 2 Buffaloes & took out their Tongues and encamped—These two Days We travelled thro Rocks and Mountains full of Laurel Thickets which We coud hardly creep thro without cutting our Way.

Wednesday 27.—Our Horses and Selves were so tired that We were obliged to stay this Day to rest, for We were unable to travel—On all the Branches of the little Cuttaway River was great Plenty of fine Coal some of which I brought in to the Ohio Company.

Thursday 28.—Set out SE 15 M crossing several Creeks of the little Cuttaway River, the Land still full of Coal and black Slate.

Friday 29.—The same Course SE about 12 M the Land still mountainous.

Saturday 30.—Stayed to rest our Horses, I went on Foot, and found a Passage thro the Mountains to another Creek, or a Fork of the same Creek that We were upon.

Sunday 31.—The same Course SE 15 M, killed a Buffaloe & encamped.

Monday April 1.—Set out the same Course about 20 M. Part of the Way We went along a Path up the Side of a little Creek, at the Head of which was a Gap in the Mountains, then our Path went down another Creek to a Lick where Blocks of Coal about 8 to 10 In : square lay upon the Surface of the Ground, here We killed a Bear and encamped.

Tuesday 2.—Set out S 2 M, SE 1 M, NE 3 M, killed a Buffaloe.

Wednesday 3.—S 1 M, SW 3 M, E 3 M, SE 2 M, to a small Creek on which was a large Warriors Camp, that woud contain 70 or 80 Warriors, their Captain's Name or Title was the Crane, as I knew by his Picture or Arms painted on a Tree.

Thursday 4.—We stayed here all Day to rest our Horses, and I platted down our Courses and I found I had still near 200 M Home upon a streight Line.

Friday April 5.—Rained, and We stayed at the Warrior's Camp.

Saturday 6.—We went along the Warrior's Road S 1 M, SE 3 M, S 2 M, SE 3 M, E 3 M, killed a Bear.

Sunday 7.—Set out E 2 M, NE 1 M, SE 1 M, S 1 M, W 1 M, SW 1 M, S 1 M, SE 2 M, S 1 M.

Monday 8.—S 1 M, SE 1 M, E 3 M, SE 1 M, E 3 M, NE 2 M, N 1 M, E 1 M, N 1 M, E 2 M and encamped upon a small Laurel Creek.

Tuesday 9 & Wednesday 10.—The Weather being somewhat bad We did not travel these two Days, the Country being still rocky mountainous, & full of Laurel Thickets, the worst traveling I ever saw.

Thursday 11.—We travelled several Courses near 20 M, but in the Afternoon as I coud see from the Top of the Mountain the Place We came from, I found We had not come upon a streight Line more than N 65 E 10 M.

Friday 12.—Set out thro very difficult Ways E 5 M, to a small Creek.

Saturday 13.—The same Course E upon a streight Line, tho the Way We were obliged to travel was near 20 M, here We killed two Bears, the Way still rocky and mountainous.

Sunday 14.—As Food was very scarce in these barren Mountains, We were obliged to move for fresh Feeding for our Horses, so We went on E 5 M, then N 20 W 6 M, to a Creek where We got something better Feeding for our Horses, in climbing up the Clifts and Rocks this Day two of our Horses fell down, and were pretty much hurt, and a Paroquete, which I had got from the Indians, on the other Side the Ohio (where there are a great many) died of a Bruise he got by a Fall; tho it was but a Trifle I was much concerned at losing Him, as he was perfectly tame, and had been very brisk all the Way, and I had still Corn enough left to feed Him—In the Afternoon I left the Horses, and went a little Way down the Creek, and found such a Precipice and such Laurel Thickets as We coud not pass, and the Horses were not able to go up the Mountain till they had rested a Day or two.

Monday 15.—We cut a Passage through the Laurels better than 2 M, as I was climbing up the Rocks, I got a Fall which hurted Me pretty much—This Afternoon as We wanted Provision I killed a Bear.

Tuesday 16.—Thunder and Rain in the Morning—We set out N 25 E 3 M.

Wednesday 17.—This Day I went to the Top of a Mountain to view the Way, and found it so bad that I did not care to engage it, but rather chose to go out of the Way and keep down along the Side of a Creek till I coud find a Branch or Run on the other Side to go up.

Thursday 18.—Set out down the said Creek Side N 3 M, then the Creek turning NW I was obliged to leave it, and go up a Ridge NE 1 M, E 2 M, SE 2 M, NE 1 M, to the Fork of a River.

Friday 19.—Set out down the said Run NE 2 M, E 2 M, SE 2 M, N 20 E 2 M, E 2 M, up a large Run.

Saturday 20.—Set out SE 10 M, E 4 M, over a small Creek —We had such bad traveling down this Creek, that We had like to have lost one of our Horses.

Sunday 21.—Stayed to rest our Horses.

Monday 22.—Rained all Day—We coud not travel.

Tuesday 23.—Set out E 8 M along a Ridge of Mountains then SE 5 M, E 3 M, SE 4 M, and encamped among very steep Mountains.

Wednesday 24.—SE 4 M thro steep Mountains and Thickets E 6 M.

Thursday 25.—E 5 M, SE 1 M, NE 2 M, SE 2 M, E 1 M, the? S 2 M, E 1 M killed a Bear.

Fi. \y 26.—Set out SE 2 M, here it rained so hard We were obliged to stop.

Saturday 27 Sunday 28 & Monday 29.—These three Days it continued raining & bad Weather, so that We coud not travel—All the Way from Salt Lick Creek to this Place, the Branches of the little Cuttaway River were so high that We coud not pass Them, which obliged Us to go over the Heads of them, thro a continued Ledge of almost inaccessible Mountains, Rocks and Laurel Thickets.

Tuesday 30.—Fair Weather set out E 3 M, SE 8 M, E 2 M, to a little River or Creek which falls into the big Conhaway, called blue Stone, where we encamped and had good Feeding for our Horses.

Wednesday May 1.—Set out N 75 E 10 M and killed a Buffaloe, then went up a very high Mountain, upon the Top of which was a Rock 60 or 70 Feet high, & a Cavity in the Middle, into which I went, and found there was a Passage thro it which gradually ascended to the Top, with several Holes in the Rock, which let in the Light, when I got to the Top of this Rock, I could see a prodigious Distance, and coud plainly discover where the big Conhaway River broke the next high Mountain, I then came down and continued my Course N 75 E 5 M farther and encamped.

Thursday 2 & Friday 3.—These two Days it rained and We stayed at our Camp to take Care of some Provision We had killed.

Saturday 4.—This Day our Horses run away, and it was late before We got Them, so We coud not travel far, We went N 75 E 4 M.

Sunday May 5.—Rained all Day.

Monday 6.—Set out thro very bad Ways E 3 M, NE 6 M, over a bad Laurel Creek E 4 M.

Tuesday 7.—Set out E 10 M, to the big Conhaway or new River and got over half of it to a large Island where We lodged that Night.

Wednesday 8.—We made a Raft of Logs and crossed the other half of the River & went up it S about 2 M—The Conhaway or new River (by some called Wood's River) where I crossed it (which was about 8 M above the Mouth of blue Stone River) is better than 200 Yards wide, and pretty deep, but full of Rocks and Falls—The Bottoms upon it and blue Stone River are very rich but narrow, the high Land broken.

Thursday 9.—Set out E 13 M to a large Indian Warrior's Camp, where We killed a Bear and stayed all Night.

Friday 10.—Set out E 4 M, SE 3 M, S 3 M, thro Mountains cover'd with Ivy and Laurel Thickets.

Saturday 11.—Set out S 2 M, SE 5 M, to a Creek and a Meadow where We let our Horses feed, then SE 2 M, S 1 M, SE 2 M to a very high Mountain up on the Top of which was a Lake or Pond about ¾ of a Mile long NE & SW, & ¼ of a Mile wide the Water fresh and clear, and a clean gravelly Shore about 10 Yards wide with a fine Meadow and six fine Springs in it, then S about 4 M, to a Branch of the Conhaway called Sinking Creek.

Sunday 12.—Stayed to rest our Horses and dry some Meat We had killed.

Monday 13.—Set out SE 2 M, E 1 M, SE 3 M, S 12 M to one Rich[d] Halls in Augusta County this Man is one of the farthest Settlers to the Westward upon the New River.

Tuesday 14.—Stayed at Rich[d] Hall's and wrote to the President of Virginia & the Ohio Company to let them know I shoud be with Them by the 15th of June.

Wednesday 15.—Set out from Rich[d] Hall's S 16 M.

Thursday 16.—The same Course S 22 M and encamped at Beaver Island Creek (a Branch of the Conhaway) opposite to the Head of Roanoke.

Friday 17.—Set out SW 3 M, then S 9 M, to the dividing Line between Carolina and Virginia, where I stayed all Night, the Land from Rich Hall's to this Place is broken.

Saturday 18.—Set out S 20 M to my own House on the

Yadkin River, when I came there I found all my Family gone, for the Indians had killed five People in the Winter near that Place, which frightened my Wife and Family away to Roanoke about 35 M nearer in among the Inhabitants, which I was informed of by an old Man I met near the Place.

Sunday 19.—Set out for Roanoke, and as We had now a Path, We got there the same Night where I found all my Family well.

CHRISTOPHER GIST.

INSTRUCTIONS GIVEN TO Mr CHRISTOPHER GIST BY THE COMMITTEE OF THE OHIO COMPANY JULY 16th 1751.

After You have returned from Williamsburg and have executed the Commission of the President & Council, if they shall think proper to give You One, otherwise as soon as You can conveniently You are to apply to Col° Cresap for such of the Company's Horses, as You shall want for the Use of yourself and such other Person or Persons You shall think necessary to carry with You; and You are to look out & observe the nearest & most convenient Road You can find from the Company's Store at Wills's Creek to a Landing at Mohongeyela; from thence You are to proceed down the Ohio on the South Side thereof, as low as the Big Conhaway, and up the same as far as You judge proper, and find good Land—You are all the Way to keep an exact Diary & Journal & therein note every Parcel of good Land, with the Quantity as near as You can by any Means compute the same, with the Breadth, Depth, Course and Length of the several Branches falling into the Ohio, & the different Branches any of Them are forked into, laying the same as exactly down in a Plan thereof as You can; observing also the Produce, the several Kinds of Timber and Trees, observing where there is Plenty and where the Timber is scarce; and You are not to omit proper Observations on the mountainous, barren, or broken Land, that We may on your Return judge what Quantity of good Land is contained within the Compass of your Journey, for We woud not have You omit taking Notice of any Quantity of good Land, tho not exceeding 4 or 500 Acres provided the same lies upon the River Ohio & may be convenient for our building Store Houses & other Houses for the better carrying on a Trade and Correspondence down that River.

1751.—Pursuant to my Instructions hereunto annexed from the Committee of the Ohio Company bearing Date 16th July 1751

Monday Nov' 4.—Set out from the Company's Store House in Frederick County Virginia opposite the Mouth of Wills's Creek and crossing Potomack River went W 4 M to a Gap in the Allegany Mountains upon the S W Fork of the said Creek—This Gap is the nearest to Potomack River of any in the Allegany Mountains, and is accounted one of the best, tho the Mountain is very high, The Ascent is no where very steep but rises gradually near 6 M, it is now very full of old Trees & Stones, but with some Pains might be made a good Waggon Road; this Gap is directly in the Way to Mohongaly, & several Miles nearer than that the Traders commonly pass thro, and a much better Way.

Tuesday 5.—Set out N 80 W 8 M, it rained and obliged Us to stop.

Wednesday 6.—The same Course 3 M hard Rain.

Thursday 7.—Rained hard and We coud not travel.

Friday 8.—Set out the same Courses N 80 W 3 M, here We encamped, and turned to see where the Branches lead to & found they descended into the middle Fork of Yaughaughgaine—We hunted all the Ground for 10 M, or more and killed several Deer, & Bears, and one large Elk—The Bottoms upon the Branches are but narrow with some Indian Fields about 2000 Acres of good high Land about a Mile from the largest Branch.

From Saturday 9 to Tuesday 19.—We were employed in searching the Lands and discovering the Branches Creeks &c.

Wednesday 20.—Set out N 45 W 5 M killed a Deer.

Thursday 21.—The same Course 5 M the greatest Part of this Day We were cutting our Way thro' a Laurel Thicket and lodged by the Side of one at Night.

Friday 22.—Set out the same Course N 45 W 2 M and cut our Way thro a great Laurel Thicket to the middle Fork of Yaughyaughgaine then S down the said Fork (crossing a Run) 1 M, then S 45 W 2 M over the said Fork where We encamped.

Saturday 23.—Rested our Horses and examined the Land on Foot, which We found to be tolerable rich & well timbered but stony and broken.

Sunday 24.—Set out W 2 M then S 45 W 6 M over the S Fork and encamp'd on the SW Side about 1 M from a small Hunting Town of the Delawares from whom I bought some Corn—I invited these Indians to the Treaty at the Loggs Town, the full Moon in May, as Col° Patton had desired Me; they treated Me very civilly, but after I went from that Place my Man informed Me that they threatened to take away our Guns and not let Us travel.

Monday 25.—Set out W 6 M, then S 45 W 2 M to a Laurel Creek, where We encamped & killed some Deer.

From Tuesday 26 to Thursday 28.—We were examining the Lands which We found to be rocky and mountainous.

Friday 29.—Set out W 3 M then N 65 W 3 M, N 45 W 2 M.

From Saturday 30 to Friday Dec. 6.—We searched the Land several Miles round and found it about 15 M from the Foot of the Mountains to the River Mohongaly the first 5 M of which E & W is good level farming Land, with fine Meadows, the Timber white Oak and Hiccory—the same Body of Land holds 10 M, S, to the upper Forks of Mohongaly, and about 10 M, N, towards the Mouth of Yaughyaughgaine—The Land nearer the River for about 8 or 9 M wide, and the same Length is much richer & better timbered, with Walnut, Locust, Poplars and Sugar-Trees, but is in some Places very hilly, the Bottoms upon the River 1 M, and in some Places near 2 M wide.

Saturday 7.—Set out W 6 M and went to an Indian Camp and invited them to the Treaty at the Loggs Town at the full Moon in May next; at this Camp there was a Trader named Charles Poke who spoke the Indian Tongue well, the Indian to whom this Camp belonged after much Discourse with Me, complained & said " my Friend You was sent to Us last Year
" from the Great Men in Virginia to inform Us of a Present
" from the Great King over the Water, and if You can bring
" News from the King to Us, why cant You tell Him some-
" thing from Me? The Proprietor of Pensylvania granted
" my Father a Tract of Land begining eight Miles below
" the Forks of Brandy Wine Creek and binding on the said
" Creek to the Fork and including the West Fork & all its
" Waters on both Sides to the Head Fountain—The White
" People now live on these Lands, and will neither let Me
" have Them, nor pay Me any Thing for Them—My Father's
" Name was Chickoconnecon, I am his eldest Son, and my
" Name is Nemicotton—I desire that You will let the Gov-
" ernor and Great Men in Virginia know this—It may be
" they will tell the great King of it, and he will make Mr Pen
" or his People give Me the Land or pay Me for it—This
" Trader here Charles Poke knows the Truth of what I say,
" that the Land was granted to my Father, & that He or I
" never sold it, to which Charles Poke answered that Chicko-
" connecon had such a grant of Land, & that the People who
" lived on it coud get no Titles to it, for that it was now
" called Mannor Lands—This I was obliged to insert in my
" Journal to please the Indian.

Sunday Dec' 8.—Stayed at the Indian Camp.

Monday 9.—Set out S 45 W 1 M, W 6 M to the River Mohongaly—at this Place is a large Cavity in a Rock about 30 Feet long & 20 Feet wide & about 7 Feet high and an even Floor—The Entrance into it is so large and open that it lets in Plenty of Light, and close by it is a Stream of fine Water.

From Tuesday 10 to Friday 13.—We were examining the Lands which for 9 or 10 M, E is rich but hilly as before described, on the E Side the River for several Miles there are fine Bottoms a Mile wide and the Hills above them are extraordinary rich and well timbered.

Saturday 14.—We had Snow.

Sunday 15.—Crossed the River Mohongaly which in this Place is 53 Poles wide, the Bottoms upon the W Side are not above 100 Yards broad, but the Hills are very rich both up and down the River, and full of Sugar Trees.

Monday 16.—Spent in searching the Land.

Tuesday 17.—Set out W 5 M the Land upon this Course hilly but very rich for about a Mile and a half, then it was level with good Meadows but not very rich for about a Mile & a half more, & the last 2 M next to Licking Creek was very good Land; upon this Creek We lodged at a hunting Camp of an Indian Captain named Oppaymolleah, here I saw an Indian named Joshua who spoke very good English; he had been acquainted with Me several Years, and seemed very glad to see Me, and wondered much where I was going so far in those Woods; I said I was going to invite all the great Men of the Indians to a Treaty to be held at Loggs Town, the full Moon in May next, where a Parcel of Goods, a Present from the King of Great Britain, would be delivered Them by proper Commissioners, and that these were the Goods which I informed them of last Year, by Order of the President of

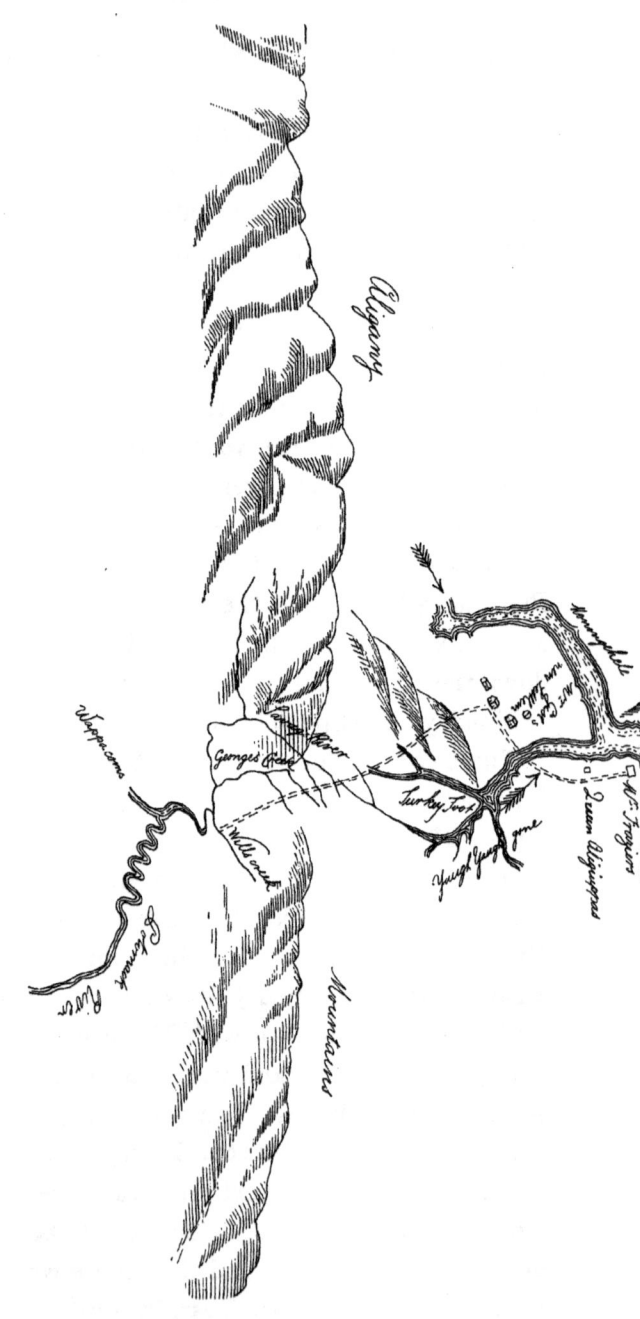

WEST PENNSYLVANIA AND VIRGINIA, 1753.

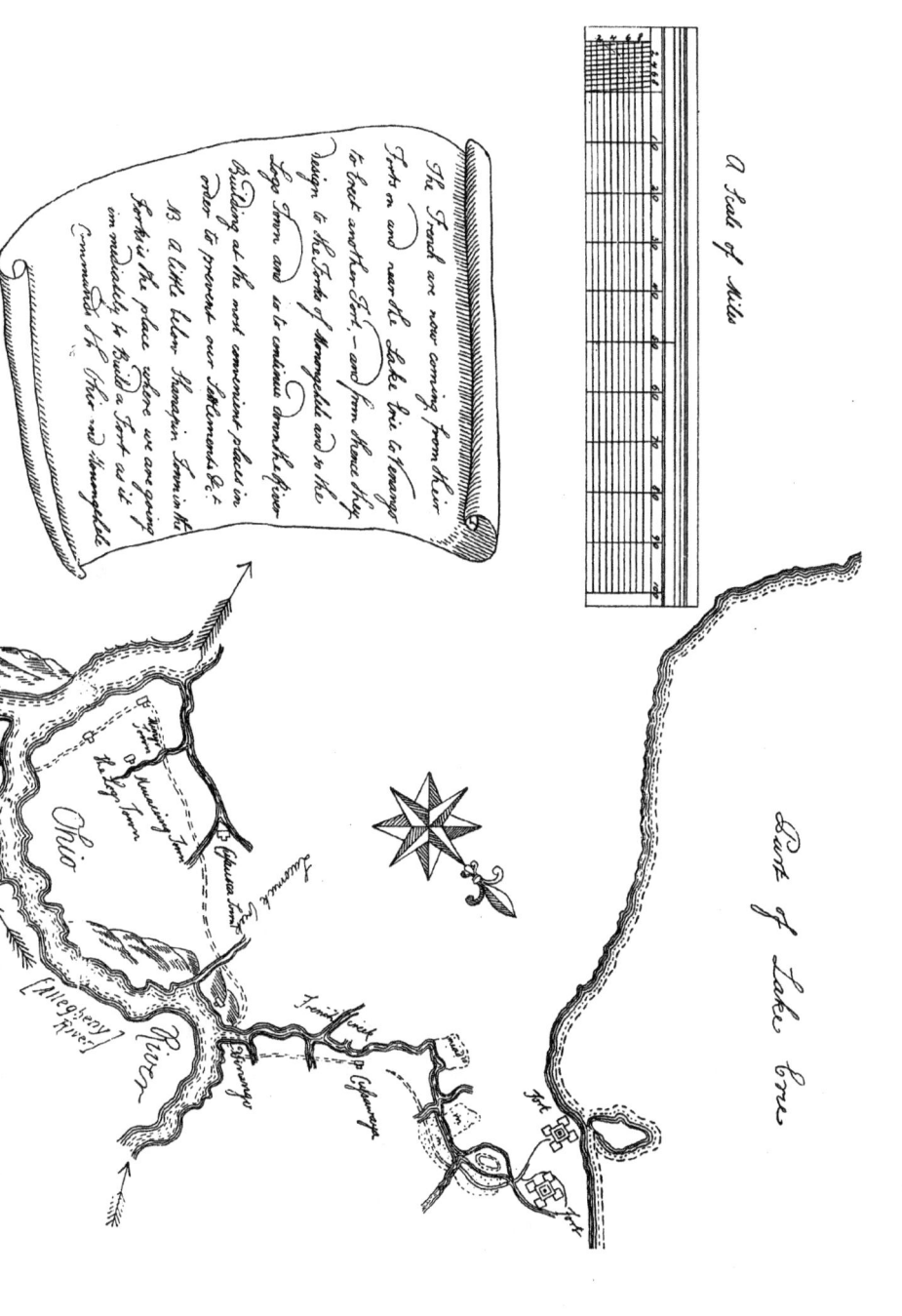

Virginia, Col° Lee, who was since dead, Joshua informed Them what I said, and they told Me, I ought to let the Beaver know this, so I wrote a Line to him by Joshua, who promised to deliver it safe, and said there was a Trader's Man who coud read it for him—This Beaver is the Sachemore or Chief of the Delawares. It is customary among the Indian Chiefs to take upon Them the Name of any Beast or Bird they ancy, the Picture of which they always sign instead of their Name or Arms.

Wednesday 18.—Stayed at the Camp.

Thursday 19,—Set out W 3 M, S 45 W 2 M, W 1 M to a Branch of Licking Creek.

Friday 20.—Set out W 1 M, S 45 W 6 M and encamped.

From Saturday 21 to Tuesday, Jan⁷ 7.—We stayed at this Place, We had a good Deal of Snow & bad Weather—My Son had the Misfortune to have his Feet frost-bitten, which kept Us much longer here than We intended however We kill'd Plenty of Deer Turkeys &c and fared very well—The Land hereabouts very good but to the W and SW it is hilly.

1752

Wednesday Jan⁷ 8—My Son's Feet being somewhat better, We set out S 30 W 5 M, S 45 W 3 M, the Land middling good but hilly—I found my Son's Feet too tender to travel, and we were obliged to stop again.

From Thursday 9 to Sunday 19.—We stayed at this Place —While We were here We killed Plenty of Bear Deer & Elk, so that We lived very well.

Monday 20.—We set out W 5 M—here we were stopped by Snow.

Tuesday 21.—Stayed all the Day in the Camp.

Wednesday 22.—Set out S 45 W 12 M, where we scared a Panther from under a Rock where there was Room enough for Us, in it We encamped & had good Shelter.

From Thursday 23 to Sunday 26.—We stayed at this Place & had Snow and bad Weather.

Monday 27.—Set out S 45 W 6 M, here We had Snow & encamped.

From Tuesday 28 to Friday 31.—Stayed at this Place, the Land upon these last Courses is rich but hilly and in some Places Stony.

Saturday Feb 1.—Set out S 45 W 3 M, S 45 E 1 M, S 2 M, S 45 W 1 M, crossed a Creek on which the Land was very hilly and rocky yet here and there good Spots on the Hills.

Sunday 2.—S 45 W 3 M, here We were stopped by Snow.

From Monday 3 till Sunday 9.—We stayed at this Place and had a good Deal of Snow & bad Weather.

Monday 10.—Set out S 45 W 8 M—The Snow hard upon the Top & bad traveling

Tuesday 11.—The same Course S 45 W 2 M, then W 1 M, S 45 W 4 M.

Wednesday 12.—Killed two Buffaloes and searched the Land to the NW which I found to be rich & well timbered with lofty Walnuts, Ash, Sugar Trees &c but hilly in most Places.

Thursday 13.—Set out W 1 M, S 45 W 2 M, W 2 M, S 45 W 2 M, W 2 M—In this Day's Journey We found a Place where a Piece of Land about 100 Yards square & about 10 Feet deep from the Surface had slipped down a steep Hill, somewhat more than it's own Breadth, with most of the Trees standing on it upright as they were at first, and a good many Rocks which appeared to be in the same Position as they were before the Ground slipt: It had bent down and crushed the Trees as it came along, which might plainly be seen by the Ground on the upper Side of it, over which it had passed—It seemed to have been done but two or three Years ago—In the Place from whence it removed was a large Quarry of Rocks, in the Sides of which were Veins of several Colours, particularly one of a deep yellow, about 3 Feet from the Bottom, in which were other small Veins some white, some a greenish Kind of Copperas: A Sample of which I brought in to the Ohio Company in a small Leather Bag N° 1—Not very far from this Place We found another large Piece of Earth, which had slipped down in the same Manner—Not far from here We encamped in the Fork of a Creek.

Friday 14.—We stayed at this Place—On the NW Side of the Creek on a rising ground by a small Spring We found a large Stone about 3 Feet Square on the Top, and about 6 or 7 Feet high; it was all covered with green Moss except on the SE Side which was smooth and white as if plaistered with Lime. On this Side I cut with a cold Chizzel in large Letters,

THE OHIO COMPANY
FEB^y 1751
BY CHRISTOPHER GIST

Saturday 15.—Set out S 45 W 5 M, rich Land but hilly, very rich Bottoms up the Creek but not above 200 Yards wide.

Sunday 16.—S 45 W 5 M thro rich Land, the Bottoms about ¼ of a Mile wide upon the Creek.

Monday 17.—The same Course S 45 W 3 M, W 3 M, S 45 W 3 M, S 20 W 3 M, S 8 M, S 45 W 2 M over a Creek upon which was fine Land, the Bottoms about a Mile wide.

Tuesday Feby 18.—S 10 M over the Fork of a Creek S 45 W 4 M to the Top of a high Ridge, from whence We coud see over the Conhaway River—Here We encamped, the Land mixed with Pine and not very good.

Wednesday 19.—Set out S 15 M, S 45 W 6 M to the Mouth

of a little Creek, upon which the Land is very rich, and the Bottoms a Mile wide—The Conhaway being very high overflowed some Part of the Bottoms.

Thursday 20.—Set out N 45 W 2 M across a Creek over a Hill, then S 80 W 10 M to a large Run, all fine Land upon this Course—(We were now about 2 M from the River Conhaway)—Then continued our Course S 80 W 10 M, the first 5 M good high Land; tolerably level the last 5 thro the River Bottoms, which were a Mile wide and very rich, to a Creek or large Run which We crossed, & continued our Course S 80 W 2 M farther & encamped.

Friday 21.—The same Course S 80 W still continued 8 M further; then S 2 M to the Side of the River Conhaway, then down the said River N 45 W 1 M to a Creek where We encamped—The Bottoms upon the River here are a Mile wide, the Land very rich—The River at this Place is 79 Poles broad.

Saturday 22.—Set out N 45 W 4 M, W 7 M, to a high Hill from whence We coud see the River Ohio, then N 45 W 12 M to the River Ohio at the Mouth of a small Run where We encamped. The Bottoms upon the River here are a Mile wide & very good, but the high Land broken.

Sunday 23.—Set out S 45 E 14 M over Letort's Creek—The Land upon this Creek is poor, broken, & full of Pines—Then the same Course S 45 E 10 M and encamped on the River Side upon fine rich Land the Bottoms about a Mile wide.

Monday 24.—Set out E 12 M up the River all fine Land the Bottoms about 1½ Miles wide, full of lofty Timber: then N 5 M crossing Smith's Creek. The Land here is level & good, but the Bottoms upon the River are not above ½ a Mile wide—then N 45 E 8 M to a Creek called Beyansoss where We encamped.

Tuesday 25.—We searched the Land upon this Creek which We found very good for 12 or 13 M up it from the River—The Bottoms upon it are about ½ a Mile wide, & the Bottoms upon the River at the Mouth of it a Mile wide, and very well timbered.

Wednesday 26.—Set out N 45 E 13 M to the River Ohio at the Mouth of a Creek called Lawwellaconin ; then S 55 E 5 M up the said Creek—The Bottoms upon this Creek are a Mile wide & the high Land very good & not much broken, & very well timbered

Thursday 27 Friday 28 & Saturday 29.—Rained and we coud not travel—Killed four Buffaloes.

Sunday March 1 and Monday 2.—Set out N 30 E 10 M to a little Branch full of Coal then N 30 E 16 M to Nawmissipia or Fishing Creek—My Son hunted up this Creek (where I had cut the Letters upon the Stone) which he said was not above 6 M in a streight Line from this Place—The Bottoms upon this Creek are but narrow, the high Land hilly, but very rich and well timbered.

Tuesday 3.—Set out N 30 E 18 M to Molchuconickon or Buffaloe Creek.

Wednesday 4.—We hunted up and down this Creek to examine the Land—The Bottoms are ¾ of a Mile wide & very rich, a great many cleared Fields covered with white Clover, the high Land rich, but in general, hilly.

Thursday 5.—Set out N 30 E 9 M to a Creek called Neemokeesy where We killed a black Fox & two Bears—Upon this Creek We found a Cave under a Rock about 150 Feet long & 55 feet wide ; one Side of it open facing the Creek, the Floor dry—We found it had been much used by Buffaloes & Elks who came there to lick a kind of saltish Clay which I found in the Cave, and of which I took a sample in a Leather Bag N . 2.

Friday March 6.—We stayed at the Cave—Not very far from it We saw a Herd of Elks near 30 one of which my Son killed.

Saturday 7.—Set out N 30 E 7 M to the Ohio River—The Bottoms here were very rich and near 2 M wide; but a little higher up, the Hill seemed very steep, so that We were obliged to leave the River & went E 6 M on very high Land; then N 9 M thro' very good high Land tolerable level to a Creek called Wealin or Scalp Creek where We encamped.

Sunday 8.—We went out to search the Land which We found very good for near 15 M up this Creek from the Mouth of it, the Bottoms above a Mile wide & some Meadows—We found an old Indian Road up this Creek.

Monday 9.—Set out N 45 E 18 M to a Creek—The same Course 3 M to another Creek where We encamped—These Creeks the Traders distinguish by the Name of the two Creeks.

Tuesday 10.—We hunted up and down these Creeks to examine the Land from the Mouths of Them, to the place where We had crossed near the Heads of Them; in our Way to the Conhaway—They run near parallel at about 3 or 4 M Distance, for upwards of 30 M—The Land between Them all the Way is rich & level, chiefly Low Grounds & finely timbered with Walnuts, Locusts, Cherry Trees, & Sugar Trees

Wednesday 11.—Set out E 18 M crossing three Creeks all good Land but hilly then S 16 M to our old Camp, where my Son had been frost-bitten. After We had got to this Place in our old Tract, I did not keep any exact Account of Course and Distance, as I thought the Rivers & Creeks sufficiently described by my Courses as I came down.

Thursday 12.—I set out for Mohongaly crossed it upon a Raft of Logs from whence I made the best of my Way to Potomack—I did not keep exactly my old Tract but went more to the Eastward & found a much nearer Way Home: and am of Opinion the Company may have a tolerable good Road from Wills Creek to the upper Fork of Monhongaly, from whence the River is navigable all the Way to the Ohio for large flat bottomed Boats—The Road will be a little to the Southward of West, and the Distance to the Fork of Mohongaly about 70 M—While I was at Mohongaly in my Return Home an Indian, who spoke good English, came to Me & said—That their great Men the Beaver and Captain Oppamylucah (these are two Chiefs of the Delawares) desired to know where the Indian's Land lay, for that the French claimed all the Land on one side the River Ohio & the English on the other Side; and that Oppamylucah asked Me the same Question when I was at his Camp in my Way down, to which I had made him no Answer—I very well remembered that Oppamylucah had asked me such a Question, and that I was at a Loss to answer Him as I now also was: But after some Consideration "my Friend" said I, "We are all one King's People and the different "Colour of our Skins makes no Difference in the King's "Subjects; You are his People as well as We, if you will "take Land & pay the King's Rights You will have the same "Privileges as the White People have, and to hunt You have "Liberty every where so that You dont kill the White Peoples "Cattle & Hogs—To this the Indian said, that I must stay at that Place two Days and then he woud come & see Me again, He then went away, and at the two Days End returned as he promised, and looking very pleasant said He woud stay with Me all Night, after He had been with Me some Time He said that the great Men bid Him tell Me I was very safe that I might come and live upon that River where I pleased—that I had answered Them very true for We were all one King's People sure enough & for his Part he woud come to see Me at Wills's Creek in a Month.

COMMITTEE OF THE OHIO COMPANY.

March — From Thursday 12 to Saturday 28. — We were traveling from Mohongaly to Potomack for as We had a good many Skins to carry & the Weather was bad We traveled but slow

Sunday 29. — We arrived at the Company's Factory at Wills's Creek.

CHRISTOPHER GIST.

THIS Day came before Me Christopher Gist & made Oath on the holy Evangelists that the two Journals hereunto annexed, both which are signed by the said Christopher Gist; the first containing an Account of his Travels and Discoveries down the River Ohio & the Branches thereof, for the Ohio Company in the Years 1750 & 1751 together with his Transactions with the Indians and his Return Home. And the other containing an Account of his Travels and Discoveries down the said River Ohio on the SE Side as low as the Big Conhaway made for the s^d Ohio Company in the Years 1751 & 1752 & his return to Wills's Creek on Potomack River (as in a Platt made thereof by the said Christopher Gist and given in to the said Ohio Company may more fully appear) are just & true except as to the Number of Miles, which the said Christopher Gist did not actually measure and therefore cannot be certain of Them, but computed Them in the most exact Manner he coud & according to the best of his Knowledge. Given under my Hand this   Day of   175

1753.

Wednesday 14 November, 1753.—Then Major George Washington came to my house at Will's Creek, and delivered me a letter from the council in Virginia, requesting me to attend him up to the commandant of the French fort on the Ohio River.

Thursday 15.—We set out, and at night encamped at George's Creek, about eight miles, where a messenger came with letters from my son, who was just returned from his people at the Cherokees, and lay sick at the mouth of Conegocheague. But as I found myself entered again on public business, and Major Washington and all the company unwilling I should return I wrote and sent medicines to my son, and so continued my journey, and encamped at a big hill in the forks of Youghiogany, about eighteen miles.

Friday 16.—The next day set out and got to the big fork of said river, about ten miles there.

Saturday 17.—We encamped and rested our horses, and then we set out early in the morning.

Sunday 18.—And at night got to my house in the new settlement, about twenty-one miles; snow about ancle deep.

Monday 19.—Set out, cross Big Youghiogany, to Jacob's cabins, about twenty miles. Here some of our horses straggled away, and we did not get away until eleven o'clock.

Tuesday 20.—Set out, had rain in the afternoon; I killed a deer; travelled about seven miles.

Wednesday 21.—It continued to rain. Stayed all day.

Thursday 22.—We set out and came to the mouth of Turtle Creek, about twelve miles, to John Frazier's; and he was very kind to us, and lent us a canoe to carry our baggage to the forks, about ten miles.

Friday 23.—Set out, rid to Shannopin's town, and down

Allegheny to the mouth of Monongahela, where we met our baggage, and swimmed our horses over Allegheny, and there encamped that night.

Saturday 24.—Set out; we went to king Shingiss, and he and Lawmolach went with us to the Logstown, and we spoke to the chiefs this evening, and repaired to our camp.

Sunday 25.—They sent out for their people to come in. The Half-King came in this afternoon.

Monday 26.—We delivered our message to the Half-King and they promised by him that we should set out three nights after.

Tuesday 27.—Stayed in our camp. Monacatoocha and Pollatha Wappia gave us some provisions. We stayed until the 29th when the Indians said, they were not ready. They desired us to stay until the next day and as the warriors were not come, the Half-King said he would go with us himself, and take care of us.

Friday 30.—We set out, and the Half-King and two old men and one young warrior, with us. At night we encamped at the Murthering town, about fifteen miles, on a branch of Great Beaver Creek. Got some corn and dried meat.

Saturday 1 December.—Set out, and at night encamped at the crossing of Beaver creek from the Kaskuskies to Venango about thirty miles. The next day rain; our Indians went out a hunting; they killed two bucks. Had rain all day.

Monday 3.—We set out and travelled all day. Encamped at night on one of the head branches of Great Beaver creek about twenty-two miles.

Tuesday 5.—Set out about fifteen miles, to the town of Venango, where we were kindly and complaisantly received by Monsieur Joncaire, the French interpreter for the Six Nations.

Wednesday 5.—Rain all day. Our Indians were in council with the Delawares, who lived under the French colors, and ordered them to deliver up to the French the belt, with the marks of the four towns, according to desire of King Shingiss. But the chief of these Delawares said, "It was true King Shingiss was a great man, but he had sent no speech, and," said he, "I cannot pretend to make a speech for a King." So our Indians could not prevail with them to deliver their belt; but the Half-King did deliver his belt, as he had determined. Joncaire did every thing he could to prevail on our Indians to stay behind us, and I took all care to have them along with us.

Thursday 6.—We set out late in the day accompanied by the French General and four servants or soldiers, and

Friday 7.—All encamped at Sugar creek, five miles from Venango. The creek being very high we were obliged to carry all our baggage over on trees, and swim our horses The Major and I went first over, with our boots on.

Saturday 9.—We set out and travelled twenty-five miles to Cussewago, an old Indian town.

Sunday 9.—We set out, left one of our horses here that could travel no further. This day we travelled to the big crossing, about fifteen miles, and encamped, our Indians went out to look out logs to make a raft; but as the water was high, and there were other creeks to cross, we concluded to keep up this side the creek.

Monday 10.—Set out, travelled about eight miles, and encamped. Our Indians killed a bear. Here we had a creek to cross, very deep; we got over on a tree, and got our goods over.

Tuesday 11.—We set out, travelled about fifteen miles to the French fort, the sun being set. Our interpreter gave the commandant notice of our being over the creek; upon which he sent several officers to conduct us to the fort, and they received us with a great deal of complaisance.

Wednesday 12.—The Major gave the passport, showed his commission, and offered the Governor's letter to the commandant; but he desired not to receive them, until the other commander from Lake Erie came, whom he had sent for, and expected next day by twelve o'clock.

Thursday 13.—The other General came. The Major delivered the letter, and desired a speedy answer; the time of year and business required it. They took our Indians into private council, and gave them several presents.

Friday 14.—When we had done our business, they delayed and kept our Indians, until Sunday; and then we set out with two canoes, one for our Indians, and the other for ourselves. Our horses we had sent away some days before, to wait at Venango, if ice appeared on the rivers and creeks.

Sunday 16.—We set out by water about sixteen miles, and encamped. Our Indians went before us, passed the little lake, and we did not come up with them that night.

Monday 17.—We set out, came to our Indians' camp. They were out hunting; they killed three bears. We stayed this day, and

Tuesday 18.—One of our Indians did not come to camp. So we finding the waters lower very fast, were obliged to go and leave our Indians.

Wednesday 19.—We set out about seven or eight miles, and encamped, and the next day

Thursday 20.—About twenty miles, where we were stopped by ice, and worked until night.

Friday 21.—The ice was so hard we could not break our way through, but were obliged to haul our vessels across a point of land and put them in the creek again. The Indians and three French canoes overtook us here, and the people of one French canoe that was lost, with her cargo of powder and lead. This night we encamped about twenty miles above Venango.

Saturday 22.—Set out. The creek began to be very low and we were forced to get out, to keep our canoe from oversetting, several times; the water freezing to our clothes; and we had the pleasure of seeing the French overset, and the brandy and wine floating in the creek, and run by them, and left them to shift for themselves. Came to Venango, and met with our people and horses.

Sunday 23.—We set out from Venango, travelled about five miles to Lacomick creek.

Monday 24.—Here Major Washington set out on foot in Indian dress. Our horses grew weak, that we were mostly obliged to travel on foot, and had snow all day. Encamped near the barrens.

Tuesday 25.—Set out and travelled on foot to branches of Great Beaver creek.

Wednesday 26.—The Major desired me to set out on foot, and leave our company, as the creeks were frozen, and our horses could make but little way. Indeed, I was unwilling he should undertake such a travel, who had never been used to walking before this time. But as he insisted on it, I set out with our packs, like Indians, and travelled eighteen miles. That night we lodged at an Indian cabin, and the Major was much fatigued. It was very cold; all the small runs were frozen, that we could hardly get water to drink.

Thursday 27.—We rose early in the morning, and set out about two o'clock. Got to the Murthering town, on the southeast fork of Beaver creek. Here we met with an Indian, whom I thought I had seen at Joncaire's, at Venango, when on our journey up to the French fort. This fellow called me by my Indian name, and pretended to be glad to see me. He asked us several questions, as how we came to travel on foot, when we left Venango, where we parted with our horses, and when they would be there, etc. Major Washington insisted on travelling on the nearest way to forks of Alleghany. We asked the Indian if he could go with us, and show us the nearest way. The Indian seemed very glad and ready to go with us. Upon which we set out, and the Indian took the Major's pack. We travelled very brisk for eight or ten miles, when the Major's feet grew very sore, and he very weary, and the Indian steered too much north-eastwardly. The Major desired to encamp, to which the Indian asked to carry his gun. But he refused that, and then the Indian grew churlish, and pressed us to keep on, telling us that there were Ottawa Indians in these woods, and they would scalp us if we lay out; but to go to his cabin, and we should be safe. I thought very ill of the fellow, but did not care to let the Major know I mistrusted him. But he soon mistrusted him as much as I. He said he could hear a gun to his cabin, and steered us more northwardly. We grew uneasy, and then he said two whoops might be heard to his cabin. We went two miles further; then the Major said he would stay at the next water, and we desired the Indian to stop at the next water. But before we came to water, we came to a clear meadow; it was very light, and snow on the ground. The Indian made a stop, turned about; the Major saw him point his gun toward us and fire. Said the Major, "Are you shot?" "No," said I. Upon which the Indian ran forward to a big standing white oak, and to loading his gun; but we were soon with him. I would have killed him; but the Major would not suffer me to kill him. We let him charge his gun; we found he put in a ball; then we took care of him. The Major or I always stood by the guns; we made him make a fire for us by a little run, as if we intended to sleep there. I said to the Major, "As you will not have him killed, we must get him away, and then we must travel all night." Upon which I said to the Indian, " I suppose you were lost, and fired your gun." He said, he knew the way to his cabin, and 'twas but a little way. "Well," said I, "do you go home; and as we are much tired, we will follow your track in the morning; and here is a cake of bread for you, and you must give us meat in the morning." He was glad to get away. I followed him, and listened until he was fairly out of the way, and then we set out about half a mile, when we made a fire, set our compass, and fixed our course, and travelled all night, and in the morning we were on the head of Piney creek.

Friday 28.—We travelled all the next day down the said creek, and just at night found some tracks where Indians had been hunting. We parted, and appointed a place a distance off, where to meet, it being then dark. We encamped, and thought ourselves safe enough to sleep.

Saturday 29.—We set out early, got to Alleghany, made a raft, and with much difficulty got over to an island, a little above Shannopin's town. The Major having fallen in from off the raft, and my fingers frost-bitten, and the sun down, and very cold, we contented ourselves to encamp upon that island. It was deep water between us and the shore; but the cold did us some service, for in the morning it was frozen hard enough for us to pass over on the ice.

Sunday 30.—We set out about ten miles to John Frazier's, at Turtle creek, and rested that evening.

Monday 31.—Next day we waited on queen Aliquippa, who lives now at the mouth of Youghiogany. She said she would never go down to the river Alleghany to live, except the English built a fort, and then she would go and live there.

Tuesday January 1, 1754.—We set out from John Frazier's and at night encamped at Jacob's cabins.

Wednesday 2.—Set out and crossed Youghiogany on the ice. Got to my house in the new settlement.

Thursday 3.—Rain.

Friday 4.—Set out for Will's creek, where we arrived on Sunday January 6.

CHRISTOPHER GIST.

CHRISTOPHER GIST was of English descent. His grandfather was Christopher Gist, who died in Baltimore County in 1691. His grandmother was Edith Cromwell. They had one child, Richard, who was Surveyor of the Western Shore and was one of the Commissioners for laying off the town of Baltimore. In 1705 he married Zipporah Murray, and Christopher was one of three sons. He was a resident of North Carolina when first employed by the Ohio Company. He married Sarah Howard. He had three sons, Nathaniel, Richard and Thomas, and two daughters, Anne and Violette. Nathaniel was the only son that married. With his sons, Nathaniel and Thomas, he was with Braddock on his fatal field of battle. Urged by bribes and the promise of rewards, two Indians were persuaded to go out on a scouting expedition. As soon as they were gone, Christopher Gist, the General's guide, was dispatched on the same errand. On the 6th both Indians and Gist rejoined the army, having been within half a mile of the fort. Their reports were favorable and the army advanced. After Braddock's defeat he raised a company of scouts in Virginia and Maryland and did service on the frontier, being then called Captain Gist.

In 1756 he went to the Carolinas to enlist Cherokee Indians for the English service. For a time he served as Indian Agent. He died in the summer of 1759, of smallpox, in South Carolina or Georgia. Richard Gist was killed in the battle of King's Mountain. Thomas lived on the plantation.

Anne lived with him until his death, when she joined her brother Nathaniel in Kentucky. Nathaniel was a Colonel in the Virginia Line, during the Revolutionary War, and afterwards removed to Kentucky, where he died early in the present century. He left two sons, Henry Clay and Thomas Cecil. His eldest daughter, Sarah, married the Hon. Jesse Bledsoe, United States Senator from Kentucky. His grandson, B. Gratz Brown, was the Democratic candidate for Vice-President in 1872. The second daughter of Colonel Gist married Colonel Nathaniel Hart, a brother of Mrs. Henry Clay. The third daughter married Dr. Boswell, of Lexington, Kentucky. The fourth married Francis P. Blair, and they were the parents of Montgomery Blair and Francis P. Blair. The fifth married Benjamin Gratz, of Lexington, Kentucky.

FIRST JOURNEY.

NOTES TO CHRISTOPHER GIST'S JOURNAL OF 1750-1.

October 31, 1750.—Colonel Cresap was an Agent and member of the Ohio Company, see Biographical Sketch in the Appendix. "Old Town." So called for a town or village of the Shawanese Indians, who abandoned the upper Potomac region in the years 1727-9, and removed to the Ohio and Allegheny rivers. It is in Old Town, District of Allegheny County, Maryland, fifteen miles southeast of Cumberland, on the north side of the Potomac, and opposite to Green Spring Station, on the Baltimore and Ohio Railway.

November 3.—Gist's route from Old Town lay by the Warrior's Path, along the base of the Great Warrior Mountain, on the eastern side, passing through the present district of Flintstone, Allegheny County, Maryland, and the townships of Southhampton, Monroe and Providence, in Bedford County, Pennsylvania, reaching the Juniata at the Warrior's Gap, near the village of Bloody Run, eight miles east of the present town of Bedford; there he entered the old Indian path leading westward. From the Juniata, where Bedford now stands, two paths led to the Ohio (Allegheny); the upper directly north to Frankstown, thence northwest to Venango (now Franklin); the lower path led west to Shannopin's Town (now Pittsburgh); the latter was the route taken by Gist.[1]

---

[1] Hutchins' Map, 1778; Scull's ditto, 1770. "Traders' Table of Distances to the Ohio;" "Colonial Records of Pennsylvania," Vol. V, p. 750. "Account of the Road to Logstown," by John Harries, in 1754, "Pennsylvania Archives," Vol. II, p. 135.

November 5–9.—In Shade Township, Somerset County, Stony Creek,[1] a branch of the Conemaugh River; the path crossed it near the present Stoyestown, in Somerset County.

November 11.—The North and East Forks of the Quemahoning, a branch of Stony Creek; these streams here flowing northeastward, misled Gist into supposing they emptied into the Susquehannah; they are so erroneously laid down from his notes on Fry and Jefferson's map of 1751. Que-Mahoning from Curoa (pine trees,) and Mahonink (a stream,) on which there is a Salt lick.[2]

November 12.—The ridge of the Alleghenies known as Laurel Hill.

November 14.—This old Indian town stood on the wide and fertile bottom land on the north side of the Loyalhanna Creek, a large branch of the Kiskiminitas River. The present town of Ligonier, in Westmoreland County, occupies the same spot, fifty-one miles east of Pittsburgh, marked "Loyal Hannin Old Town—fifty miles to Shannopin's Town," on a map presented to the Governor and Council of Pennsylvania, by John Pattin (Indian Trader), and Andrew Montour (a Six Nation Chief and Interpreter), March 2, 1754.[3] Laurel-hanne, signifying the middle stream in the Delaware tongue.[4] The stream here is half way between the Juniata at Bedford and the Ohio at the Forks.

November 16.—The path here left the Loyalhanna and by a northwest course passed through the Chestnut Ridge, at

[1] In the Delaware tongue "Ach'sin-hanac" or "Stony Stream."
[2] Delaware.
[3] "Colonial Records," Vol. V, pp. 747, 750.
[4] Heckwelder in "Transactions of the Moravian Historical Society for 1872," p. 28. McCullough, "Narrative and Incidents of Border Life," Lancaster, 1841, p. 81. See also "Trumbull on Indian Geographical Names," Vol. II, p. 12. "Collection of the Connecticut Historical Society."

the Miller's Run Gap, and reached the creek again, at the Big Bottom, below the present town of Latrobe, on the Pennsylvania Central Railway; there the trail forked, one branch led northwest down the creek to the Kiskiminitas River, at Blacklegs Indian town, by the mouth of the creek of the same name; thence it continued down to the Kiskiminitas Old Town, at Old Town Run, about seven miles from the Allegheny River. The other branch, or main trail (travelled by Gist), led directly westward to Shannopin's Town, by a course parallel with and a few miles north of the Pennsylvania Railroad. The courses stated by Gist for the 16th and 17th November are manifestly wrong; the distances are given much more correctly.[1]

November 17.—This camp was Cockey's Cabin, its owner a Delaware Indian, well known by the traders. It was on Bushy Run, a branch of Turtle Creek, near the place of the two days' battle between the army under Colonel Bouquet and the Indians, led by Guyasuta (Kiashuta), August 5th and 6th, 1763, about three miles north of Penn Station, on the Pennsylvania Railroad, and twenty-three miles east of Pittsburgh.[2] Shannopin's Town, on the bank of the Allegheny River, now in the city of Pittsburgh, between Penn Avenue, Thirtieth Street and the Two Mile Run, in the Twelfth Ward. It was small, containing about twenty wigwams, fifty or sixty natives and twenty warriors.[3] It was much frequented by the traders. By it ran the main Indian trail from the east to the west. In April, 1730, Governor Thomas,

---

[1] See "Colonial Records," Vol. V, p. 750-1. "Pennsylvania Archives," Vol. II, p. 135. Scull's Map, 1770. Hutchins', 1778. Evans and Mitchell's, 1755.

[2] "Pennsylvania Archives," Vol. II, p. 135. "Bouquet's Expedition, Philadelphia, 1765." "Virginia State Papers, 1875."

[3] "Colonial Records," Vol. V, p. 702; id., Vol. VII, p. 561.

at Philadelphia, received a message from "the Chiefs of ye Delewares at Allegaeniny, on the main road," taken down (written) by Edmund Cartledge, and interpreted by James Le Tort, both noted traders. Among the names signed to the message is that of "Shannopin his X mark." The message of the chiefs was to explain the cause of the death of a white man, named Hart, and the wounding of another, Robinson, down the Ohio, occasioned by rum. The bringing of such great quantities of liquor into the woods they desired the Governor to prevent, as well as to limit the number of traders. Shannopin's name appears signed to several documents in the State Archives.[1] He made a speech to Conrad Weiser, at Logstown, September 15, 1748.[2] He was present at the Conference held at Philadelphia, August 1, 1740, between the Proprietary, Thomas Penn, Governor Thomas, the Provincial Council, and the Delaware and Mingoe Indians, from Ohio, Allegheny, Shamokin, etc.[3] Shannopin died about the year 1749.[4]

November 21.—The width of the river here is about the same as stated in the journal, although the banks have been partly washed away by freshets.

November 24.—"At Shannopin's there is a fording place in very dry times and the lowest down the river."[5] In the first half of the last century the Allegheny River was gener-

[1] "Pennsylvania Archives," Vol. I, p. 255; do., p. 341.

[2] "Journal of Weiser," Historical Society of Pennsylvania Collection, Vol. I, p. 29; "Colonial Records," Vol. V, p. 355.

[3] "Colonial Records," Vol. IV, p. 441.

[4] "Colonial Records," Vol. V, p. 519. See also "Journals of Assembly," 1754, pp. 295 and 299. "Colonial Records," Vol. V, pp. 746, 751, etc. *London Magazine* for June, 1754. Evans and Mitchell's Maps, 1755. Fry and Jefferson's Maps, 1751.

[5] "Analysis of Map of the Middle Colonies," by Lewis Evans, 1775, p. 25.

ally called the Ohio, of which it is the head branch. "The Ohio" by the Senecas. Allegheny is the name of the same river in the Delaware language. Both words signify "the fine or fair river." Post was a Moravian missionary amongst the Ohio Indians for many years.[1] He was twice married among them and thoroughly understood various Indian dialects. He was often employed on Indian affairs by the colonial authorities. On the map prefixed to "Washington's Journal of 1753-4, London, 1754," reprinted by Joseph Sabin, New York, 1865, the Allegheny is marked "The Ohio or Allegheny River," and the main stream "The Ohio or the Fair River."[2] In the language of the different tribes of the Iroquois, or Six Nations, there are some variations of the word Ohio, none of its meaning. In the Seneca, Cayuga and Mohawk dialects it is O-heéyo; in the Onondago and Tuscarora O-heé-yee; in the Oneida O-heé, the same as Allegheny—"fair or beautiful"— which the French rendered "La Belle Rivière."[3] The early traders in Kentucky and on the Ohio called it Allegheny, or Ohio, as they happened to trade most with the Iroquois or Delawares. On the map of Cornelli, "North America with the New Discoveries of the Year 1688," published at Venice in 1690, the main part of the Ohio is laid down and inscribed "R Ohio or la Belle Rivière, said by the savages to have its source near the Lake Frontenac" (Ontario). In the "Procés Verbal" (Declaration) of the taking possession of Louisiana, at the mouth of the Mississippi, by the Sieur de la Salle, April 9,

---

[1] Christian F. Post in his Second Journal, 1758, London, 1759, p. 17, reprinted in Appendix to Proud's "History of Pennsylvania," 1798, Vol. II; also in Craig's "Olden Time," Vol. I.

[2] See also "Weiser's Journal, 1748." "Colonial Records," Vol. V, p. 349. "Collection Pennsylvania Historical Society," Vol. I, p. 23.

[3] "Morgan's League of the Iroquois," p. 394. "Collection of the Connecticut Historical Society, Vol. II, p. 13."

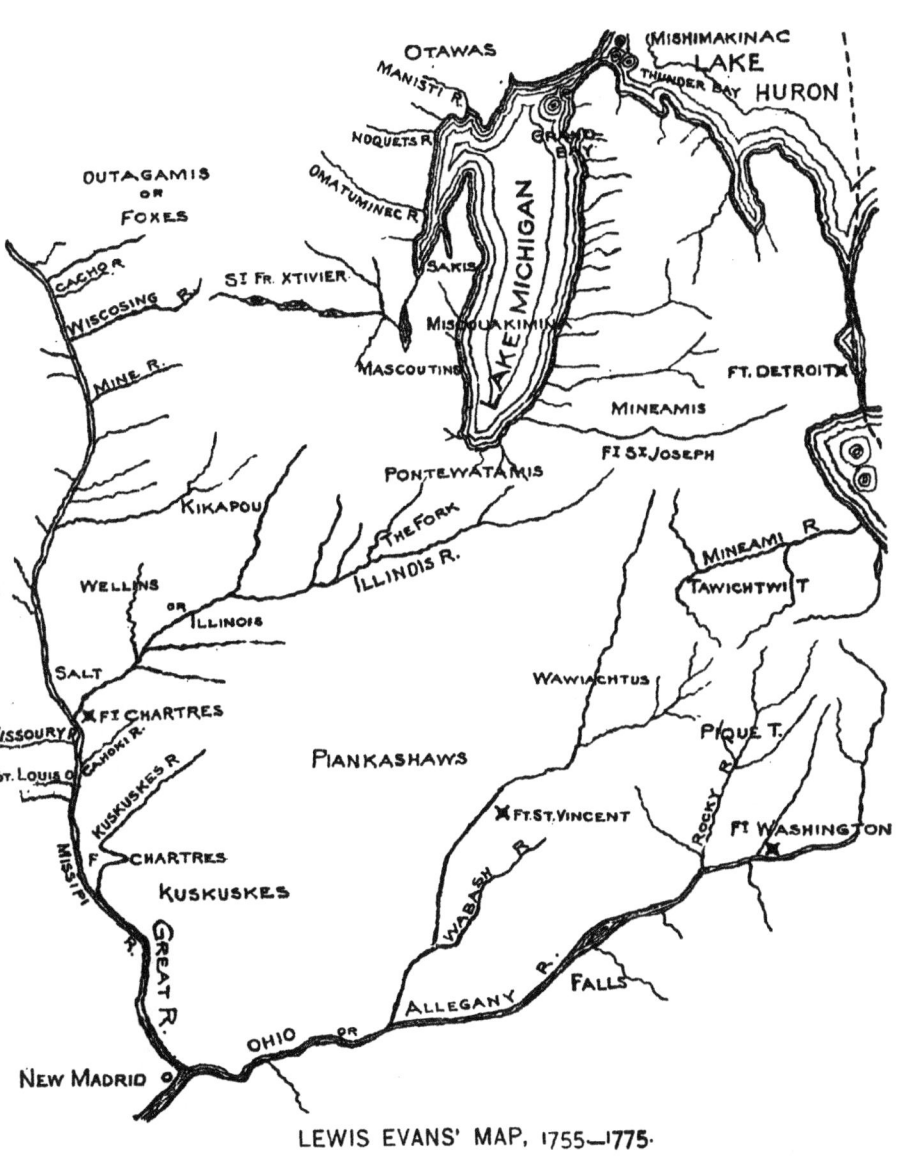

LEWIS EVANS' MAP, 1755—1775.

NOTES TO CHRISTOPHER GIST'S JOURNAL OF 1750-51. 95

1682, the names "Ohio" and "Alighin" are both evidently given to the same stream.[1] After crossing the river from Shannopins, Gist's route was by the old path which ran by the line occupied now by East and West Ohio Streets, in Allegheny City, to Beaver Avenue, thence along it and down the river bank to Sewickley, twelve miles below Pittsburgh.

November 25.—Logstown. This once noted Indian and French town stood on the first and second bank on the north side of the Ohio River, immediately below the present town of Economy, eighteen miles from Pittsburgh, in Beaver County, Pennsylvania; the well-known German settlement, of which George Rapp was the head, established there in 1824. Logstown Run, a small stream, and the bar in the river perpetuate the name and locality. The town was first described by Conrad Weiser in the Journal of his visit to it in August, 1748.[2] William Franklin (son of Benjamin), afterwards the Royal Governor of New Jersey, was one of Weiser's company.[3] The Shawanese established themselves here, probably soon after their migration from the Upper Potomac country and Eastern Pennsylvania, in 1727-30. In the summer of 1749 Captain Bienville de Celeron, in command of a detachment composed of eight subaltern officers, six cadets, an armorer, twenty soldiers, one hundred and

---

[1] This document, preserved in the French Archives at Paris, is printed in Sparks' "Life of La Salle," Appendix, p. 194. "American Biographies, New Series, 1864, Vol. I; also in "Monette's Valley of the Mississippi," Vol. I, p 144. "Historical Collection of Louisiana," by B. F. French, 1846, p. 49, Vol. I.

[2] "Collection of the Pennsylvania Historical Society," Vol. I. p. 23, etc. "Colonial Records of Pennsylvania," Vol. V, p. 348, etc.

[3] "Pennsylvania Archives," Vol. II, pp. 10-15. Evans' "Analysis of Map of the Middle Colonies, 1755," p. 10.

eighty Canadians, thirty Iroquois and twenty-five Abanakis, descended the Allegheny and Ohio rivers, from Canada, for the purpose of taking military possession of the country.[1] Their route from Lake Erie to the Allegheny was by the old Portage to the head of Chautauqua Lake; thence down the lake to the outlet, through to the Chenango Creek, and by it to the Allegheny. In evidence of the French king's claim, leaden plates, with suitable inscriptions, were deposited at various points along the rivers. A number of them were found in after years.[2] The French arrived at Logstown on the 9th or 10th of August, encamped and remained about two days.

Contrecœur, to whom Ensign Ward surrendered the little fort at the Forks of the Ohio, April 17, 1754, where Pittsburgh now stands, and who named it Du Quesne, was one of Celeron's officers. Coulon de Valliers, to whom Washington capitulated at Fort Necessity, in June of the same year, was another. He was a brother of Jumonville, killed in a previous contest with Washington's troops. George Croghan arrived at Logstown just after the French departed.[3] He had a Trading House there, in which Weiser lodged during his visit the previous year.[4] Washington and Gist remained here five days while on their way to Venango and Le Bœuf, in 1753.[5] Washington was again here in 1770 on his way to the Kanawha.[6] In June, 1752, a treaty was

[1] See "Fort Pitt."

[2] See fac-simile of one in Craig's "Olden Time," Vol. II; of another in "New York Colonial History," Vol. VI, p. 611, also in Hildreth's "Pioneer History" and De Hass' "Indian Wars of Western Virginia," 1851. "Magazine of American History," March, 1878.

[3] "New York Colonial History," Vol. VI, p. 531; do., Vol. VII, p. 267.

[4] "Weiser's Journal."

[5] Journals of Washington and Gist, 1754.

[6] Journals in Sparks' "Life of Washington," Vol. 2, Appendix; also in Craig's "Olden Time," Vol. I.

made here between the Indians and the Commissioners of Virginia, Fry, Lomax and Patton. Gist was present, George Croghan also. Arthur Lee, in his "Journal of 1784," mentions Logstown as "formerly a settlement on both sides of the Ohio."[1] A settlement on the south side of the river is called Indian Logstown in "Western Navigation," edition of 1814, p. 76.[2] George Croghan, in his Journal of 1765, describes Logstown as "an old Settlement of the Shawanese, situated on a high bank on the north side of the Ohio River, a fine fertile country around it." An error in printing "south" for "north" has occasioned some controversy. His description better applies to the north side, and is so written in the manuscript.[3] The tract on the south side appears to have been surveyed for Alexander M'Kee in 1769,[4] and was advertised for public sale by the agents of the State "at Pittsburgh, on the 12th day of October next." Three hundred acres of land, on the south side of the Ohio, located by Alexander McKee, including his house and improvements opposite Logstown and confiscated as the property of the said Alexander McKee.[5] Tanacharison, the Half King, with Monakatoocha and a number of that tribe (Six Nations) lived at Logstown in 1753-4.[6]

On December 2, 1758, soon after the capture of Fort Du Quesne, the Moravian Missionary, Christian Frederick Post, arrived there and found it deserted by its late inhabitants. "In this town," he states, "there is forty houses, all built

[1] "Life of Lee," Vol. II, p. 384.
[2] See also Cumming's "Western Tour," Pittsburgh, 1816, p. 80.
[3] Craig's "Olden Time," Vol. I, p. 403. Butler's "History of Kentucky," second edition. Appendix, p. 459.
[4] "Pennsylvania Archives," Vol. IV, p. 346.
[5] *Pennsylvania Gazette*, September 8, 1784.
[6] "Washington's Journal, 1754."

for them by the French and lived in by about one hundred and twenty warriors."[1] In Post's original Journal, London, 1759, p. 57, reprinted in Proud's "History of Pennsylvania," Vol. II, Appendix, and in Craig's "Olden Time," Vol. I, he relates, December 2, 1758: "I with my Companion Kekuscund's son came to Logstown situated on a high hill. On the East End is a great Piece of low land where the old Logstown used to stand. In the new Logstown the French have built about thirty Houses for the Indians. They have a large Corn Field on the South Side where the Corn stands ungathered." (Extract from the "Deposition" of Major Edward Ward, taken at Pittsburgh, March 10, 1777, before the Commissioners of Virginia, Wood and Simms.) In the year 1752, and before his surrender to the French, "that about one-third of the Shawanese Inhabited Logstown on the West side of the Ohio and tended Corn on the East side of the river—and the other part of the nation lived on the Scioto river."[2] The reader will observe on the Map that the Ohio River here makes a bend and runs in its course nearly due north. The traders' stores, here and elsewhere in the Ohio Valley, were sacked and plundered by the Indians on the outbreak of Pontiac's War, in 1763. Some of the traders were killed.[3] In the original manuscript account and affidavit of losses suffered by George Croghan and Company, in 1753, appears the item: "One Store House at the Logstown Twelve miles from Fort Du Quesne on the north west side of Ohio £150."

After the capture of Fort Du Quesne and erection of Fort Pitt, in 1758, Logstown dwindled to insignificance, although some traffic was carried on there with the Indians. General

[1] Journal in "Pennsylvania Archives," Vol. III, p. 560.
[2] "Virginia State Papers Calendar," p. 278.
[3] "Colonial History of New York," Vol. VII, p. 724. "Plain Facts," p. 59. Parkman's "Conspiracy of Pontiac," Vol. II, pp. 6, 10.

John Gibson had a small trading establishment there in 1777.[1] From the beginning of the war of the Revolution it had neither trade nor inhabitants; Fort Pitt absorbed both.

The site of the town and the surrounding scenery is very picturesque. In the account of Colonel Bouquet's Expedition against the Ohio Indians, in 1764, occurs this passage: "Friday, October 5.—In this day's march, the Army passed through Loggstown, situated seventeen miles and an half, fifty seven perches by the path from Fort Pitt. This place was noted before the last war for the great trade carried on there by the English and French, but its inhabitants abandoned it in the year 1758. The lower town extended about sixty perches over a rich bottom to the foot of a low, steep ridge, on the summit of which, near the declivity, stood the upper town, commanding a most agreeable prospect over the lower and quite across the Ohio, which is quite five hundred yards wide here, and by its majestic, easy current adds much to the beauty of the place."[2]

Remains of many of the houses are noted in the draught of the survey executed for the State of Pennsylvania.[3] Portions of some of the most substantial buildings were visible in the early part of the present century. For the location of Logstown see Evans' Map of 1755. Fry and Jefferson's ditto, 1751. Hutchins' Map in "Bouquet." Large Map of ditto, 1778. Map of the Ohio River, by General Victor Collot, 1796.

A town named Montmorin was laid out on a large scale on the site of Logstown in 1788. It only existed on paper. Adver-

[1] "McDonald's Sketches," p. 202. Arnold's "Campaign Against Quebec," Munsell's edition, 1877, p. 6.

[2] "Historical Account of Bouquet's Expedition," Philadelphia, 1765, p. 10. Robert Clarke Co's. Reprint, Cincinnati, 1869, p. 45.

[3] Land Office Records. Tracts numbers 18 and 19 in Leet's "District of Depreciation Lands." Howell's Map of Pennsylvania, 1792.

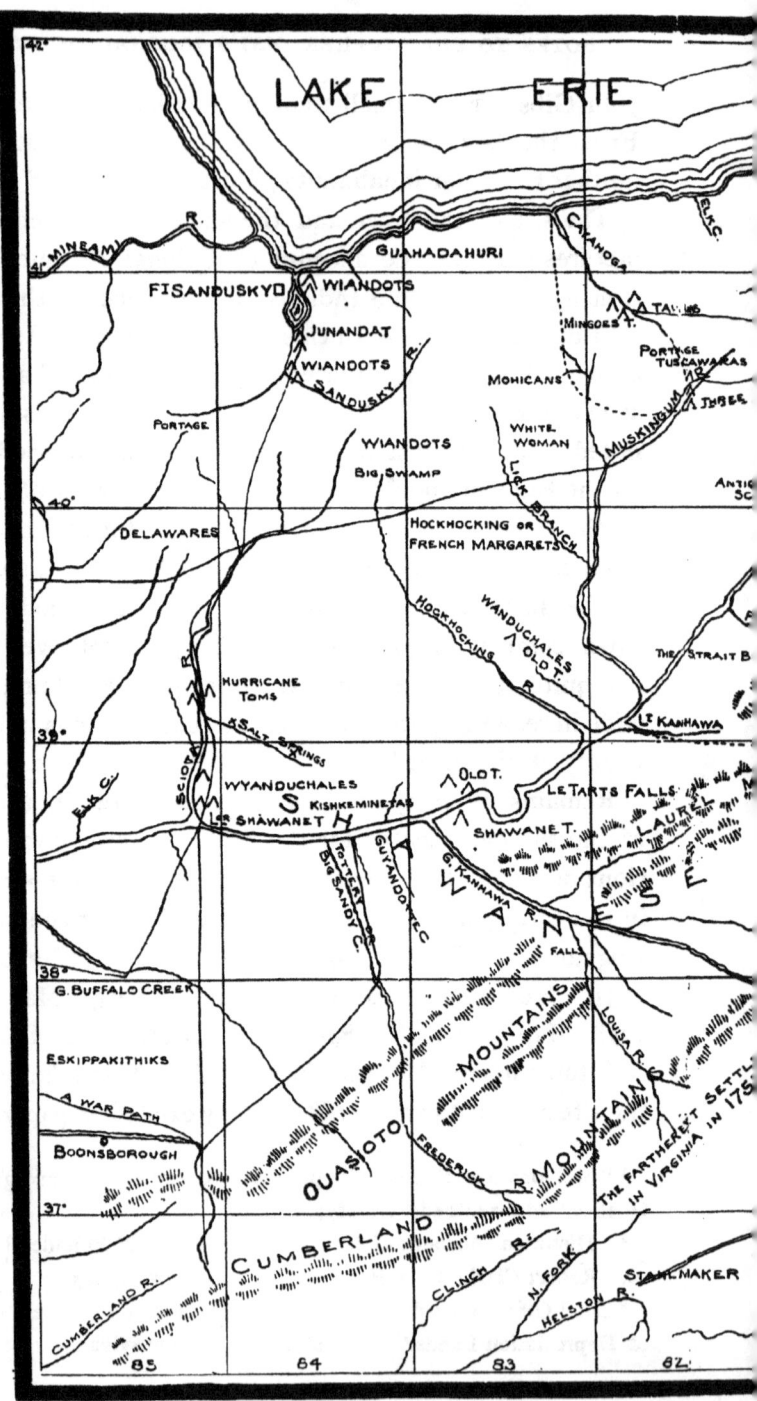

LEWIS EVANS' MAP, 1775.

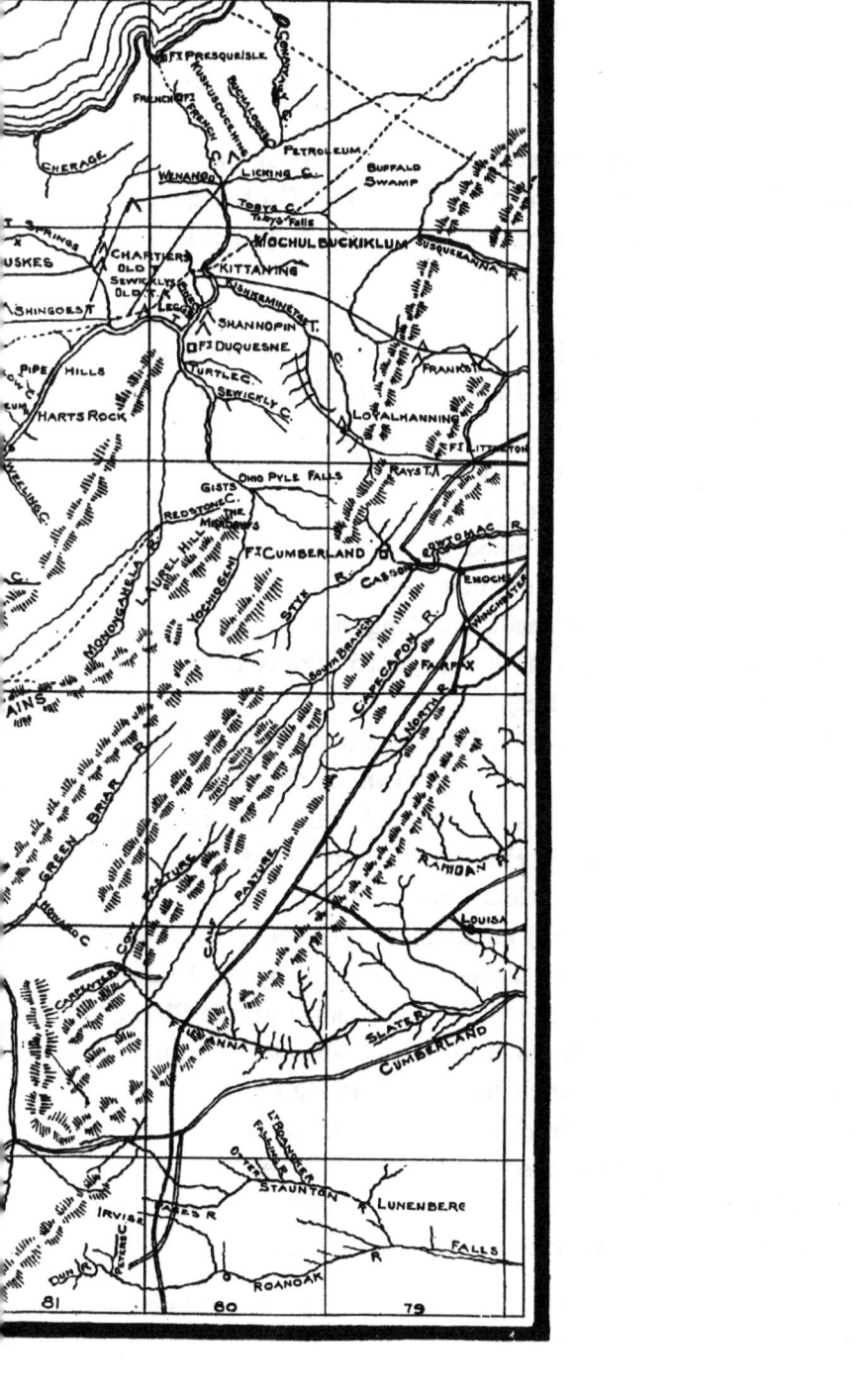

tisement in the *Pennsylvania Gazette*, No. 3,005, March 12, 1788.

On the plain, a short distance below, the army under General Wayne, known as the "Legion of the United States," encamped from November, 1792, to the 30th of April, 1793. The place was called Legionville.

November 26.—Where the town of Rochester now stands, on the east side of the Beaver, at its junction with the Ohio. Barny Curran was an old Indian trader. He was employed by Washington on his mission to Venango, in 1753.[1] Great Beaver Creek, named for King Beaver; in the Delaware tongue Amahkhanne or Beaver Stream.

November 27.—Gist crossed the Beaver to the west side, where, on the bottom land, now occupied by the town of Bridgewater, stood the small, but long noted, Indian town, Sarikonk or Soh-kon, a Delaware word signifying "at the mouth of a stream" (outlet).

On the elevated table-land adjoining the bottom, and at the west end of the present county town of Beaver, another Indian village was built by the French, in 1756. Both are thus described in the "Historical Account of Bouquet's Expedition," original edition, 1765, p. 10: "About a mile below its (Beaver Creek) confluence with the Ohio stood formerly a large town, on a steep bank, built by the French, of square logs, with stone chimneys, for some of the Shawanese, Delawares and Mingo Tribes, who abandoned it in the year 1758, when the French deserted Fort Du Quesne. Near the fording of Beaver Creek stood about seven houses, which were deserted and destroyed by the Indians after their defeat at Bushy Run," August 6, 1763, "when they forsook all their remaining settlements in this part of the country."

---

[1] Journal, 1754, p. 2, "Colonial Records,"Vol. V, p. 440. "History of Western Pennsylvania," 1846, p. 40.

King Beaver and Shingiss, his brother and successor, and noted warrior and war chief of the Delawares, resided here until the Spring of 1759, after the erection of Fort Pitt, when they removed to Kuskusky.[1] They afterwards removed to Muskingum. "Shingis Old Town" is mentioned in the deed from the Six Nations to the State of Pennsylvania, executed at Fort Stanwix, October 23, 1784, and now in the State Archives; also printed in the Minutes of the General Assembly for 1784-5, p. 320.

The Act of Assembly of September 28, 1791, authorized the Governor to have surveyed, at the mouth of Beaver Creek, "two hundred acres of land in town lots, at or near the ground where the old French town stood," now the Borough of Beaver.

Fort McIntosh was built here in 1778, by the troops under General Lachlan McIntosh. These Indian towns, Soh-kon and Shingoes, were prominent places of rendezvous for warriors, and the scene of much cruelty and bloodshed during the Indian and French wars. The Indian trail from Shannopins here divided, the lower (taken by Gist) led to Tuscarawas, the upper, along the west bank of the Beaver to Kuskuskis town, on the Mahoning, six miles above the forks of Beaver, where Edenburgh, Lawrence County, now stands. Old Kuskuskis stood on the Shenango, between the Forks and the mouth of the Neshannock (where New Castle now stands), on the wide bottom on the west side. Kuskuskis was divided into four towns, some distance apart.[2] Portions

---

[1] Letter of Colonel Hugh Mercer to R. Peters, "Colonial Records," Vol. VIII, p. 305; id., pp. 307, 309, 313. "Pennsylvania Archives," Vol. III, p. 634.

[2] "Christian Fred. Post's Journal," September, 1758. Hugh Gibson's "Narrative," Massachusetts Historical Collection, Vol. VI, Third Series, p. 144. General Wm. Irvine's Letters in "Pennsylvania Archives," Vol. XI, p. 518, etc. "Western Annals," p. 358.

of the path along the west bank of the Beaver and Mahoning, worn deep into the soil, were plainly visible and often seen by the writer about thirty years since, and some he is credibly informed yet remain.

Christian Fred. Post, Moravian Missionary, sent by the Governor of Pennsylvania and General Forbes to prevail on the Indians of the Upper Ohio to withdraw from the French interest, was at Soh-kon, in August, 1758, and again in the following month of November. At first roughly received, he was finally successful. (See his first and second Journals, published in 1759; reprinted in Proud's "History of Pennsylvania," 1798, Appendix to Vol. II. Also, in Craig's "Olden Time," Vol. I, and (but not so full) in "Pennsylvania Archives," Vol. III, pp. 520, 560, 563.)

Post states: "At Beaver Creek there is thirty-eight houses, all built by the French for the Indians; some with stone chimneys. When all their men are at home they can send out one hundred warriors." Hugh Gibson was a prisoner at Soh-kon in 1757. Narrative before referred to. (See also Hutchins' Map, 1778. Map in "Bouquet." Evans' Map, 1755. Howell's Map, 1792. Heckwelder in "Bulletin of Pennsylvania Historical Society," Vol. I, p. 129.)

November 27.—From Shingis town the trail left the river, taking a northwest course, passing near the present village of West Salem, Pennsylvania, to a point a little southeast from New Lisbon, Columbiana County, Ohio, on nearly the same line as the present road from Beaver to New Lisbon.[1]

Captain Hutchins was the chief-engineer in the army of Bouquet, and has laid down the line of each day's march and

---

[1] See Howells' and Hutchins' Maps, especially the beautiful map of Hutchins in the original, a Philadelphia edition of "Bouquet's Expedition Against the Ohio Indians, in 1764."

encampment minutely. The route of the army was by the old Indian trail travelled by Gist.

November 30.—To the northwest corner of the present Wayne township, Columbiana County, Ohio, after crossing the west or "last branch" of the Little Beaver Creek, having crossed the middle and east branches the preceding day. Little Beaver Creek, or Tank-amahk-hanne, in the Delaware tongue.

December 1, 1750.—To a point near Hanover, on the Pittsburgh and Cleveland Railway, in Columbiana County.

December 2.—A little south of Bayard, in the same county.

December 4, 5.—Near Oneida, in Carroll County, now known as Big Sandy Creek, a branch of the Tuscarawas. The Indians applied one name, "Elk's Eye," to the three streams; in modern times known as the Big Sandy, Tuscarawas, and Muskingum. On Evans' Map of 1755 and Hutchins' of 1778 the Big Sandy is named Lanianshicolas, now the Nimishicolas, and correctly applied to a branch. "The Delawares say the elks were so plenty on that river and so tame the Indians could come so near as to see into their eyes, so they called the river Mooskingung or Elk's Eye." Zeisberger, the Moravian Missionary, in the "Bulletin of the Pennsylvania Historical Society," Vol. I, p. 34: Elk's Eye, on account of the number of elks feeding on its banks. Loshiel's "History of Moravian Missions, 1794," p. 6: "Mooshingung, that is Elk's Eye River. Elk in their language being called Moos."[1] The words are mostly Narragansett, "Moos-soog"—the great ox, or rather a red deer. Muskingum is usually but incorrectly defined—water clear as an elk's eye.

December 7.—This town of the Ottoways stood near the

---

[1] Rev. David Jones' Journal, 1772; original edition, pp. 68, 84. Sabin's Reprint of ditto, New York, 1865, pp. 90-111, etc.

junction of the Big Sandy and Tuscarawas, on the west side of the latter and just above the present town of Bolivar. At this period but a small number of the Ottawa tribe remained in Eastern Ohio. By Hutchins' Maps of 1764 and 1778, and Evans' Map of 1755, they appear to have had a village on the Cuyahoga River, and "Ottowas Old Fort" is marked on the head of a branch of the White-woman's Creek, in the northern part of Richland County, from which was a four-mile portage to the waters of the river Huron. About fifty years since the Ottawa tribe held large reservations of land on the waters of the Maumee. In 1760 this village was known as King Beaver's Town, its occupants being Delawares.

Major Robert Rogers, on his way from Detroit to Fort Pitt, arrived there on January 13, 1761. He mentions "the number of warriors in this town is about one hundred and eighty."[1]

Bouquet's army, in 1764, made their twelfth encampment here, after leaving Fort Pitt, from which Captain Hutchins computed the distance to be one hundred and sixteen miles. They found "Tuscarawas a place exceedingly beautiful in situation, lands rich, and on the northwest side an entire level plain, upwards of five miles in circumference," and "from the number of ruined houses, supposed the Indians who inhabited the place and are with the Delawares to have had about one hundred and fifty warriors."[2] This is a noted spot in the early history of Ohio. Christian Fred Post, the Moravian Missionary, established a station on the north side of the Tuscarawas, in the present Stark County, in the year 1761, and erected, it is claimed, the first house in Ohio.[3] Fort

---

[1] Journal, 1760-1, p. 234.

[2] "Journal of Bouquet's Expedition, 1765," p. 13, original edition.

[3] "Heckwelder's Narrative," p. 61. "Life of Zeisberger," by De Schweinitz, p. 256. "Beatty's Journal," 1766, p. 40.

Laurens, the most western military post erected by the Americans during the Revolution, stood just below the site of Tuscarawas town.

The Greenville Treaty Line, of 1795, extended from the mouth of Cuyahoga "to the crossing place above Fort Laurens, thence westerly to Laramie's store," on a branch of the Great Miami, in the present Shelby County. It marked the boundary between the lands of the Indian tribes and those they ceded to the United States.[1] The great Indian trails radiated from this point in various directions.

December 9.—Margaret's Creek. The trail crossed it in the present Franklin Township, Tuscarawas County, near Strasburgh. This stream was named for Margaret Montour, usually called "French Margaret," the daughter of Madame Montour. This stream was afterwards called Sugar Creek; it empties into the Tuscarawas at Dover.

December 10.—A branch of Margaret's Creek.

December 11.—To a point in Buck's Township, Tuscarawas County.

December 12.—Near the mouth of White Eyes Creek, in Coshocton County.

December 14.—This was a large and important town of the Wyandots, on the Tuscarawas, the head branch of the Muskingum River, within a mile from the "Forks," where Coshocton now stands. Marked "Old Wyandot Town" on Hutchins' Map, in Bouquet, 1764; Owendot's Town on Dr. Mitchell's Map of 1755. This town was abandoned by the Wyandots prior to 1760, probably soon after the capture of Fort Du Quesne, in 1758. They were there in 1756.[2] Gist

---

[1] "Treaty of Greenville, August 3, 1795." American State Papers, Vol. V, p. 562. State Maps of Ohio, 1815, 1831 and 1869.

[2] Letter of Colonel John Armstrong to Governor Denny, December 22, 1756. Pennsylvania Archives, Vol. III, p. 83.

mentions Muskingum as though it was the name of the town. He should have written "a town of the Wyandots at the Muskingum," the latter being an Algonquin or Delaware word. The Indians do not, like the whites, give every town or village a name, but they are known by the name of the place, the locality, head chief, etc. "They preferred to describe a man or a river or town, by some quality or remarkable feature rather than designate the object by a name.[1] Thus Chillicothe towns in Ohio—Upper, Lower and Old—simply meant towns of the Chillicothe tribe of the Shawnese.[2] Soh-kon, outlet (a village) at the outlet. Shannopin, from the head chief, Kittanning. Kittan, great, ung-on, or at the great river.[3] The Wyandots, or Hurons, were ancient occupants of Central and Eastern Ohio and Northwestern Pennsylvania, to which region they retreated from Canada, to escape the fury of the conquering Iroquois, or Five Nations, in the middle of the seventeenth century.[4] The Wyandots are called Tiononaties, Petuns or Petuneuæ, Tobacco Indians, from their industrious habit of cultivating that plant. Petun (obsolete French for tobacco derived from the Brazilian) being a nickname given to them by the French traders.[5] In the Mohawk dialect of the Iroquois the name for tobacco is O-ye-aug-wa.[6] In the Huron of La Hontan, Vol. II, p. 103, Oyngowa; and in Campinus "History of New Sweden," in the Mingo.

---

[1] "Transactions of the Historical and Philosophical Society of Ohio," Vol. I, p. 235.

[2] John Johnson, in Butler's "Kentucky," last page, Appendix.

[3] See Trumbull on "Indian Geographical Names," Connecticut Historical Society, Vol. II, p. 43, etc.

[4] "American Antiquarian Society Transactions," Vol. I, p. 271-2; id. Vol. II, p. 72. Charlevoix's "History of New France."

[5] "Historical Magazine." Vol. V, O. S., 1861, p. 263.

[6] Gallatin's "Synopsis American Aboriginal Archives," Vol. II, p. 484.

The flotilla of Céleron, before mentioned as on its way down the Ohio, arrived at the mouth of the Muskingum on the 15th of August, 1749, and on the 16th they buried a lead plate in the western bank of that stream, bearing the inscription " Rivière Yenangue," and on the map of Father Bonnecamp —a Jesuit mathematician who accompanied the expedition— the Muskingum is marked " R. Yanangué konan. " On Bellin's Map, in Charlevoix's original edition, 1744, it is named Chenangue. The meaning clearly is from the Iroquois ; from Ynango—tobacco—and Konan people, or river on which the tobacco people—Wyandots or Petuns—have a town, referring to the town at which Gist had now arrived.

Colonel John Johnston, for many years United States Agent for the Ohio Indians, in his valuable "Specimens of the Wyandot Language," gives the signification of Muskingum as " a place of residence ;" but again erroneously states it to mean a town on the river side in the Delaware. " The Shawnese," he adds, "call it Wakitama Sepe, which has the same signification."[1]

De Witt Clinton, in a letter to the American Antiquarian Society, in 1827, erroneously supposed the town, to which allusion is made, to be "the celebrated remains of an ancient town at Marietta." He is also in error, in the same letter, in the supposition that the leaden plate deposited at the mouth of the Muskingum, found and dug up in 1798, to " have been originally deposited at the mouth of the Venango (French Creek) above Pittsburgh." He was misled by the similarity of the name Yznangue with Venango, as it is now written. The date on the plate should have undeceived him. However, Venango was an old village of the Wyandots, or Tobacco Indians. Washington, in his Journal of 1753, mentions it as the

---

[1] American Antiquarian Society, Vol. I, pp. 297, 298.

site of an old Indian town;[1] and it is probable that wherever the name Chenango occurs in early times or on early maps, it indicates the site of a town of the tobacco tribe—Wyandots —or of a place where Indian tobacco was cultivated.[2]

The claim of the Wyandots to Central Ohio was admitted by the United States, who made them compensation therefor.[3]

The Wyandots released to Pennsylvania, at the latter mentioned treaty, their claim to the western portion of that State. There was a Wyandot town on the Big Beaver, on the east side, nineteen miles above its mouth. On its site the Moravians, in 1770, erected their town of Friedenstadt.[4]

The name of "Little Mingoes," applied by Gist to the Wyandots, I have not observed elsewhere. The Wyandots, or Hurons, were of the original Iroquois stock (or Mengine changed to Mingo).

Croghan's Trading House, here mentioned, was afterwards (1753) with the goods stored in it, seized by the French. In the original MS. account of losses suffered by George Croghan & Co., occasioned by the French, during his trades in the Ohio country, appears this item: "One store House at Muskingum £150." Croghan's affidavit is attached to it, dated at Carlisle, April 24, 1756. Four traders were captured— Joseph Falkner of New York, Luke Erwin of Pennsylvania, Thomas Burk of Lancaster, Pennsylvania, and John Pattin of

[1] Journal, original edition, p. 17.
[2] See "Transactions American Antiquarian Society," Vol. II, p. 535. Hildreth's "Pioneer History of Ohio," 1848, p. 22. "American Magazine," March, 1878, in which is the map of Céleron's Route, by O. H. Marshal, of Buffalo.
[3] Declaration annexed to the Treaty at Fort Harmar, in 1789. "American State Papers, Indian Affairs," Vol. I, p. 7. Treaty of September 29, 1817, Vol. II; do., Treaty at Fort McIntosh, etc.
[4] Lochiel's "History of Missions." De Schweinitz's "Life of Zeisberger."

Chester County, Pennsylvania. The first two were in the employ of George Croghan & Co. Pattin was seized at Fort Miami. Erwin, Burke, and Falkner, were captured at a place called "Argentout" (Wyandot), near the little Lake Otsanderkat (Sandusky Bay), the former stronghold of the Huron Chief Nicholas, who in 1747 rebelled against the French and built himself a Fort there.[1]

The traders were captured by orders of Céleron, Commander at Detroit,[2] to which place they were taken and confined in the fort for five months, then taken to Niagara and Quebec At the latter place Falkner was left, on account of sickness ; the other three were sent to Rochelle, France, and there imprisoned for three months, then liberated and returned to America. Pattin's goods, to the value of eight or nine hundred pounds, were seized when he was captured.[3]

December 17.—The "New Fort" which the French were building on one of the branches of Lake Erie, and to which Croghan supposed the French took the captives, is erroneously stated by Mr. Bancroft to be Fort Sandusky. There has been much uncertainty respecting the location of the

---

[1] Letter of the Marquis de la Jonquière to M. Rouille. Also from same to Governor Clinton of New York. New York: Colonial History, Vol. VI, p 733; ditto, Vol. X, p. 240. Pennsylvania Colonial Records, Vol. V, p. 556. See the examination and depositions of the prisoners, by the Governor of Canada, La Jonquière, at Montreal, in June 1751, in "The Conduct of the Ministry, a Memorial, etc.," pp. 92-106. English edition, 1777. French original edition, 1756, pp. 89-100. See Pennsylvania Colonial Records, Vol. V, p. 522.

[2] New York Colonial History, Vol. X, p. 251.

[3] See his petition to the Assembly of Pennsylvania for relief. Journals of Assembly, October 17, 1752. Letter of Earl of Albemarle, from Paris, March 1, 1752, to the Earl of Holderness. New York Colonial History Vol. X, p. 241. John Pattin's "Narrative of his Captivity, 1750," Pennsylvania Historical Society.

French Fort Sandusky and also of the British Post subsequently erected. In the French official reports, from 1748 to 1763, there is no mention of any fort at Sandusky (excepting that of the Huron Chief Nicholas), while the Posts at Detroit, Miami and Niagara are frequently referred to, and detailed accounts of their condition given.[1]

There is no mention of a fort at Sandusky in Colonel James Smith's Narrative. He lived and hunted with the Indians along the south shore of Lake Erie, from the Cuyahoga to the Maumee, during the five years of his captivity—1755 to 1760.[2] Nor is there anything said of Fort Sandusky in the journals of Major Robert Rogers, who was sent with a detachment of troops, by General Amherst, in 1760, to Detroit, to receive the surrender of that and all other western posts held by the French, in accordance with the terms of the capitulation of Canada, by Governor Vaudreuil.[3]

The Fort of the Huron (Wyandot) war chief, Nicholas, was probably on what is now called Cherry Island, in the marshes, between Green Creek and the Sandusky River, about two miles above the mouth of the latter. It now contains but a few acres of good land, above overflow, and is the most inaccessible of the islands in the vast Sandusky marshes, and only to be reached by canoes or small boats. Nevertheless, Nicholas, apprehensive of French attack, with the assistance of their Indian allies, early in the Spring of 1748,

---

[1] "Memorial of De Galissonière on the Canadian Posts, December 10, 1752;" New York Colonial History, Paris, Vol. X, p. 230. "Dispatch of Longueil to Rouille, April, 1752;" id., pp. 245-'51.

[2] "Smith's Narrative" Ohio Valley, Historical Series: R. Clarke & Co., 1870.

[3] Journals of Rogers, London, 1765; also, " Journals of George Croghan, Fort Pitt to Detroit, 1760-1,"in Massachusetts Historical Collection; Fourth Series, Vol. IX, pp. 362, 366.

burned his fort and village, and with 119 warriors of his nation, men, women and baggage, took the route to White River.[1] This probably is the fort "Junundat, built in 1754," marked as on the east side of the Sandusky River, near the Bay, on Evans' Map of 1755, and Pownall's of 1776. If this location is correct, the Wyandot fort and village must have been on Peach and Graveyard Islands, directly at the mouth of the river, on the east side. On these same maps Fort Sandusky is laid down on the west side, opposite Junundat. Both river and bay being very erroneously delineated on Dr. Mitchell's Map, published by authority of the British Government, in 1755: "Sandusky usurped by the French in 1751 is marked at the river's mouth on the west side; the river itself is named Blanc."

On the map of D'Anville, Paris, 1755, "Sandousche" is marked on the west side of the river Blanc, at its mouth, and on the English map of the same date, the location is the same, marked "Fr. Fort Sanduski." On the map of M. Bellin, the French Geographer Royal, Paris, 1755, the "Fr. Ft. Sanduski" is placed at the west side of the mouth of the river and noted as an old or "Ancient Fort abandoned;" and in the "Remarques sur la Carte," published with the Atlas, the author, in describing the country around Lake Erie, observes that "where the river flows into the end of the Bay of Sandusky, we (the French) have a fort and habitation." "The French go in three days from Fort De Troit to Fort Sandoskes, which is a small pallisaded Fort with about twenty men, situated on the south side of Lake Erie and was built in the latter end of the year 1750." From narrative of John Pattin, Indian trader, of his captivity in 1750.[2] Among the "King's Maps and Drawings," in the Library of the

[1] "French Journal of Occurrences in Canada," 1747-8; "New York Colonial History," Vol. X, pp. 162, 178; id., Vol. VI, pp. 706, 733.

[2] Historical Society of Pennsylvania.

British Museum, the writer found and had copied a large and finely executed MS. map of Lake Erie and the Allegheny River, with the British Posts of Presque Isle, Le Bœuf, Venango, and Fort Pitt, made about 1760.

A fort destroyed is laid down on the northwest shore of Lake Sandusky, about two miles east of the entrance to the Little Portage, or Indians' carrying place, and a half mile in length between Sandusky Bay and the mouth of the Portage River, where Port Clinton now stands. This was on the usual route taken by the Indians and French from and to Detroit and the North. "The French erected a post here (Sandusky) in the year 1754 and abandoned it in the year 1759. This post was established principally with a view of keeping up the communication with Detroit, Fort DuQuesne and Presque Isle and of assisting parties of warriors residing northward of Lake Erie, when on their way to, and returning from, the frontiers of the different States."[1] The earlier date of the erection of the French Fort at Sandusky, 1750, as stated by Pattin, seems to be the correct one, as well as its location near the "Little Portage," where a "Fort destroyed" is marked on a small sketch of the bay, the location of the Indian villages and the British block-house, made by an officer, in 1761, and now with the "Bouquet" MSS. in the Library of the British Museum.

In the latter part of 1761 the British erected a block-house on the south shore of Sandusky Bay, at the mouth of Mills Creek.[2] "The block-house at Sandusky is finished; Lieutenant Meyer and Ensign Paully remain yet there with thirty

---

[1] MS. account of the country and "Route from Fort Pitt to Sandusky and thence to Detroit," by Captain Thomas Hutchins, 1761. Library of Pennsylvania Historical Society, Philadelphia.

[2] Letter of Colonel Bouquet to General Amherst, from Fort Pitt, December 2, 1761.

men."[1] Lieutenant Meyer commanded during the erection of the fort. Its location is correctly marked on the map of Captain Thomas Hutchins, of 1778. Also on his map in the historical account of Bouquet's Expedition of 1764. Captain Hutchins was then an engineer in the British service. He was at Fort Sandusky in 1762.[2]

The reader doubtless remembers that the British Fort Sandusky shared the fate of many of the western posts, being captured and destroyed by the Indians during the 'Pontiac War of 1763.

December 25, 1750. Christmas Day.—This, no doubt, was the first Protestant religious service ever held within the limits of the present State of Ohio. The first Protestant sermon was preached by the Rev. Charles Beatty, on the 21st of September, 1766, at Newcomerstown, about sixteen miles farther up the Muskingum. The Rev. George Duffield preached in the afternoon of the same day, at the same place. These ministers were Presbyterian Missionaries, sent out by the Synods of New York and Philadelphia.[3] On the 14th of March, 1771, the Rev. David Zeisberger, Moravian Missionary, preached his first sermon in Ohio, in the same town.[4] The Rev. David Melluse, Missionary from Connecticut, preached here in September, 1772.[5]

[1] " Diary of Sir William Johnson," in Appendix to Stone's Life of Sir William, Vol. II, p. 466. Letter of Colonel Bouquet to General Monckton, from Fort Pitt, July 24, 1761. Massachusetts Historical Collection, Vol. IX, Fourth Series, p. 434, and same to the same, August 12, 1761, id., p. 438.

[2] Letter of Colonel Bouquet to Ensign Paully, April 3, 1762. in *Gazette*, Philadelphia, April 27, 1791. Treaty of Greenville.

[3] "Beatty's Journal of a Two Month's Tour West of the Allegheny Mountains in 1766," London, 1768, pp. 55-56.

[4] " Life of Zeisberger," by E. DeSchweinitz, 1870, p. 366.

[5] " Journal of Missions, Hartford, 1773," of Thomas Burney, see note to February 24.

January 4, 1751.—Michael Taaf, or Teaff, was a partner in the Indian trade with William Trent and George Croghan. He resided on the Susquehanna, a little below Harris' Ferry.[1]

January 9, 1751.—This English trader captured was John Pattin, taken at Fort Miami.[2]

January 14.—The answer of the King and Council was given to George Croghan and Andrew Montour for the Governor of Virginia, at Logstown, May 29, 1751. They say, they are now at war with the Southern Indians; may be soon struck by the French, so that it is not in their power to go down to hear what their great Father, the King of Great Britain has to say. They expect that their Father's speeches will be sent here where their brothers of Pennsylvania have kindled a Council Fire.[3]

January 15.—Reaching the Whitewoman's Creek, about four miles west of the present town of Coshocton. Mary Harris, the white woman, doubtless was the same person who was captured at the assault and burning of Deerfield, Massachusetts, by the French and Indians from Canada, February 29, 1704. A list of the killed and prisoners is given in the Appendix to the fourth edition of the "Captivity and Deliverance of the Rev. John Williams, of Deerfield, Massachusetts, 1758." The name of Mary Harris is marked among those still absent. It appears she left the village, where Gist saw her, and returned to Canada, as in a "Memoir of the Rev. John Williams, by his grandson, Stephen W. Williams, Northampton, Massachusetts, 1853," it is stated, on page 121, that "as lately as the year 1756 Mary Harris, who was one of the female prisoners and a child at the time of the capture of the town, resided at Cahnawaga" (near Montreal).

[1] "Colonial Records," Vol. VI, p. 150.
[2] See note to December 17th, *ante*.
[3] "Colonial Records," Vol. V, p. 537.

"She was at that time a married woman and had several children, one of whom was an officer in the service of France." The Cahnawagas, or French Mohawks, frequented the country, both north and south of the Ohio. Their chief town was at the rapids of St. Louis, near Montreal, where a number of the tribe yet reside, 1879.[1] Whitewoman's Town is marked on Dr. Mitchell's Map of 1755 as well as Gist's route, from his notes referred to in the sketch of the Ohio Company. The town is also marked on the Map of Evans, 1755, and appears to have been situated about opposite the mouth of Killbuck Creek, in the present County of Coshocton, which location agrees with Gist's. Whitewoman's Creek is also called the Walkending—a Delaware name.

January 16.—The trail led in a southwesterly direction, through the present Coshocton County, passing near Dresden, in the County of Muskingum; thence to the Licking Creek, crossing it at Clay Lick Station, Hanover Township, Licking County, on the Central Ohio Railroad, six miles east of Newark.

January 17.—In the southern part of Licking County. At the time of Gist's visit this swamp was of great extent, part of the locality is known as the Licking Reservoir of the Ohio Canal, the construction of which commenced here in 1825.[2] This was the "Great Buffalo Swamp" of Smith's narrative, where he hunted with the Indians in 1755 or 6 and where they made salt.[3]

[1] See "Narrative of Colonel James Smith," pp. 16, 32, 52, 107 and Appendix, p. 172. "Bouquet's Expedition," R. Clarke & Co., pp. 63, 75, 153. Deposition in appendix to these notes.

[2] Ohio Canal Doc., 1828, p. 105. Niles' Register, Vol. XXVIII, p. 22.

[3] "Colonel James Smith's Captivity," page 21. See also "Historical Sketch of Licking Township," by Isaac Smucker. Pioneer Paper, No. 3, Licking County Pioneer Association, Newark, Ohio, 1869.

January 19.—Hockhockin, now Lancaster, Fairfield County, the "Standing Stone" or Ach-sin-sink of the Delawares, is a rocky eminence near the town. Visited by the Missionary, the Rev. David Jones, in 1773. He mentions in his Journal: "February 9th, at the Standing Stone. This town consists chiefly of Delaware Indians. It is situated on a creek called Hock-hock-in.[1] Hack-hack is a Delaware word, and signifies a gourd with a neck; also applied to bottles.[2] Hockhocking, from the shape of the creek,[3] resembling that of a bottle. John Brickell's account: he was for five years a prisoner among the Delawares in Ohio.[4] Marked "Hockhocking or French Margaret's," town on Evans' Map of the Middle Colonies, 1755. Mitchell's ditto, Pownall's of 1776, ditto. French Margaret was a daughter of Madame Montour. It is probable she resided here at one time.

January 20.—Maguck. In the Pickaway plains, between Scippo Creek and the Scioto River, in Pickaway County and township, three and one-half miles south of Circleville; "the small rising in the middle" was called "Black mountains" by the natives.[5] William Trent got to the Maguck July 3, 1752.[6] "The Delawares informed me the lower Shawanese had removed off the river (Ohio) up the Sciota to a great plain called Moguck."[7] At the time of Gist's visit only

[1] Journal, p. 64, original edition, Burlington, New Jersey, 1774. Sabin's reprint, New York, 1865, p. 86.

[2] Heckwelder, "Historical Account of the Indian Nations," p. 56. Narrative of ditto, p. 144.

[3] About six miles above Lancaster.

[4] American Pioneer, Vol. I, p. 38–43. Howe's "History of Ohio," pp. 161–600.

[5] Howe's "Ohio," p. 402.

[6] Journal, R. Clarke & Co., 1871.

[7] "Journal of Christopher F. Post, November 28, 1758," Pennsylvania Archives, Vol. III, p. 560.

a portion of the Delaware tribes had removed to the Ohio country from Pennsylvania.

The Shawanese occupied the land on the Scioto in the latter part of the preceding century and also the country along the lower Cumberland River, in Kentucky, first called the Shawnee River; they were compelled to remove in their wars with the Iroquois or Five Nations. Some of the tribe went south, but the greater part emigrated to the upper Potomac and to Pennsylvania, along the Susquehanna and its branches.[1] "You Shawanese look back toward Ohio the place from whence you came and return thitherward for now we shall take pity on the English and let them have all this land." "The Delaware Indians sometime ago bid us Depart for they was Dry and wanted to drink ye land away, whereupon we told them Since some of you are gone to Ohioh we will go there also, we hope you will not Drink that away too."[2]

They gradually removed westward, Delawares and Shawanese from 1728 to 1755, first to the Allegheny and Ohio rivers and thence to the Muskingum and Scioto, by permission however of the Wyandots.[3]

The wild rye was a coarse, natural grass, much used for fodder by the early settlers.[4] Scioto, deer. Where deer are

---

[1] Pennsylvania Colonial Record, Vol. IV, p. 337. Hazard's "Pennsylvania," Vol. V, p. 115.

[2] "Shawnee Chief's Message to Governor Gordon, 1732," Pennsylvania Archives, Vol. I, p. 329. Report of Committee, November 22, 1755. Journals of Pennsylvania Assembly, p. 517.

[3] "Treaty of the United States with the Wyandots at Fort Harmar, in 1789." American State Papers, Indian Affairs, Vol. I, p. 7. New York Colonial History, Vol. IX, p. 1035. Albert Gallatin in "Transactions of American Antiquarian Society," Vol. III, pp. 49, 68, 69. Shea's "Discoveries in the Mississippi Valley," 1853, p. 41, note.

[4] Ohio Gazetteer, 1841, p. 360.

plenty.[1] Deer, Scaenoto, Magua.[2] Zeisberger and other Moravian Missionaries.[3] The language of the Hurons and Wyandots comes near the Magua.[4] John Johnston observes in "Howe's History of Ohio," p. 600, that "the Sci-on-to River was named by the Wyandots, who formerly resided on it; signification unknown." On p. 599 of the same volume he gives specimens of the Wyandot language; in the list deer is—Ough—Scanoto.[5] In the Onondaga tongue deer is Skan-o-do.[6] The Wyandots or Hurons, and Iroquois or Five Nations, were of the same original stock.

The Rev. David Jones, in his Journal of 1772, p. 4, says: "The name which the Shawnese give Sciota has slipped my memory, but it signified Hairy River. The Indians tell us deer were so plenty when they came to drink, the stream would be thick of hairs. The name Ona-Sciota, mountains in Southeastern Kentucky, on Evans' Map of 1755 and Hutchins of 1778, doubtless meant mountains where deer are plenty.

January 24.—It is evident from the text of the Journal that Gist did not cross to the west side of the Scioto, where he states Harrickintom's town to be located, and such is the conclusion of Governor Pownall in his edition of Evans' Map, 1776, on which Gist's route is laid down and this town placed on the east side of Scioto. On Dr. Mitchell's Map of 1755 the same. On Evans' original Map of 1755 and Hutchins' of 1778 it is

---

[1] "Lagard's Dictionary of the Huron Language," Paris, 1632.

[2] Mohawk.

[3] Vocabulary in the "Bulletin of the Pennsylvania Historical Society," Vol. I, p. 42.

[4] Id., p. 31.

[5] Also in Transactions American Antiquarian Society, Vol. I, pp. 293-298.

[6] Schoolcraft, Gallatin's Vocabulary.

placed on the west side. It seems to have stood a little below the site of the present city of Chillicothe and nearly opposite the mouth of Paint Creek.

January 25.—Salt Lick Creek empties into the Scioto, on the east side, in Jefferson township, Ross County. The "Scioto Salt Works," the first and for several years the only manufactory of salt in this part of Ohio, were on this creek.[1] "This river (Scioto) is furnished with salt on an eastern branch."[2]

January 27.—This town stood on the east branch of the Scioto, in the present Clay township, Scioto County. Windaughalah was a great war chief during the French wars. His name implies an ambassador. He was a prominent counsellor in peace times. He lived at Tuscarawas in 1762, where he had the figure of a water lizard tatooed on his face above the chin; he was then named Swe-gach-shasin.[3] This chief appeared at a Conference, held at Pittsburgh, July 5, 1759, between George Croghan, Deputy of Sir Wm. Johnston, Superintendent of Indian Affairs in North America, Colonel Hugh Mercer, Commander of the Garrison of Fort Pitt, officers, etc., and the Indian chiefs and warriors of the Six Nations, Shawanese, Delawares, and Wyandots.[4] Also at a Conference held at Lancaster, Pennsylvania, between Governor Hamilton, the Council of the Province and the chiefs of the Ohio Delawares, Shawanese, Tuscarawas, Ottawas and Miamis, and the Six Nation chiefs and others from the North, in August, 1762.

At Pittsburgh, with "White Eyes" and other chiefs, in June, 1774.[5] He was present at the Treaty of Fort McIntosh,

---

[1] "American Pioneer," Vol. I, p. 97.
[2] Evans, Analysis of Map, 1755, p. 30.
[3] Heckwelder's "Indian Nations," p. 198.
[4] Colonial Records of Pennsylvania, Vol. VIII, p. 383, etc.
[5] Pennsylvania Archives, Vol. IV, p. 531.

on the Ohio, where Beaver, Pennsylvania, now stands, in January, 1785, and then with other chiefs, representing the Delawares and Wyandots, executed a deed to the State of Pennsylvania for the remainder of their lands within that State. Being the oldest, Chief Windaughalah, or the "Council Don," signed first.[1] He also appeared at the Treaty held at Fort Finney, at the mouth of the great Miami, in January, 1786, between the United States and the Shawanese. Windaughalah being active in persuading that tribe to make terms with the Government.[2] At this time this distinguished chief must have been quite old. The famous head chief and warrior of the Delawares, Buckongahelas, was his son.

January 29.—The lower Shawanese Town was situated where the present town of Alexandria, opposite Portsmouth, at the mouth of the Scioto, now stands, and also on the south shore of the Ohio River, directly opposite,[3] to which the Shawanese on the north side were compelled to remove, within a few years after Gist's visit, in consequence of a great flood in the Scioto destroying the town at its mouth. George Croghan was there at the time; the water was near fifty feet above the ordinary level.[4] This town was a noted place for Indian trade.[5]

In the original MS. account of "losses occasioned by the French and Indians, driving the English Traders off the Ohio," in 1754, made by George Croghan, at Carlisle, April 24, 1756, appears this item of property seized belonging to William Trent, George Croghan, Robert Callender and Michael Teaff, Traders in Company:

[1] See "Minutes of the Pennsylvania Assembly, 1785," p. 327.
[2] Craig's "Olden Time," Vol. II, p. 455, etc.
[3] In the present Green County, Kentucky.
[4] Croghan's Journal, in Appendix to "Butler's History of Kentucky," Second Appendix, p. 462.
[5] "Evans' Analysis of Map of 1755," p. 30.

"One large store House on the Ohio opposite to the mouth of the River Scioto where the Shawanese had built their new Town called the Lower Shawanese Town, which House we learn by the Indians is now in the possession of a French Trader £200."

The Shawanese removed to the plains of Scioto in 1758 and sent for those of their tribe, at Logstown, to join them.[1] On Hutchins' large Map of 1778 the town at the mouth of the Scioto is marked "Old Lower Shawnee Town," and the place to which they removed is laid down "Lower Shawnee Town," situated on both sides of the Scioto, on the "Plains." There it became known as Upper Chillicothe, or Old Chillicothe and "Pluggy's Town," four miles below Circleville, on the west side of the river.[2] Some of the log cabins and stone chimneys of the town, on the Kentucky side of the Ohio, were standing in June, 1773, when Captain Bullit and the McAfee Company passed down the Ohio.[3] Dr. Davidson mentions it as a French village.[4] Traces of this town were visible in 1820.[5]

"We are glad that the Shawanese who were our enemies did make their application to you last fall, for protection and that you sent them hither to endeavour to make peace with us."[6]

---

[1] "Post's Journal." Dr. Franklin's Tract, "The Walpole Grant; or, Ohio Settlement, 1772," original edition, p. 22.

[2] Pownall's Map, 1776. Evans' ditto, 1755. Dr. Mitchell's ditto. Note in Appendix to Colonel Smith's Narrative.

[3] Note on p. 53, Davidson's "History of the Presbyterian Church in Kentucky."

[4] "Evans' Analysis of Map of 1755," p. 30.

[5] See Collins' "History of Kentucky, 1874." Palmer's "Travels in the United States and Canada, 1817," p. 65.

[6] "Answer of the Five Nations to Governor Fletcher, at Albany, July 4, 1693." New York Colonial History, Vol. IV, p. 42.

January 30.—The two prisoners were Maurice Turner and Ralph Kilgore, in the employ of John Frazer, a trader, living at the old Indian town of Venango, on the Allegheny River.[1] They were captured about twenty-five miles from the Miami Town, in May, 1750, by seven Indians in the French interest, who took them to Detroit, which "then had one hundred and fifty houses, stockaded all around." They were set to work for a farmer in the neighborhood, for three months, when the commander of the Fort being superseded, by Céleron, he took them with him to Niagara. While there they saw Jean Cœur with the goods intended for Ohio. On their way to Quebec they escaped from the guard in the night, between Niagara and Oswego, reached the English fort at the latter place and thence got to Sir William Johnston's "in a miserable condition," and thence by way of New York to Philadelphia.[2] In the original MS. deposition of Turner,[3] taken at Philadelphia, June 28, 1756, he states that "he and Kilgore were taken by seven French Indians who robbed him of fifty Pounds worth of Wampum and Silver work," and Turner was again captured and robbed, in April, 1753, below the Falls of the Ohio; he escaped, with a French deserter, after being taken to Logstown.[4]

February 11.—Marriage and cohabitation with women amongst the savage tribes throughout the world present many similar features, curious, and often beastly, customs. A temporary interchange of wives is not uncommon among the

---

[1] "Pennsylvania Colonial Records," Vol. V, p. 659, 660.

[2] Examination of Turner and Kilgore, by the Governor and Council, October, 1750. "Pennsylvania Colonial Records," Vol. V, p. 482. Letter of Sir William Johnston to Governor Clinton, id., p. 481, and also in "New York Colonial History," Vol. VI, p. 599.

[3] Among Colonel F. Etting's ";Traders' Papers."

[4] MS. deposition.

Indians of the far North.[1] A similar dance, etc., by a small party of Iroquois near Fort Cumberland, in 1755, is described in Sargent's "History of Braddock's Expedition," p. 376. It is stated [2] that in the Iroquois Canton of Tsonnontonon [3] a plurality of husbands prevails.

February 12 to 17.—To make the courses and distances stated in the Journal reconcilable, Gist passed through the present counties of Scioto, Adams, Highland, Fayette, Madison, Clarke and Champaign to West Liberty, in the northern part of Logan County, about 140 miles from the mouth of the Scioto; there he crossed the Mad River,[4] thence southwest to the Twigtwee town—about twenty-five miles as he gives it. His object being to examine the country occasioned his not taking a more direct course, which would have been forty miles less. The Twigtwees, or Pickawillamy Town, stood on the west bank of the Great Miami, at the mouth of Laramie's Creek, on the south side, in the present county of Miami, about two and a half miles north of the present town of Piqua.[5] Howe erroneously places it at the point where Laramie's store, or Fort Laramie, afterwards stood, fourteen miles farther north. By the French accounts the Miamis, in 1718, had a thousand warriors.[6] In 1736 about six hundred fighting men.[7] At the Treaty of Greenville, in 1795, the Miamis claimed to have had undisputed occupation from time immemorial of all

[1] Mackenzie's Voyages.

[2] Jeffry's "History of the French Dominions in America," London, 1750, p. 71.

[3] Senecas.

[4] Supposed by him to be the Little Miami, which heads about forty miles farther south.

[5] Evans' and Mitchell's Maps, 1755. Pownall's, 1776. Hutchins', 1778.

[6] Memoir in the "Colonial History of New York," Vol. IX, p. 891.

[7] Id., p. 1057.

the country between the Scioto and the Wabash and from Detroit to Chicago.[1]

In the Fall of 1747 the Miamis seized the French Fort Miami, plundered and partly burned it.[2] In July, 1748, the chiefs and deputies from the Miamis held their first Conference and Treaty with Pennsylvania at Lancaster. A number of the Six Nations, Delawares, Shawanese and chiefs of other tribes were present. The Miamis then claimed to have, with their allies, twenty towns and one thousand warriors.[3] Dispatches received from Governor Vaudreuil by the French Ministry state that the English have succeeded in carrying a revolt among the Miami tribes settled on the Rock River[4] and the Wabash.[5]

February 18.—This fort was an Indian fortification, not a traders'; they, however, used it for their protection, as many as fifty of them sometimes lodging within it.[6] Pattin and near sixty other traders lodged in "cabins" within a fort belonging to the Miamis, whose chief's name was La Demoiselle. It is probable the cabins and the Long or Council House were stockaded, making a very defensible structure. It was called La Demoiselle Fort in the dispatches of the Marquis de Longuere to the Minister.[7] "You told us you discovered on the Great Miami traces of an old Fort. It was not a French Fort, Brother, it was a Fort built by me."[8]

[1] Speech of Little Turtle, American State Papers, Vol. I, p. 570.

[2] "New York Colonial History," Vol. X, p. 140.

[3] "Pennsylvania Colonial Records," Vol. V, pp. 307-9, September 18, 1750.

[4] Big Miami.

[5] Paris Document, "New York Colonial History," Vol. X, p. 220.

[6] French Memorial, Paris edition, 1756, p. 97. London edition, 1758, p. 103.

[7] "New York Colonial History," Vol. X, p. 245.

[8] That is, "By my Tribe or Nation."

NOTES TO CHRISTOPHER GIST'S JOURNAL OF 1750-51. 125

Reply of the Miami chief, Little Turtle, to General Wayne, at the Treaty of Greenville, August, 1795.[1] The ruins of this fort were observed by the army under General Harmar, which crossed the Miami here on October 10, 1790.[2] At the Treaty at Fort Harmar, in 1789, this point is referred to as "at the mouth of the branch of the Big Miami," where the fort stood which was taken by the French in 1752.[3]

February 22.—The Treaty referred to in the biographical sketch of George Croghan was dated as executed this day.[4]

February 24.—This fort was attacked and captured by a force of about two hundred and forty Indians, led by two Frenchmen, June 22, 1752. The old King, called Brittain, was taken, killed and eaten, near the fort, in the presence of his tribe. In the attack one white man and fourteen Indians were killed, and five whites were taken prisoners.[5] Thomas Burney and Andrew McBryar, traders, were in the fort at the time of the attack, but escaped in the night. The other whites were captured. Burney was afterward killed at Braddock's defeat, July 9, 1755, and McBryar taken prisoner.[6]

"The Indians are not habitual Cannibals';" after a victory, however, it often happens that the bodies of their enemies are consumed at a formal feast. A superstitious rite to incite them to warlike deeds.[7] The British Ministry made much of

[1] American State Papers, Indian Affairs, Vol. I, p. 576.
[2] Letter of General Harmar to the Secretary of War, Nov. 23, 1790.
[3] American State Papers, Vol. I.
[4] See "Pennsylvania Colonial Records," Vol. V, p. 524, and see post March 1.
[5] Thomas Burney's Account and Message from the Twigtwees to Governor Hamilton, August, 1752. Colonial Records, Vol. V, p. 599. Assembly Journals of Pennsylvania, p. 234.
[6] "MS. Accounts of George Croghan & Co., 1750," in which it is stated that they lost goods, in the hands of Burney and McBryar at the taking of the Twigtwees Town, to the value of £331, 15s.
[7] Parkman's "Pontiac," Vol. I, second edition, p. 234-257.

this affair in all of their statements respecting the origin of the war of 1754. On Dr. Mitchell's official Map of 1755, Pickwaylinees is described as an "English Fort, established in 1748."[1] It is obvious, as the "French Royal Geographer" observed, that the French established in the neigborhood[2] would not have permitted the erection of an English post here.[3] The hostile force did not keep possession of the fort. William Trent was in it a few days afterwards.[4] The Miamis afterwards returned to the French alliance; and it is stated their fort was again attacked, although unsuccessfully, by the Shawanese, Delawares and other Indians, in the English interest, assisted by a few traders. Soon afterwards the Miamis left the Big Miami, retiring to the Wabash and the Maumee. The Shawanese took their place, since known as Upper Piqua.[5]

February 25.—The Wawaughtanneys, or as the French called them, Ouatemeous—the most ancient of the Miami tribes.

February 26—Twigtwees—as the Six Nations called the Miamis, the French called them Ouitaneous.[6]

February 27.—The French fort, Miami; about forty-five miles from Pickwaylinees and where the City of Fort Wayne, Indiana, now stands.[7]

March 2.—This point on "Mad Creek" is about seven miles west of Springfield, in Bethlehem township, Clarke

---

[1] See also "Contest in America," by an impartial hand, 1757, pp. 221-237. Evans' Map, 1755; Hutchins', 1778.

[2] At Fort Miami, etc.

[3] Remarques sur la Carte de l'Amérique, Paris, 1755, p. 120.

[4] Journal, Logstown to Pickawillamy, 1752. Clarke & Co., 1871.

[5] Howe's Ohio, Miami County, p. 363.

[6] Shea's "Charlevoix, American Antiquarian Collection," p. 63, Vol. II.

[7] "French Memoire," 1756, p. 98; English edition, p. 103. See also Dillon's "History of Indiana." Brice's ditto of Fort Wayne. Hutchins' Map, 1778. Arrowsmith's, ditto, 1796.

County, at the junction of the old road from Laramie's store, with the Springfield and Dayton road, or turnpike, where the village of West Boston stood, five miles west of Springfield. Piqua, a town famous in Shawanese Indian annals, was built here, subsequently. It was destroyed by the army under George Rogers Clarke, in 1780. Tecumseh was born here about 1768.[1] The traders captured here, were those before mentioned, January 30, Turner and Kilgore.

March 3-8.—It seems probable Gist did not leave the valley of the little Miami until in the present County of Warren, thence Northeast to the mouth of Scioto. The Mingoes, a name generally applied to Indians of the Iroquois tribes or Six Nations. The Menguaes, or Mengwe, were, however, a distinct but kindred tribe of the Iroquois, with whom they were continually at war, for over a century, until their final subjugation in 1672-5, when their remnant, known as Conestogas, was incorporated with their conquerors.[2] Their country extended between the lower Susquehanna and the Delaware. They were known by the different names of Minguaes, Susquehannas, Andastes and Gandastogues or Conestogas.[3] Dr. O'Callaghan, editor of the "New York Colonial History," erroneously restricts the name "Mingo" to the "Iroquois of the Ohio." Dr. Shea also, in note to "Private Diaries of Washington; Tour of the Ohio," p. 224, N. Y. 1860: "The Conestogas were formerly a part of the Five Nations, called Mingoes, and speak the same language to this day."[4]

[1] According to Drake's "Life of Tecumseh."
[2] Speech of Cannesatego at the treaty of Lancaster, 1744. "Colonial Records of Pennsylvania," Vol. IV, p. 708, etc. Colden's "History of the Five Nations," third edition, 1755, Vol. II.
[3] "The Fall of the Susquehannocks," by S. F. Streeter; "Historical Magazine," Vol. I, 1857, p. 65. Alsop's "Maryland," 1666.
[4] "Colonial Records of Pennsylvania," Vol. III, pp. 101-204. Proceedings of Provincial Council, at Philadelphia, October 3, 1722; and in Evans' "Geographical Essays," an analysis of Map, 1755, p. 11. Note.

"The Confederates, otherwise called Iroquois, Five Nations, Six Nations, Minguaes and Mingoes." As Dr. Shea correctly observes,[1] "Gallatin erroneously placed them, (the Andastes or Mingues), on the head waters of the Ohio, and having been followed by Bancroft has misled many."[2]

March 12.—Crossed the Ohio to the south shore, in the present County of Greenup, Kentucky, thence to a point near the present town of Vanceburgh.

March 13.—Hugh Crawford's name first appears in the list of Indian traders licensed in 1747-8.[3] He was trading among the Miamis in the winter of 1749-50. They sent a message by him to the Governor of Pennsylvania.[4] In 1755 he made the first settlement, or improvement at the "Standing Stone," now the town of Huntingdon, Pennsylvania.[5] Crawford's House is marked at the mouth of Standing Stone Creek, west side, on Scull's Map of Pennsylvania, 1759.[6] He was an Ensign in the 1st Battalion, 1st Pennsylvania Regiment, 1757.[7] Served in General Forbes' campaign, 1758. In March, 1759, he was in command of a detachment of

[1] "Historical Magazine," for 1857, Vol. II, p. 294.

[2] See "History of United States," Vol. III, p. 245, and Map; also "Transactions of American Antiquarian Society," Vol. II, p. 73, and Map. See also "Discoveries in New Netherlands," and Map. "Report of Captain Hendrickson," 1616. "Holland Documents; New York Colonial History," Vol. I, p. 13. Vocabulary of the Minguae's Language, and note in Campanius' "History of New Sweden," original edition, Stockholm, 1702, p. 182, etc.; Du Ponceus' translation, Philadelphia, 1834, p. 148. "Captain John Smith's Explorations," 1608, and Map, in his "General History of Virginia," 1629, Richmond edition, 1819, p. 182, etc., of Vol. I. Map of Virginia, De Laet, 1640.

[3] "Pennsylvania Archives," Vol. II, p. 14.

[4] "Colonial Records," Vol. V, p. 437.

[5] Lytle's "History of Huntingdon County," p. 71.

[6] See also Judge Huston's "Land Titles of Pennsylvania," p. 338.

[7] Pennsylvania Archives, Vol. II, p. 336.

troops at the "Breastworks," on the branch of Stony Creek, now known as "Breastworks Run," near Stoyestown, Somerset County, Pennsylvania.[1] At the outbreak of the Pontiac War, in the Spring of 1763, he and a boy were captured by the Indians at Cedar Point, Maumee Bay, Lake Erie. Six men of the party were killed.[2] He was interpreter and conductor of the Indians in running the western part of Mason and Dixon's line, in 1767.[3] For his services in that business he received a "grant of preference" for five hundred acres of land, in January, 1768, from Governor Penn. It was one of the "Gist Tracts," in the present Fayette County.[4] Crawford died in 1770. Salt Lick or Spring, since known as the Big Bone Lick, in Boone County, Kentucky, about one and one-half miles from the Ohio River, at the mouth of the creek, twenty-five miles below the great Miami and eighty-six miles above Louisville. So called from the bones of the Mastodon, or Mammoth, found there, first by the French, in 1729.[5] George Croghan visited the Lick in 1765.[6] He removed some of the bones and sent them to Peter Collinson in London.[7] See also letter from Dr. Wm. Clarke, of Cincinnati, to Thomas Jefferson, in 1806, in refer-

[1] MS. letter, March, 1759, to Colonel Bouquet, from Hugh Crawford, respecting the health of his men. "Bouquet Papers."

[2] Letter from Thomas Calhoon, at Tuscarawas, May 28, 1763.

[3] Manuscript Journal of Mason and Dixon, Library Pennsylvania Historical Society. "History of Mason and Dixon's Line," by James Veech, 1857, p. 42.

[4] Note to p. 96 of "Monongahela of Old," James Veech.

[5] Bellin's Map of 1754, in Charlevoix's "History of New France," Vol. I, and Bellin's "Remarques sur la Carte de l'Amérique," 1755, p. 121 note.

[6] Journal in Butler's "History of Kentucky," second edition, Appendix.

[7] "Description of the Mastodon, or Mammoth, of Ohio," pamphlet by A. C. Bown, M.D., Amsterdam, 1809.

NUREMBERG, 1756.

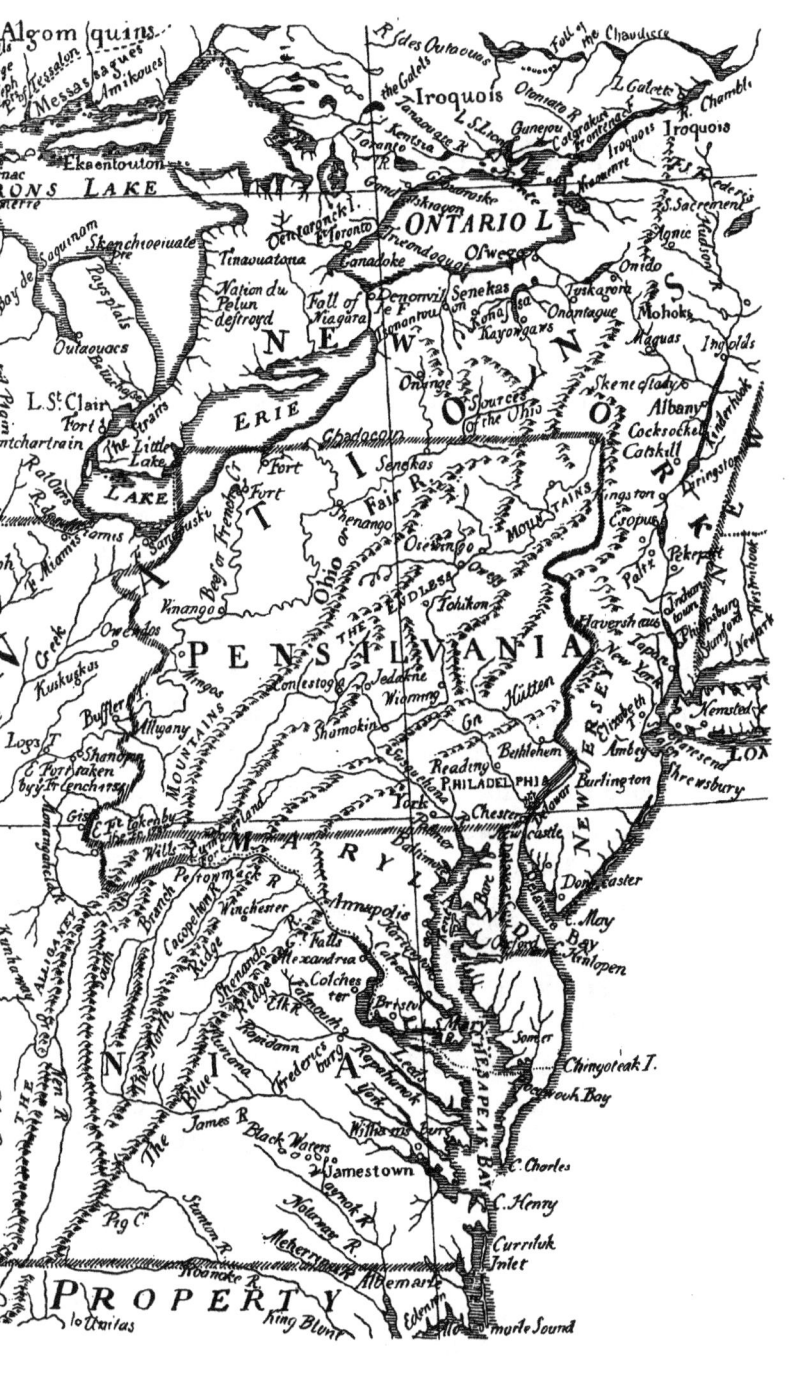

ence to his explorations here. He states that he had at one time five tons of the bones.[1] Renewed and deep explorations in 1876 brought to the surface quantities of these remains.

March 14.—About the site of Washington, Mason County, four miles south of Maysville.

March 15.—Probably the Licking River at the Lower Blue Licks. He had travelled thus far by an old trail from the Ohio.

March 16.—Through the present counties of Hamilton, Nicholas, Scott, and Franklin, to the Kentucky River, or near it, above Frankfort.

March 18.—The Lower Salt Lick, now known as Salt River. It is possible Gist reached it at the Licks, since called Bullit's Licks, three miles from the river, in Bullit County, near Shepherdville, and about eighteen miles southeast from Louisville, at the Falls. The courses he gives in the Journal would take him to this point, although his distances do not. He must also have misunderstood Smith, as Salt River is below and not above the Falls. It seems more probable that the farthest point he reached westward was the branch of Salt River, since known as Floyd's Fork; there was a Salt Lick on it in early times, where Floydsburgh, in Oldham County, now stands.[2] The ridge of mountains he ascended is a low range or elevation, extending from Oldham eastward to the Kentucky River.

March 19.—The creeks he crossed are now named Bullskin, Gist's, and other branches of Brashear's Creek, in Shelby County; their course is southwest. He reached "the little Cuttawa," or Kentucky River, about where the city of Frankfort now stands, crossed at the island above, thence southeast

---

[1] Appendix to Cramer's "Navigator," Pittsburgh, 1814. Cuming's "Western Tour in 1807-9." Pittsburgh, 1810, p. 409.

[2] See Munsell's State Map of Kentucky, 1816.

through the present counties of Woodford and Fayette to the border of Clark. The Kentucky River is here called the "Little Cuttawa,"[1] and such appears to be the name by which it was first known, from the fact that the Indian trail or war-path to the Country of the Catawbas, in the Carolinas, led from the lower Shawnee town, opposite the mouth of the Scioto, southward to the Warrior Branch, or North Fork, of the Kentucky River, thence up the river to the "war gap" in the mountain ridge,[2] thence southwest to the Shawnee or Cumberland River, thence south to the Cumberland Gap, thence to and by way of the French Broad River to the Catawba country.[3] Kentucky or Kentuckgin, Kantuchy, Kentucke, from Ken-ta-ke, a Mohawk[4] word signifying "among the meadows,"[5] so applied with the usual correctness of descriptive names by the Indians to the country through which the Kentucky River flows—the woodland meadows being its characteristic feature.[6] John Johnston, who was for many years Agent for Indian Affairs in Ohio, states that "Kentucky is a Shawnee word, meaning, at the head of a river."[7] In the Shawnee language Meadows is M'shish-keè-we-kut-uk-ah.[8] In Evans' "Analysis of Map of 1755," p. 29, this river is described as "having high clay banks,

[1] Catawba.

[2] In Clay and Perry counties.

[3] See Lewis Evans' Map, 1755. Pownall's, 1776. Hutchins', 1778. Filson's Map of Kentucky, 1784. Munsell's State Map of ditto, 1816.

[4] Iroquois or Six Nations.

[5] List of names of places given to Dr. Hough, by an intelligent Indian of the Cahnawagas, or French Mohawks, of the tribe near Montreal. Hough's "History of St. Lawrence County," New York, 1858.

[6] In a Mohawk Vocabulary, in the "American Aboriginal Archives," Vol. II, p. 486, Meadows is Ye-e-an-ty-yk-ta.

[7] "Archives Americana," Vol. I, p. 279. Howe's "Historical Collection of Ohio," p. 600.

[8] Vocabulary in Schoolcraft's "American Aboriginal Archives," Vol. II, p. 474.

abounds in Cane and Buffaloes and large Salt Springs, its navigation interrupted with some shoals, but passable with Canoes to the Gap where the war path goes through the Ouasiota mountains," which Evans deems "a very important pass." Evans' information respecting the country was obtained from Alexander Maginty and Alexander Lowry, well-known and intelligent traders from Pennsylvania.[1] The name Kentucky first appears in the Deposition of Alexander Maginty, taken at Philadelphia, before William Allen, Chief Justice of Pennsylvania, on the 12th of October, 1753, wherein he states that on the preceding 16th of January, when returning with six other traders from the Cuttawas, in Carolina, they were attacked and taken prisoners by seventy Cahnawagas, or French Praying Indians, from the river St. Lawrence, at a place about twenty-five miles from the Blue Lick town and on the south bank of the Cantucky River, which empties itself into the Allegheny River, about two hundred miles below the lower Shawnee Town.[2] The captives were beaten and plundered of their goods, taken to Fort Miami, thence to Detroit, Niagara and Montreal. Two of their number were sent to France; one escaped. Maginty, with the three remaining prisoners, were redeemed by Colonel Schuyler and the other commissioners of Indian affairs, at Albany, paying the Indians about seventy-two pounds. In Maginty's petition to the Pennsylvania Assembly for relief, the river is called "Kantucqui," a western branch of the Ohio.[3] In the Treaty of Greenville, 1795, Article III, it is mentioned as the Cuttawa or Kentucky River; also on Hutchins' Map, 1778, and in Morse's Gazetteer of North America, 1798, Kentucky River "is

---

[1] Analysis, p. 10.

[2] "Colonial Records of Pennsylvania," Vol. V, pp. 627, 663. *New York Mercury*, August 19, 1754.

[3] Assembly Journal of Votes and Proceedings for 1753, October 16, p. 272.

sometimes called Cuttawa," p. 260. In the Walpole Grant of Vandalia, in 1773, it is mentioned as the "Louisa Catawba, or Cuttawa."[1] By the "Great Cuttawa River" Gist probably means the Cherokee River, now the Tennessee. Hendrick Apamans, a Mohican chief, speaks of the "Cherokees or Kuttoohwoh" in his interesting "Narrative," 1794, Vol. II, part 1, p. 128. Memoirs of the Pennsylvania Historical Society, 1827. On the map, in the Tract attributed to General Oglęthorpe, London, 1733, the Tennessee River is marked "Cussetaolias Hochelepe" River. George Croghan, in his Journal, on May 31, 1765, mentions, "passed the mouth of the river Kentucky or Holsters River," "A fine level country;" so Daniel Boone described it. The beautiful level of Kentucky.[2]

March 20.—This mountain is the low ridge in Clarke County.

March 21.—To the Kentucky River, near the mouth of Red River, between Clarke, Estill and Madison Counties. The "shining stones" doubtless were iron ores, with a little sulphur, abundant here.[3] This was the point reached by Daniël Boone on his first visit to Kentucky, in 1769, eighteen years after Gist.[4]

March 24.—Along the North Fork of the Kentucky River, in the present counties of Lee, Perry and Letcher, coal abundant.[5]

April 1.—Through the Pound Gap, or Stony Gap, as some call it, about twelve miles southeast of Whitesburgh, in Letcher

---

[1] MS. and "Plain Facts," 1781, p. 156. Butler's "History of Kentucky," second edition, pp. 24, 504. Hall's "Sketches of the West," Vol. I, p. 251, and Introductory Chapter to this volume, part relative to Dr. Thomas Walker's explorations.

[2] "Narrative" in Filson's "History of Kentucky," 1784, p. 326.

[3] See Collins' "History of Kentucky."

[4] Boone's "Narrative," in Filson, p. 326. Collins' "History," Vol. II, p. 495.

[5] Collins' "History of Kentucky," Vol. II, pp. 462, 579.

County, Kentucky; then he struck the head of the Pound Fork of the Big Sandy River, in Wise County, Virginia. Coal is abundant in this county and has many surface indications.[1]

April 3.—On the stream called Indian Creek, the middle head fork of the Big Sandy, in Wise County. The Crane was a totem or badge of one of the Miami tribes;[2] also of the Wyandots.[3] A common practice among the Indian tribes, with war parties at a distance from home, was to paint on trees or a rock figures of warriors, prisoners, animals, etc., as intelligible to other Indians as a printed handbill among whites.[4]

April 7.—On Guesse's Creek or River, a branch of Clinch, in Wise County, Virginia. This stream was probably named for our explorer—Gist being often mispronounced "Guess." On the map of Kentucky, in Imlay's "History," third edition, 1797, Gist's Creek, a branch of Brashear's, in Shelby County, is marked Guesse's Creek.[5]

April 23.—Along the New Garden ridge, dividing Buchanan and Russell counties.

April 27-29.—In Baptist Valley, Tazewell County. From the 7th to this day—the 29th—Gist was slowly toiling along on his general course, east and northeast, in the valley of Clinch River, on the south side of the ridge dividing the heads of the Big Sandy from the Clinch, which stream he evidently supposed to be the Cuttawa or Kentucky.

[1] Madison's Map of Virginia. State Map of Virginia. Lloyd's Map, etc.
[2] "New York Colonial History," Vol. IX, pp. 621, 1057.
[3] Howe's "History of Ohio," Wyandot County. Kirchval's "History of the Valley of Virginia," p. 67. Howe's Historical Collection of Virginia, Tazewell County. Morris' "Narrative," p. 491.
[4] For a curious instance of their conveying defiant notice in this manner to their enemies, the French, see Schoolcraft, "American Aboriginal Archives," and Colden's "History of the Five Nations," Vol. II, Chapter XII.
[5] See Martin's "Geographical Gazetteer of Virginia," pp. 434-35, and map.

April 30.—The Blue Stone River, in Abbs Valley, Tazewell County, northeast of Jeffersonville. In 1756 and subsequent years the Indians from north of the Ohio made frequent incursions against the settlers in Western Virginia, by way of Kentucky or Big Sandy rivers, and then by the Blue Stone to the Kenhawha or New River.[1]

May 1.—In Mercer County, the "very high mountain," upon the top of which was a rock, sixty or seventy feet high, to the top of which he climbed, is on the west side of New River. The eminence Gist paused to climb was not the "Hawk's Nest," as erroneously stated by Mr. Bancroft.[2] That grand precipice overhangs the east bank of New River, in Fayette County, at least fifty miles north of the ridge ascended by Gist. The Kanawha "breaks through the next high mountain below the mouth of Greenbrier River, in Raleigh and Greenbrier counties."

May 7.—This stream is usually called "Kanhawha" below the junction of the Gauley and New Rivers. Respecting the origin of the names Kanhawha and New River or Woods River, see note to Gist's second "Journal."

May 8.—He reached and crossed the New River, below the mouth of Indian Creek,[3] which is eight miles in a direct line above the mouth of the Blue Stone.

May 9.—On the stream well known as Indian Creek, at the mouth of Drooping Lick Creek, in Monroe County, about midway from the Red to the Salt Sulphur Springs.

May 10.—Peters' Mountain.

May 11.—Big Stony Creek, in Giles County. The "Lake or Pond" is on the summit of Salt Pond Mountain, in the

---

[1] Howe's "Historical Collection of Virginia," p. 490. Bickley's "History of Indian Wars of Tazewell County," 1852, p. 191.

[2] "History of the United States," Vol. IV, p. 82.

[3] In Monroe County.

same county, and about ten miles east of Parisburgh. "The water is fresh, clear and inhabited by fine trout."[1] Produces but few fish.[2] "The Lake is three-quarters of a mile long and will average a third of a mile in width.[3] This agrees with Gist's estimate of its dimensions. Pollard also states that "it has never been inhabited by fish . . . all placed in it disappeared."[4] Sinking Creek is also in Giles County; this stream sinks, a mile or more before reaching the New River, by an underground passage or channel.

May 13.—Richard Hall's, at or near where Christiansburgh now stands, in Montgomery County.

May 14.—Thomas Lee was the President of the Council of Virginia.

May 15.—This day he reached a point at or near Little River, in the present Floyd County.

May 16.—"Beaver Island Creek." He encamped by its main branch, now called Big Reedy Island Creek, in the present Carroll County.

May 17.—At the "Flower Gap," on the dividing line between the present counties of Carroll, in Virginia, and Surry, in North Carolina.

May 18.—On the north side of the Yadkin River, and on the west side of the stream marked Saw Mill Creek, near and west of Reddies River, near the present town of Wilkesbarre, in Wilkes County, North Carolina,[5] on which Gist's place of residence is marked.[6]

[1] Howe's "Historical Collection of Virginia," p. 278. Boyes' State Map of Virginia, 1859. "Gazetteer of Virginia," p. 346.

[2] Kirchval's "Valley of Virginia," p. 343, where it is also stated that "the pond has risen twenty-five feet since 1804."

[3] Pollard's "Virginia Tourist," 1870, p. 146.

[4] Id., p. 141.

[5] See Fry & Jefferson's Map of Virginia, 1751-55.

[6] See also map engraved for Jefferson's "Notes on Virginia," and Price & Strothers' State Map of North Carolina, 1808.

NOTES TO GIST'S SECOND JOURNAL, 1751-52.

November 4, 1751.—The Ohio Company's store-house stood on the south bank of the Potomac, directly opposite to the present city of Cumberland, Maryland, in Frederick (now Hampshire) County, Virginia. It was built in the year 1750, by Hugh Parker, the Factor of the Company, on land purchased for them from Lord Fairfax by Parker and Colonel Thomas Cresap. The main building was constructed of timber, a double house and two stories in height; it stood on the bank, a short distance east of the present residence[1] of Captain Perry, fronting and near the river.[2] The name of "Caicutuck or Wills' Creek" first appeared on Fry & Jefferson's Map of Virginia and Maryland, 1751. It is accurately laid down, but not named, on Mayo's Map of the Survey of the Potomac in 1736. The gap in the Allegheny Mountains is four miles west of Cumberland, where the Baltimore & Ohio Railroad crosses the National Road at "Braddock's Run," as the southwest fork of Wills' Creek has been called since 1755; Braddock's route and the National Road as at first constructed being on the same track as that of Gist.[3]

November 5.—To a point about three miles west of the present town of Frostburgh, in Garrett County, Maryland, on the National Road.

[1] 1877.
[2] Copy of drawing in the King's Library, British Museum, made for W. M. Darlington, 1874. London Board of Trade MS. Fry & Jefferson's Map of Virginia, 1751. Sparks' "Washington Letters," Vol. II, p. 15. "Pennsylvania Archives," Vol. II, p. 134.
[3] "Braddock's Expedition."

November 8.—Little Meadow Run and other small streams, heads of Castleman's River, or the middle fork of the Youghiogheny; on the west side or foot of Little Meadow Mountain, and about twenty miles west of Cumberland, in Garrett County, Maryland, and Elk Lick Township, Somerset County, Pennsylvania.

November 20-21.—Crossing Negro Mountain into Addison Township, Somerset County, Pennsylvania.

November 22.—The Youghiogheny River has three heads or forks: the main, or south fork, rises in Preston County, West Virginia, near the spring-head of the Potomac; the middle fork, or Castleman's River, rises in Garrett County, Maryland, and the north fork, or Laurel Hill Creek, rises in Somerset County, Pennsylvania. The name first appears, marked "Spring heads of Yok-yo-gane river a south branch of the Monongahela," on a "Map of the Northern Neck in Virginia, the Territory of Thomas Lord Fairfax according to a late survey drawn in the year 1737 by Wm. Mayo."[1] It next appears on Fry and Jefferson's Map of Virginia and Maryland, of 1751, as the "Yawyawganey River." Gist seems to have reached the middle fork this day, above Lost Run, in the northwest part of Addison Township, Somerset County, Pennsylvania, thence crossed into Upper Turkey-foot Township.

November 24.—Crossed the south fork at Turkey-foot, or Three Forks, near the present town of Confluence, in Somerset County, where the three branches of the Youghiogheny unite; thence proceeding, he encamped about the head of "Gabriel's Run," in Henry Clay Township, Fayette County. The name Youghiogheny—Youghanné—was evidently given to this stream by the Indian tribe of the Kanhawhas, Conoys or Canawese, who, in the beginning of the last century, inhabited the country around the heads of the Potomac and

[1] "History of the Dividing Line," and other Tracts, Richmond, 1866, Vol. II, p. 117, etc.

back of the great mountains in Virginia.¹ They were of the same nation and language as the Nanticokes, of the Algonquin, Lenape or Delaware stock. Yough—four—and hanne—stream or rapid-flowing stream. As before mentioned, the three head branches of this river join at the point and form a fourth or main stream.²

November 25.—To the Licks, on Stony Fork of Big Sandy Creek, in Wharton Township, Fayette County, and near the National Road.

November 26-29.—In George's and South Union townships, Fayette County.

December 6.—The upper forks of the Monongahela are formed by the junction of Cheat River, in Fayette and Green counties, near the southern boundary-line of the State. The general course of Gist from Wills' Creek to the Monongahela was to the north of the road subsequently opened for the Ohio Company, in 1752-53, by Gist and Cresap, they employing Indians for that purpose. The troops under Washington, in 1754, greatly repaired it as far as Gist's plantation, and in 1755 it was widened and completed by General Braddock's army to within about six miles of Fort Du Quesne.³ The reader will readily observe that Gist deviated continually from a direct path, in

---

[1] See notes on the Kanawha Post.

[2] Smith's "History of Virginia," 1629. Richmond edition, 1819, Vol. I, p. 147. "Hakluyt Society," 1849, p. 96. "Roger Williams' Key," p. 22. Heckwelder, "History of the Indian Nations," 1819, pp. 26-74. John Eliot's "Indian Grammar," Massachusetts Historical Collection, Vol. IX, Series 2, p. 260. Dr. Edwards' "Indian Language," id., Vol. X, p. 129, Connecticut Historical Society, Vol. II, pp. 4-12, etc. Gallatin's "Synopsis of the Indian Tribes." "Transactions of the American Antiquarian Society," Vol. II, pp. 52-56, and Vocabulary, same volume, p. 359.

[3] Resolutions of the Ohio Company, at a meeting held at Stafford Court House, June 21, 1749. Also at Ocquoquan Ferry, December, 1750, and in March, 1753. MS.

order to explore the country thoroughly, pursuant to his instructions.

December 7.—This Indian owner of this camp was the well-known Delaware, Nemacolin. The creek was called by his name in early times, but subsequently changed to Dunlap's.[1] It empties into the Monongahela, at Brownsville.[2] Nemacolin was the principal of the Indians employed by Gist and Cresap to blaze and clear the road before mentioned. He was intelligent and trustworthy.[3] A letter from his father, Checochinican, the chief of the Indians on the Brandywine, to Governor Gordon, June 24, 1729, is in the "Pennsylvania Archives," Vol. I, p. 239. It seems the Indians had sold their lands on the Brandywine, reserving a part on the head of the creek, by a writing, which was burned, with the cabin wherein it was deposited. The mill-dams of the white settlers destroyed their fishing, and they were otherwise "crowded out"—as usual to the present day.[4] Charles Pokes's name appears in the list of Indian traders in 1734.[5] On Mayo's Map, of 1737, his name is marked, with those of four other settlers, at the north bend of the Potomac, where Hancock, Maryland, now stands.[6] In 1774 he lived on Cross Creek, West Virginia, about sixteen miles from the Ohio River,

---

[1] An old trader.

[2] "Pennsylvania Archives," Vol. XII, p. 347. "Shippen Papers," p. 163. "American Pioneer," Vol. II, p. 60.

[3] Jacobs' "Life of Cresap," 1828, p. 28.

[4] See "Pennsylvania Archives," Vol. XII, p. 281. "Colonial Records," Vol. III, p. 269. "Votes of Assembly," 1726, Vol. II, p. 481. Smith's "History of Delaware County," pp. 235, 240. Gordon's "History of Pennsylvania," p. 194. Hazard's "Pennsylvania Register," Vol. I, p. 114.

[5] "Colonial Archives," Vol. I, p. 425.

[6] See also "Colonial Records of Pennsylvania," Vol. V, p. 760.

where Wellsville is now situated. He was still living in Shelby County, Kentucky, in 1799.[1]

December 9.—River Monongahela, said to be from the Shawnee Mehmonauangehelak. Falling-in-Bank River.[2] "The Cavity in a Rock" was probably on the river bank, on the east side, six miles from Brownsville, up the river, on the farm now owned by Captain Jacobs; in the original patent it is called the Cave Tract, "Menangihilli;" this word implies "high banks breaking off in some places and tumbling down."[3] The correctness of these definitions is doubtful, the banks of this river do not "fall in" or "break off" more than those of the Ohio, Allegheny, and many other streams, nor is it known that they ever did, and the Indians invariably gave accurate descriptive names. It may be, however, that the banks at some point on the river "fell in" on some occasion, to commemorate which, the Indians applied the name.[4]

December 15.—Crossed the Monongahela to the west side, below the mouth of the Youghiogheny.

December 17.—Oppaymolleah, a Delaware Chief, appeared at the conference held at Fort Pitt, in April and May, 1768, by George Croghan, Deputy Agent for Indian Affairs, the Commissioners of Pennsylvania, Alexander McKee, the Commander, and officers of the garrison, with the chiefs and warriors of the Six Nations, Delawares, Wyandots and others residing on the waters of the Ohio. 1103 Indians were present, besides their women and children.[5]

[1] See his Deposition in Appendix to Jefferson's "Notes on Virginia," edition of 1801, p. 368.

[2] See note to "Washington's Tour to the Ohio," p. 244.

[3] John Heckwelder, "American Philosophical Society," Vol. IV, new series, 1834, p. 376.

[4] The name Monongahela first appears on the map of William Mayo, in 1737, and next on the map of Fry and Jefferson, 1751.

[5] "Colonial Records," Vol. IX, p. 54, etc.

Joshua was a Delaware also. In December, 1759, he and Tangoochqua (Wissameek) or Catfish, were sent as messengers from the Delawares on the Ohio, to Philadelphia, with a message to the Governor and Council of Pennsylvania.[1] The Beaver, or Tamaquè, was the King or Head Chief of the Delaware tribe on the waters of the Ohio. He resided at Soh-kon, (mouth of Beaver Creek), afterwards at Kuskuskis, near the Forks, and in 1764, at the Forks of Tuscarawas.[2] He frequently appeared at conferences held at Fort Pitt, and also at Philadelphia. He was the brother of Shingiss and Custaloga. He died about 1770, on the Muskingum, where the Moravian town of Gnadenhutten was built two years afterwards, near the present town of New Philadelphia.[3]

January 8, 1752.—To head of Fish Creek, Marshall County, West Virginia, and Green County, Pennsylvania.

January 22.—To a point in Wetzel County, West Virginia, between Little and Big Fishing Creek.

January 27.—To a point over south side of Fishing Creek, Wetzel County.

February 1.—At Middle Island Creek, near Middlebourne, Tyler County.

February 2.—Three miles south of Middlebourne.

February 10.—On McKun's Fork of Middle Island Creek, Pleasants County.

February 11.—Hughes River, near Hainesville, Ritchie County.

February 14.—This stone stood on the creek bottom, opposite the slip in the hill, on the left hand or Parish Fork of Standing Stone Creek. Within the past ten years[4] oil having been found there the stone was broken up to make

[1] "Colonial Records," Vol. VIII, p. 415. "Archives," Vol. III, p. 575.
[2] Journals of C. F. Post, 1758. " Bouquet's Expedition Against the Ohio Indians," 1765.
[3] Pennsylvania Historical Society, Vol. I, pp. 147–153.
[4] 1877.

walls for steam boilers. The inscription cut on it no doubt, had long previous been effaced by the lapse of time or incrusted over by lime. The date cut by Gist, February, 1751, was in accordance with the old style of computation, by which the year began on the 25th of March, instead of the 1st of January, to which it was changed throughout the British Dominions, by law, in 1751, the new style to commence on January 1, 1752. Why Gist cut the date 1751 instead of 1752 is not easy to explain, especially as his Journal is kept by the new method of computing time.

February 15.—Near Wirt, C. H., (Elizabeth,) the creek is the Little Kanawha.

February 16.—On the head of Lee's Creek, Wirt County.

February 17.—To Poplar Fork of Thirteen-Mile Creek of the Big Kanawha, after passing through Jackson County. The Kanawha River derived its name from a tribe of Indians, who formerly inhabited the country on its waters, and also on the upper Potomac. These tribes were destroyed by the Iroquois or Five Nations about the close of the seventeenth century, and their remnants incorporated with their conquerors. At the Treaty of Lancaster, in 1744, the Iroquois Chief, Tachanoontia, said: "All the world knows we conquered the several nations living on Susquehannah, Cohongownton, (Potomac), and on the back of the great mountains in Virginia. The Conoy-uch-rooch (people), the Coh-no-was-ronaw, feel the effect of our conquests being now a part of our nations and their lands at our disposal," and, again, "as to what lies beyond the mountains, we conquered the nations residing there, and that land, if the Virginians ever get a good right to it, it must be by us."[1] Mr. Gallatin

---

[1] "Treaty of Lancaster," printed by B. Franklin, at Philadelphia, 1744, Vol. II, pp. 57-71; also in Colden's "History of the Five Nations," 3d edition, 1755, Vol. II, pp. 57, 71. "Pennsylvania Colonial Records," Vol. IV, p. 712. Albert Gallatin's "Synopsis of the Indian Tribes."

supposes the tribes on the Potomac and Kanawha to be distinct or different, although their names are near alike. Evidently they were kindred tribes of the same nation. John Heckwelder says: "The Conoys are the people we call Canais, Conoys, Canaways, Kanhawas.[1] In Pennsylvania they were called Canawese."

February 18.—Over the Southern Fork of Big Mill Creek, thence to the top of the ridge near the Spruce Fork of Thirteen-Mile Creek.

February 19.—Probably Big Buffalo Creek, in Putnam County.

February 20.—Across Little Buffalo Creek to head of Arbuckle's Creek, thence north, across Thirteen-Mile Creek, in Mason County.

February 21.—Probably encamped at the mouth of Ten-Mile Creek.

February 22.—High Hill, the Kanawha Ridge, about eight miles northeast from Point Pleasant, at the mouth of the Kanawha River, thence to the river Ohio, at the mouth of Ten-Mile Creek.

February 23.—Le Tort's Creek, a small stream, empties into the Ohio, thirty miles above Point Pleasant, so called for James Le Tort, an early trader with the Indians on the Ohio. He was a French Huguenot, and lived near Philadelphia in his childhood; afterwards on the banks of the Susquehanna, and built a cabin about 1720, at Le Tort's Spring, where Carlisle, Cumberland County, Pa., now stands.[2] He was often employed as interpreter by the Provincial authorities. Trading on the Allegheny and Ohio, from 1729 to 1739, he appears

---

[1] "Historical Sketch of the Indian Nations," p. 26.

[2] "Rupp's History of Cumberland County," p. 389. "Hazard's Register of Pennsylvania," Vol. IV, p. 389, also Vol. XV, p. 82.

to have had a trading camp or station at this point, since well known as Le Tort's Rapids or Falls.[1]

February 24.—Smith's Creek. Big Mill Creek, in Jackson County. Probably so named for Robert Smith, the trader, met by Gist, on the Miami, in the month of March. He had been trading in the Ohio country for some years previous.[2] The creek here called Beyansoss is Big Sandy Creek, in Jackson County.

February 26.—"Lawwellaconin." Pond Creek, in Wood County.

March 1.—"The little branch full of coal" is probably the head of the middle fork of Tygart's Creek, in Wood County. Naumissippia or Fishing Creek, another name for the Little Kanawha. Naemas, Fish, Sipia River or Creek, in the Delaware tongue.[3]

March 3.—Molchuconickon or Buffalo Creek, now Middle Island Creek, in Pleasants and Tyler Counties. The name Buffalo is yet applied to one of its branches; the distance is greater to this stream from the little Kanawha than it is here given.[4]

March 4.—Probably reached a point near the present Middlebourne, Tyler County.

March 5.—Neemokeesy,[5] now Fishing Creek.

March 7.—To the Ohio River, probably a few miles below Fish Creek, in Marshall County; then east and north across Big Grave Creek to Wheeling Creek, about the junction of the North and South Forks. Wheeling is from a Delaware

---

[1] "Pennsylvania Archives," Vol. I, pp. 255-301, etc. "Rupp's History of Lancaster County," p. 512. "Colonial Records," Vol. IV, p. 237.

[2] See Gist's first Journal, March 1st, 13th.

[3] See Fry and Jefferson's Map.

[4] See Gist's statement relative to distances at the end of the Journal.

[5] Naemas, Fish.

Indian word "Wihe," or "Wie," (a head), ung or unk, (place or locality), place of a head. A prisoner taken and put to death by the Indians and his head stuck upon a sharpened pole.[1] There was another "Wheeling" on the upper branch of the Mahoning Creek in Armstrong County, Pennsylvania.[2]

March 9.—The first creek here mentioned is now called Buffalo Creek. It empties into the Ohio at Wellsburg, in Brooke County. The second is Cross Creek. Directly opposite to it, on what was formerly called "The Indian side of the Ohio," is "Indian Cross Creek." These were the two creeks of the Indians and traders. A noted Indian path led down along the creek on the west side to the crossing place at its mouth. There the Indians crossed to the creek on the east side of the Ohio and took the path along its shore, hence the name of Cross Creeks. At a later time, these creeks were by some known as the "Two Upper Creeks," while "Short Creek," above Wheeling and "Indian Short Creek," opposite, were called the "Two Lower Creeks."[3]

March 10.—In Brooke County, West Virginia, and in Washington County, Pennsylvania.

March 11.—"Crossing Three Creeks," branches of Buffalo Creek in Washington County; thence south to the "camp" of December 21 to January 8, near the heads of Dunkard and Ten-Mile Creeks, in Greene County, Pennsylvania.

[1] Pennsylvania Historical Society, Vol. I, p. 131. American Antiquarian Society, Vol. II, p. 312. Schoolcraft, "American Aboriginal Archives," Vol. II, p. 470.

[2] Hutchins' Map.

[3] Hutchins' large Map, 1778. George Croghan's Journal, 1765, in Appendix to Butler's "History of Kentucky," second edition. Winterbotham's "America," Vol. I, p. 189.

NOTES ON CHRISTOPHER GIST'S THIRD JOURNAL, 1753.

November 14. Wills Creek empties into the Potomac.

November 15.—Conegocheague, a branch of the Potomac; signifying, "indeed, a long way."

November 23.—Shannopins Town, now Pittsburgh.

November 24.—King Shingiss, a noted Indian warrior, "a terror to the frontier settlements of Pennsylvania."

November 27—Half King Scarrooyady, often mentioned by Croghan, Montour and others. He died at Paxton, October 5, 1754. His friends imputed his death to French witchcraft. Letter of Governor Morris to Governor Dinwiddie.

December 11.—Fort Le Bœuf.

A JOURNAL DESCRIPTIVE OF SOME OF THE FRENCH FORTS.

HAD FROM THOMAS FORBES, LATELY A PRIVATE SOLDIER IN THE KING OF FRANCE'S SERVICE.[1]

January, 1755.

ABOUT a Year and a half ago I with 120 private Soldiers and our officers embarked in old France for Canada.

Our Vessell was a Frigate of forty Guns and another Frigate of 30 Guns sailed at the same time with a company of Soldiers to relieve the Garrison at the Mouth of the Mississippi. After a short Voyage we disembarked at Quebeck, where we were permitted to stay three weeks to refresh ourselves.

The regular Troops in that City did not exceed 300, but I was told that there were many Parties and Detachments quartered up and down the Country all round that Place.

Being joined by a Company of 50 Men from that Garrison we went in Batteaus to Montreal under the Command of Lieut. Carqueville and there we spent the last Winter.

At our arrival there was a Company of 50 men in the City where we were quartered, so that in all we made 220 exclusive of Officers. Very early in the Spring we were joined by near 400 more who were drafted out of the several Companies that Garrisoned the Forts and were posted on the Frontiers of Canada. Easter Tuesday we embarked to the number of six or 700 in about 300 Batteaus or Canoes (not Barken) and took with us a large quantity of Barreled Pork and Meal in Baggs; the Bags weighed sixty or 70 lb each, and I believe there

---

[1] MSS. "America and West Indies." P. R. O.

might have been 1500 of them, how many of the Pork there were I never heard nor could I guess, but I believe the Canoes that were not laden with Flour carried five or six Barrels at least, each of them, and the Batteaus received 17 or 20. We were three weeks going from Montreal to Lake Ontario keeping the shore close on board because of the rapidity of the Stream, and at Night we went ashore, excepting a few that were left with the canoes, that were fastened to stakes or trees on the shore.

Then we had our Biscuit, which was laid in for the Voyage, delivered to us, with 1 lb of Pork to each, and kindling large fires we cooked our Provisions for next day and slept around the Fires, each of us being provided with a blanket. We kept along the southeast shore of Ontario Lake, and passed so near to the English Fort called Conquen or Oswego that we could talk to the Centinels.

When we came to the Fort at the Falls of Niagara, we landed all our Provisions in which service the Garrison at the Fort assisted and carried them on sleds that were there at the fort, to a little Log House (called le petit Fort de Niagara) three Leagues beyond Niagara Fort, where we put them aboard other Batteaus and Canoes that were there ready to receive them. At our arrival at Niagara there were at that Fort 25 private men, commanded by Lieut. de la Perrie, but Monsieur Contrecœur was also then in the Fort, and had the Chief command, there was also a Sergeant's Guard at the little Fort. The Fort at Niagara is no more than an Emmenence surrounded with Stockadoes or Palisades, which stand about fourteen feet above the ground very close together, and are united or fastened together by three pieces of long scantling that is put transversly on the inside at the distance of three feet or so from each other. These Stockadoes enclose an Area near 300 paces square on which is built a

House for the Commandant, Barracks for the Men and a Smith's Shop, it is not rendered defensible by any out work or even a Ditch and there are not mounted in it more than four Swivel Guns. As soon as we had put our Provisions on board at the little Fort that I mentioned, we proceeded to Lake Erie with Captain Contracœur, who had himself now taken the Command of all the Troops in those Canoes. We kept along the Eastern Coast of this Lake to Fort Presqu' isle which I apprehend is about 50 Leagues from Niagara.

This Fort is situated on a little rising Ground at a very small Distance from the water of Lake Erie, it is rather larger than that at Niagara but has likewise no Bastions or Out Works of any sort. It is a square Area inclosed with Logs about 12 feet high, the Logs being square and laid on each other and not more than sixteen or eighteen inches thick. Captain Darpontine Commandant in this Fort and his Garison was 30 private Men. We were eight days employed in unloading our Canoes here, and carrying the Provisions to Fort Bœuff which is built about six Leagues from Fort Presqu' isle at the Head of Buffaloe River. This Fort was composed of four Houses built by way of Bastions and the intermediate Space stockaded. Lieut St Blein was posted here with 20 Men. Here we found three large Batteaus and between two or 300 Canoes which we freighted with Provisions and proceeded down the Buffaloe river which flows into the Ohio[1] at about twenty Leagues (as I conceived) distance from Fort au Boeuff, this river was small and at some places very shallow so that we towed the Canoes sometimes wading and sometimes taking ropes to the shore a great part of the way. When we came into the Ohio we had a fine deep water and a stream in our favour so that we rowed down that river from the mouth of the Buffaloe to Du Quesne Fort on

[1] Allegheny.

Monongehela which I take to be 70 Leagues distant in four days and a half.

At our arrival at Fort Du Quesne we found the Garison busily employed in compleating that Fort and Stockadoing it round at some distance for the security of the Soldiers Barracks (against any Surprise) which are built between the Stockadoes and the Glacis of the Fort.

Fort Du Quesne is built of square Logs transversly placed as is frequent in Mill Dams, and the Interstices filled up with Earth; the length of these Logs is about sixteen Feet which is the thickness of the Rampart. There is a Parapat raised on the Rampart of Logs, and the length of the Curtains is about 30 feet, and the Demigorge of the Bastions about eighty. The Fort is surrounded on the two sides that do not front the Water with a Ditch about 12 feet wide and very deep, because there being no covert way the Musqutteers fire from thence having a Glacis before them. When the News of Ensign Jumonville's Defeat reached us our company consisted of about 1400. Seven hundred of whom were ordered out under the command of Captain Mercier to attack Mr. Washington, after our return from the Meadows, a great number of the Soldiers who had been labouring at the Fort all the Spring were sent off in Divisions to the several Forts between that and Canada, and some of those that came down last were sent away to build a Fort some where on the Head of the Ohio, so that in October the Garison at Du Quesne was reduced to 400 Men, who had Provisions enough at the Fort to last them two years, notwithstanding a good deal of the Flour we brought down in the Spring proved to be damaged, and some of it spoiled by the rains that fell at that Time. In October last I had an opportnnity of relieving myself and retiring, there were not then any Indians with the French but a considerable number were expected and said to be on their March thither.

THE MONTOURS.

ABOUT the year 1667 a French gentleman named Montour settled in Canada. By a Huron Indian woman he had three children—one son and two daughters. The son, Montour, lived with the Indians, and was wounded in the French service, in a fight with some Mohawks, near Fort La Motte,[1] on Lake Champlain, in 1694. He deserted from the French, and lived with "the farr Indians"—the Twightwees (Miamis) and Diondadies (Petuns or Wyandots). By his assistance Lord Cornbury prevailed on some of these tribes to visit and trade with the people of Albany in 1708. For his endeavors to alienate the "upper nations" from the French, he was killed in 1709 by the troops under Lieutenant le Sieur de Joncaire, by orders of the Marquis de Vaudreuil, Governor of Canada, who wrote that he would have had him hanged, had it been possible to capture him alive.

Of the two daughters of the Frenchman, Montour, one became conspicuously known as Madame Montour.[2] She was born in Canada about the year 1684, captured by some warriors of the Five Nations when she was but ten years old, taken to their country and brought up by them. It is probable that she lived with the Oneidas, as, on arriving at maturity, she was married to Carondawana, or the "Big Tree," otherwise Robert Hunter, a famous war-chief of that nation.

[1] "New York Colonial History:" Fort St. Anne, or La Motte, erected 1666, on the upper part of Lake Champlain.

[2] "Massachusetts Historical Collection." "New York Historical Collection."

He was killed in the wars between the Iroquois and Catawbas, in the Carolinas, about the year 1729.[1]

The Proprietaries of Pennsylvania, John and Thomas Penn, expressed much concern for his death to some of the Indians who visited Philadelphia in September, 1734. Madame Montour was there also, and, for having underrated the rank or station of the Oneida visitors, she seems to have been angrily and unjustly charged by a prominent chief of the Six Nations, Hetanguantagetchy, before the Council at Philadelphia, in the month of October following, with spreading false reports. He said, further, that her "old age only protected her from punishment," and that they "must resent it and hope to get rid of her."

Madame Montour first appeared as interpreter at a conference held at Albany, in August, 1711, between the sachems of the Five Nations and Robert Hunter, the royal Governor of New York (from 1709 to 1719). Probably at that time Carondawana received, or took, the Governor's name, by which he was frequently known afterward. To adopt the name of a prominent white man was, by the Indians, considered a high compliment and a bond of friendship.

The war between the Tuscaroras and the people of North Carolina, commenced in September, 1711, was still raging in the summer of the following year. The Five Nations in New York became restless and uneasy; it was feared by the Governor and Assembly that, instigated by the French, the Northern Iroquois would join the Southern, and embroil the colonies in a general Indian war.[2]

The Five Nations informed the Governor that they desired "to interpose amicably in the matter." Distrusting their sincerity, and to "dissuade them from this fatal design," by

[1] Marshe's Journal.
[2] "New York Colonial History."

means of "presents and promises," the Assembly and Governor, in June, 1712, directed Colonel Peter Schuyler to "proceed to the Onondaga Country forthwith, taking with you Laurence Clause the Interpreter, Mrs. Montour and her husband and such others as you shall see fit."

At Onondaga he was to assemble all of the Indian sachems who could be got together for a conference on the subject of his mission. Any fresh "Surmises or Jealousies of the Indians" were to be overcome by his "own wisdom, with due regard to her Majesty's interest and honour and ye quieting ye minds of ye Indians."

The complete subjugation of the Tuscaroras, after a protracted struggle of two years' duration, removed all apprehension of trouble with the Five Nations. In the year 1714 the Tuscaroras migrated north, and were received into the Iroquois Confederacy as the Sixth Nation.[1]

The influence of Madame Montour among the Indians was so great, and adverse to the French, that the Governor of Canada repeatedly endeavored to persuade her to withdraw from the English and remove to his Dominion, offering higher compensation as an inducement, but without success until the year 1719, when he sent her sister to prevail on her to remove to Canada. Apprehensive of her doing so, to the injury of the province to which she had been so serviceable, the Commissioner of Indian Affairs sent for her to Albany, when it appeared that she had not received a farthing of her stipulated pay for twelve months. The Commissioners promised that she should receive thereafter "a man's pay from the proper officer of the four Independent Companies posted in the Province,"[2] and the business was thus satisfactorily settled.

[1] Dr. Hank's "History of North Carolina."
[2] MS., Secretary of State's office, New York.

Madame Montour was present at Philadelphia in July, 1727, as interpreter, at a conference held by Governor Gordon with several chiefs of the Five Nations. Again, in October, 1728; her husband, Carondawana, otherwise Robert Hunter, was there also. She retained her father's name after marriage, and was usually mentioned as "Mrs. Montour, a French woman, wife to Carondawana, or Robert Hunter." She appears to have lived among the Miamis, at the west end of Lake Erie, at one time prior to 1728.[1] To one of that nation her sister was married. Her residence in 1734 was at the village on the Susquehanna, at the mouth of the Loyalsock Creek, on the West side, where Montoursville, Lycoming County, Pennsylvania, now stands. It was known as Otstuago,[2] Ots-on-wacken, or French Town.

On Evans' Map of Pennsylvania, of 1749, the village is marked "French T.," and the creek, the "Ostuega." There, in March, 1737, Conrad Weiser, Indian agent and interpreter, on his way to Onondaga with a message from the President of the Council of Pennsylvania, James Logan, lodged at Madame Montour's, who, he states, is a "French woman by birth, of a good family, but now in mode of life a complete Indian." She treated Weiser and his companions kindly, supplying them with food, although she had but little to spare.

In the fall of 1742 Count Zinzendorf, the Bishop and head of the Moravian Church, with a large party, and among them Conrad Weiser, visited the village of Oztenwacken, where he was received with military salutes and hospitably welcomed by Madame Montour and her son, Andrew. "He preached there in French to large gatherings." Madame Montour was deeply affected when she saw Zinzendorf and learned the

[1] "Colonial Records."
[2] Otsteara, "Rock," in the Iroquois tongue.

object of his visit. She had entirely forgotten the truths of the Gospel, and, in common with the French Indians, believed the story originated with the Jesuits, that the Saviour's birthplace was in France, and His crucifiers Englishmen. Count Zinzendorf appears to have visited Oztenwacken subsequently.

In June and July, 1744, the great treaty between the Six Nations and the provinces of Pennsylvania, Maryland and Virginia was held at Lancaster. Madame Montour was present with two of her daughters. Witham Marshe, Secretary to the Maryland Commissioners, relates in his journal that he visited her at her cabin and obtained the particulars of her life. She told him that she had several children by the famous war captain, who had been killed in the war with the Catawbas fifteen years previous, that since she had not married.[1] Marshe describes her as genteel, of polite address, and had been handsome. Her two sons-in-law and only son were away south, to war against the Catawbas. In June, 1745, Spangenburgh, Zeisberger, and other missionaries of the Moravians, accompanied by Conrad Weiser on their way to Onondaga, stopped for a few days at Shamokin (now Sunbury), on the Susquehanna. They visited Madame Montour, who was living on the island with one of her daughters.[2] She appears to have left Oztenwacken permanently, as there is no evidence of her residing there afterwards. Zeisberger found that village deserted and in ruins in 1748. The smallpox had desolated the valley. There is no further direct account of Madame Montour. It seems, however, that she was not living in 1754. Some time prior to that year she became blind, but was sufficiently vigorous to ride on horseback from Logstown, on the Ohio, to Venango in two days, a distance by the path

[1] Massachusetts Historical Society.
[2] Moravian Historical Society.

of over sixty miles, her son Andrew on foot, leading her horse all the way. Of her children but three can be identified with any certainty; one of the two daughters who were with her at the treaty of Lancaster in 1744, and two sons, Andrew, alias Henry, and Louis. Her daughter, known as "French Margaret," was wife to Keterioncha, alias Peter Quebec, and living near Shamokin when Shikillimy lived there in 1733, probably on the island where Zeisberger and Spangenburgh visited her and her mother in 1745, as before related. Another of her daughters is mentioned as a sister of Andrew Montour's, and one of the converts at the Moravian Mission, at New Salem, Ohio, April 14, 1791, and that she was a living polyglot of the tongues of the West, speaking English, French and six Indian languages. She must have been at least seventy years of age at that time.

Madame Montour evidently was older than she told Marshe, at Lancaster in 1744, as she was at Albany in 1711 as Mrs. Montour—her old age referred to in 1734 as her protection—and blind before 1754.[1] "It is probable that she was captured prior to 1696, after which year the raids of the Iroquois into Canada ceased for some time. That she was very young when captured, is clear. She could not have been less than sixty years old at the time of the treaty of Lancaster in 1744, and probably was older, and if but ten years of age when taken, as she said, the year of her captivity was 1694, and of her birth 1684. Of the many errors respecting this noted woman, the most prominent are, first, the frequently repeated statement that she was the daughter of a former governor of Canada."[2] This story originated with herself, or it may have been told by her savage captors to enhance the value of their prize. There never was a governor of Canada named Mon-

[1] Dussieux, Canada.
[2] Marshe's Journal.

tour, and the letter of Lord Cornbury, of August 20, 1708, before cited, is conclusive as to her origin, taken, of course, in connection with her own statement to Secretary Marshe. Second, that she was living at the time of the American Revolution, and also confounding her with her granddaughter, Catherine of Catherine's Town, near the head of Seneca Lake, New York, destroyed by the army under General Sullivan in 1779. She is not mentioned in any work of original authority, as Catherine, but invariably as Mrs. or "Madame Montour." Highly colored accounts have been given respecting her association with the ladies of Philadelphia, who evidently, owing to her intelligence and previous history, treated her with considerate kindness and nothing more. From the authorities of the province she received such presents and compensation for services as were usually given to prominent Indian visitors. Those who knew her best, related that she was habited and lived like the Indians [1] Her French blood doubtless imparted a vivacity of manner to her, the like of which is observed at this day among the people of mixed French and Indian ancestry in Canada and along our northern frontier.

[1] Colonial Records.

ANDREW MONTOUR.

ANDREW MONTOUR, eldest son of Madame Montour, first appears as captain of a party of Iroquois warriors marching against the Catawbas of Carolina in 1744. He fell sick on his way to James River and was obliged to return to Shamokin.[1] In May, 1745, he accompanied Weiser and the Chief Shichillany to Onondaga with a message and instructions from the Governor of Pennsylvania, to induce the Six Nations to send deputies to a Peace Conference with the Catawbas at Williamsburgh, Virginia; also to urge them to compel the Shawnese, with Peter Chartier at their head, to make restitution for the robbery of Pennsylvania traders, incited thereto by the French.[2] In June, 1748, he was introduced by Weiser to the President and Council of the Province at Philadelphia, and highly commended as "faithful and prudent;" "lives amongst the Six Nations between the branches of the Ohio and Lake Erie."[3]

In July, following, he was interpreter at a Treaty at Lancaster, between the Provincial Authorities and the Six Nations, Shawnese, Miamis, etc.[4] In August, 1748, he accompanied Weiser on his mission to Logstown. In May, 1750, arrived at George Croghan's House at Pennsboro, Cumberland County, from Allegheny, and joins in the Conference held on the 17th with some Six Nation and Conestoga Chiefs.

[1] Marshe's Journal, Vol VII. Letter of C. Weiser to James Logan.
[2] Colonial Records, Vol. IV, p. 778.
[3] Colonial Records, Vol. V, p. 290.
[4] Colonial Records, Vol. V, p. 307., id., p. 349.

Governor Hamilton recommended him to the Assembly as a discreet person of influence with the Indians in keeping the French from alienating them from the British and deserving of recompense, to which the Assembly assented. He received £92 15s. On September 20, a message to the Governor from the Miamis and Hurons was delivered to Secretary Peters by Andrew Montour. The Assembly having voted a present of £100 to be given to the Twigtwees (Miami) Indians, the Governor directed Croghan and Montour to hasten to Ohio with it, which he called a small present; but they were both sick and therefore detained. Before they were able to start on their journey news came of active French movements and of their capturing two English traders, Turner and Kilgore, in the Ohio country, and also of the death of Conestoga, the great Chief of the Six Nations, an Onondaga and firm friend of the English, while his successor was strong in the French interest and a Roman Catholic. Therefore, the Governor gave orders to Croghan and Montour to stay until he should learn the resolution of the Assembly, to whom he communicated the alarming information. That body responded by voting £100 as a present of condolence to the Six Nations on the death of Conestoga, £100 more to be given to the Miamis, and £500 "to the natives at Ohio" in suitable goods and to be sent as soon as possible.

Croghan and Montour set out on their journey, arriving at Logstown on the Ohio on November 15. Of course, they took no goods for the present; they were yet to be purchased and the Indians to be notified to assemble to receive them.

Not later than March Croghan arrived and wrote that the French, under Jean Cœur, had five canoe loads of goods up the Allegheny, and was, the Indians said, very generous in making presents to all the chiefs he met with. At Logstown they found thirty warriors of the Six Nations on their way to war with the Catawbas. But few of the chiefs of the Indians were seen, being absent hunting. He further wrote to the Governor that "Montour takes a great deal of pains to promote the English interest among the Indians, and has great sway among all those nations." The Indian goods were purchased; the transportation to the Ohio cost £230—very costly—but it could not be done for less, as the Governor informed the Assembly. Pack-horses then, and for near half a century afterward, were the only means of transportation.

Croghan and Montour proceeded on to the Muskingum River, where, at a large Wyandot town (near the site of the present Coshocton, Ohio) Croghan had a trading house. Here they remained some weeks and were joined by Christopher Gist, the agent of the Ohio Company of Virginia. Croghan and Montour held frequent councils with the Indians, delivering the message from the Governor of Pennsylvania promising the presents to be delivered in the Spring at Logstown. They proceeded to the Shawnee towns at the mouth of the Scioto, and also on the south, or Kentucky, side of the Ohio, where, at a Council with the Shawnese, Croghan delivered speeches from the Governor of Pennsylvania to the chiefs of the nation and informed them that the escaped traders who had been in prisons of the French, brought news that the French had offered a large reward for Montour and himself if alive, or for their scalps if dead. Montour also informed them, as he had done the Wyandots and Delawares, that the King of Great Britain had sent them a large present of goods.[1]

Montour was called by the French, a French Canadian deserter. Croghan, Montour, Gist and Robert Callender then proceeded to Pickawillamy, chief town of the Miamis.[2] It was situated on the Big Miami. Among other proceedings, Cro-

[1] "Conduct of the Ministry."
[2] "Conduct of the Ministry."

ghan presented them with a gift of the value of £100. Montour delivered them a message from the Wyandots and Delawares. On March 3 Gist left them for the lower Shawnee Town, while they took the path to Hockhocking.

While at the Miami Town, articles for a treaty of peace and alliance were entered into between the English and Miamis, drawn up by Gist, signed, sealed and delivered on both sides.[1]

Conrad Weiser was selected to deliver the goods at Logstown, but declined, and, highly recommending Croghan and Montour as every way qualified, the Governor appointed them to transact the business. The goods were valued at £700.

When Croghan reported the matter of the treaty of peace and alliance made with the Miamis, he said it was done at the request of the Indians, he consenting rather than discharge them at so critical a time. The Governor reproved him for acting in public matters without authority, but received it and ordered its entry on the Books of Minutes.

On May 18, 1751, Montour and Croghan arrived at Logstown with the promised presents for the Indians, of whom a great number were assembled—Six Nations, Delawares and Shawanese. They welcomed the messengers by firing guns and raising the English colors. Two days afterward Jean Cœur, with one other Frenchman and forty Six Nation warriors, arrived from the head of the Ohio. Jean Cœur held a council with all the Indians in the town on the following day, and urged them to turn away all the English traders from their country, otherwise they would be visited with the displeasure of the Governor of Canada.[2] To which a Six Nation chief directly replied, emphatically refusing the proposition of the French. On the 27th Croghan and Montour held a conference with the chiefs of the Six Nations, and agreed upon

---

[1] "Colonial Records."

[2] "Virginia State Papers," p. 245.

the speeches to make the day following to the Delawares, Miamis, Wyandots and Shawanese, when the promised presents were to be delivered. Accordingly, on the 28th, the treaty was held; George Croghan delivered the speeches; Andrew Montour acted as interpreter for Pennsylvania. Some ten traders were present. The Beaver, of the Delawares, and chiefs of other tribes responded, among other things saying they hoped "our brother would build a strong-house on the River Ohio," that, in case of war, a place of security might be ready.

Croghan and Montour left on the 30th. On his arrival at Pennsboro, Croghan wrote to the Governor, sending a copy of the treaty, with an account of the proceedings. All, he said, had been conducted to the great satisfaction of the Indians. Mr. Montour, he wrote, had exerted himself very much on this occasion. "He is very capable of doing business, and is looked upon by all the Indians as one of their chiefs." He adds that, as Andrew has devoted all his time to the business he hopes the Governor will recommend him to the Assembly for proper recompense, and that "Mr. Montour is now at my house and will wait on you when a time is appointed."

In communicating the account of the proceedings of Croghan and Montour to the Assembly, the Governor said Mr. Montour was in town by his orders, to receive a recompense for his services, and that he must do him the justice to say that it appears he has well performed the business entrusted to him, and hopes the Assembly will pay him to his satisfaction. Montour was paid £80 in full for his services.

Montour, being very desirous of living "over the Blue Hills," had often applied to the Governor for permission, which was given after a good deal of consideration and consultation with Mr. Weiser and Mr. Peters.[1] It was thought

---

[1] "Colonial Records."

proper, as numbers had lately gone to settle there, and others were daily crowding into those parts, that Andrew Montour should be furnished with a commission under the Lesser Seal to go and reside there, in order to prevent others from settling or from dealing with the Indians for their consent to settle. Montour was granted a commission under the Lesser Seal to go and reside over the Kittochtinny Hills, at such place as he might judge most central and convenient. His duty was to warn all settlers off and report them to the Governor. The place fixed upon by Montour was at the mouth of the stream called Montour's Run, in the present Perry County. On the same day that Montour received his commission he waited on the Governor, and requested permission to interpret for the Governor of Virginia at the ensuing treaty, to be held at Logstown, on the Ohio. The leave was granted, together with a kind message from the Governor, to be delivered to the Indians at Ohio.

In May following, the Commissioners of Virginia—Joshua Fry, L. Lomax and James Pattin—held a treaty with the Indians at Logstown. Christopher Gist, George Croghan and Andrew Montour were present, the latter as interpreter. The object of the treaty was to obtain from the Indians, if possible, a confirmation of the treaty of Lancaster of 1744, by which, the Virginians claimed, the Indians had ceded to the King of Great Britain the right to all the lands in the colony of Virginia.[1]

The Indians afterwards hearing the construction put upon this deed, disowned it, and it was the object of the Conference at Logstown to have the treaty explained and their objections removed. In a private Conference held on the 9th of June, with the Half King and the other chiefs, they acknowledged themselves satisfied. For Montour's services

[1] "Plain Facts." pp. 38-42.

in this transaction, the Ohio company, at a meeting at Alexandria, September, 1752, resolved "to allow him thirty pistoles for his trouble at Logstown, in May last, on account of the company, and that if he will remove to Virginia and settle on the company's lands, and use his interest with the Indians to encourage and forward our settlements, that the company will make him a present of one thousand acres of land to live on, and will make him a legal title for the same." [1]

In 1753, the Six Nations of Ohio chose him as one of their counsellors, and observed all the ceremonious forms usual on admitting members of council. He visited Onondaga early this year, 1753, by request of the Governor of Virginia, to invite the Six Nations to send a deputation to a treaty to be held at Winchester. He returned, and being in Philadelphia, informed Secretary Peters that the Six Nations were averse to either the French or English settling or building forts at Ohio, and wished them to quit their country. He said he was going a second time to Onondaga by request of the Governor of Virginia and Mr. Peters. In August, 1753, Montour was with Captain William Trent, at the forks of the Ohio, when Captain Trent viewed the ground, selecting the spot on which to build the fort. "Captain Trent and French Andrew, the heads of the Five Nations, the Picts, the Shawanese, the Owendats, and the Delawares, for Virginia," writes John Frazer, Indian trader, then residing at Turtle Creek, near the ground to become so famous two years later as "Braddock's Fields." In September a treaty was held at Winchester, Virginia, between Col. Fairfax and Chiefs of the Six Nations. Lord Thomas Fairfax was present the first day, when the Indians, over eighty in number, were received with considerable ceremony. Col. Gist, William Trent and George Croghan were present. Andrew Montour was interpreter,

[1] "Colonial Records."

and also efficient in arranging the business.[1] The Indians, by the Half King, Scarrooyady, declaring that they took back the consent they had given at Logstown, in May, to any settlement of their country, but they desired a strong house to store goods in. The Virginia authorities promised the Indians to supply them with ammunition to defend themselves against the French. George Croghan, William Trent and Andrew Montour were appointed to distribute it at the Ohio. After the close of the Conference at Winchester, the Indians took their way to Carlisle, where they met the Commissioners of Pennsylvania, Mr. Peters, Isaac Morris and Benjamin Franklin, and held a conference with them, having been encouraged to make the visit by the frequent solicitations of Andrew Montour.[2] The Conference at Carlisle lasted four days, with the usual ceremonies; the Indians repeated their determination given at Winchester, respecting keeping settlements from extending west of the mountains, and as to the strong house which the Governor of Virginia intends to build on the Ohio, they thought that intention occasioned the Governor of Canada to invade their country, but as soon as they knew his intention, "as he speaks with two tongues, they (the Indians) well know what to do;" evidently they were unsettled in their minds respecting the "strong house," but as to settlements west of the Allegheny hills, there could be no doubt they were decidedly opposed to it. Towards the close of the Conference Scarrooyady, the Oneida chief, said it was with a great deal of pleasure he informed them "that you may believe that what Andrew Montour says to be true between the Six Nations and you, they have made him one of their counsellors and a great man among them and love him dearly." Scarrooyady gave a large belt to Andrew Montour, and the

[1] "Plain Facts."
[2] Report of Commission.

Commissioners agreed to it. In January, Montour was at Shannopin's Town and Logstown with Croghan and James Pattin, where, between the drunkenness of the Indians and the presence of a detachment of French soldiers, with whom they had high words, their situation was dangerous. In February, Montour was at Philadelphia and underwent a close examination by the Governor and Committee of Assembly relative to the location of Shannopin, Logstown and Venango.

1754.—George Washington, having sent for Montour to meet him at Ohio, the latter wrote to Secretary Peters, from his residence on Sherman's Creek, on the 16th of May, 1754, urging the immediate necessity of Pennsylvania sending men and arms to join the Indian Allies, to resist the impending French invasion. Ward had surrendered the little fort at the Forks of the Ohio, on the 17th of April, to Contrecœur. Croghan and Montour proceeded to the Monongahela, and there on the 9th of June found Washington; and Montour was with him at his surrender of Fort Necessity, July 3, 1754. He had a company under Washington, of both Whites and Indians. On the 21st of July, Montour wrote to the Governor of Pennsylvania, from Winchester, saying that the Half King and Monakatootha, with a body of Six Nations,[1] had gone to Aucquick to settle, where the other Indians, as fast as they can get off from the French, are to join them; and as there is a large body of them and no ground there to hunt to support their families, they expect the Governor to provide for their families, as their men will be engaged in the war. On August 31st he met Weiser at Harris' Ferry, on his way to a great meeting at Aucquick.

1755.—During the campaign of Braddock, that General wrote, on May 20, to Governor Morris, that he had engaged between forty and fifty Indians from the frontier of the pro-

---

[1] "Colonial Records."

vince, to go over the mountains, and would take Croghan and Montour into service.[1] Montour was at Philadelphia on the 8th of August, acting as interpreter with Weiser and a few Indians, who had been in the fatal defeat of Braddock. Scarroyady commented, with great severity, on the pride and ignorance of the great English General. On the French and Indian invasion of the settlements, in 1755, after Braddock's defeat, Montour was active and zealous in gaining intelligence of their movements.

He was at Shannopin, with Scarroyady, in October, and warned John Harris of his great danger; "there were forty Indians out many days, and intended to burn my house, and destroy myself and family." At Shamokin,[2] "painted as the rest" of the Indians, he warned the inhabitants, that an attack might very soon be expected. He had been at the Big Island, with Manoquetotha, at the request of the Delawares.

1756.—Andrew Montour, with Scarroyady, one of the chiefs of the Oneida Nation, was sent on a mission, to the Six Nations, by Governor Morris. They passed up the Susquehanna, to Onondaga; on their way, while among the hostile Delawares, their lives were in great danger. Montour and Scarroyady met the Provincial Council, in their chamber in Philadelphia, on March 27th, when they made full report of their mission to the Six Nations. They had been present at Fort Johnston, at a conference held with the Six Nation chiefs, and Sir William Johnston, February, 1756. The chiefs expressed great resentment at the conduct of the Delawares, etc. The Council decided to offer rewards for Indian scaips. The Provincial Assembly highly commended the conduct of Montour and Scarroyady.

[1] "Colonial Records."
[2] Shamokin is at the Forks of the Susquehanna, on the east side.

On the 19th to the 21st of April a conference was held at Philadelphia, at the house of Israel Pemberton, between the Quakers of Philadelphia and the heads of the Six Nations. Weiser and Montour were interpreters. On the 20th the Indians had a long conference with the Governor. "They put Andrew Montour's children under his care; as well the three that are here, to be independent of the mother, as a boy of twelve years old, that he had by a former wife, a Delaware, a grand-daughter of Allompis." They added that he had a girl among the Delawares called Kayodaghscroony, or Madelina, and desired she might be distinguished, enquired after, and sent for, which was promised. John Montour's name (one of Andrew's children, in the care of the Province) appears in the "Items of Accounts, votes of Assembly,". 1758, p. 75; this boy was the same, afterwards living on, and claiming the Island, near Pittsburgh, now Neville; possibly the same who died in 1830.

On May 10th, Montour was interpreter, at a meeting at Fort Johnston, between Scarroyady and other Oneida chiefs, and Sir Wm. Johnston. In June, he was at the camp on Lake Onondaga, as interpreter.

On the 25th of July Sir William Johnston held a conference, at Fort Johnston, with the chiefs of the Six Nations, Shawnese, Delawares, Mohickons, etc. After the usual ceremonies, he told them, that as Lord Loudon, the new Commander-in-Chief, had not arrived, he would have some Six Nation warriors go to Canada, to try whether the edge of the hatchet he sharpened at Onondaga would cut. Some chiefs sang the war song. Montour was appointed the captain of a party of Indians. He rose up and sang his war song. Some warriors joined his party, and the war dance was danced.[1] Some of these warriors, forty-eight in number,

[1] "New York Colonial History."

indulging too freely in rum, squandered all of their outfit. Scarroyady and Montour came to the council room, at Fort Johnston, on the 14th of August, and Sir William Johnston, for the second time, fitted them out with arms and clothes, in place of those they had sold to some River Indians and Tuscarawas. News having arrived of the capture of Oswego, by Montcalm's army, Sir Wm. Johnston spoke to the two war parties, and desired them to march to General Webb's rendezvous, at the Oneida carrying place. August 26th that General, however, beat a rapid retreat to the Flats. On the 10th of September, Montour appears as interpreter at Fort Johnston. On the 20th of September Sir Wm. Johnston, with all the Indians he could gather, with Croghan and Montour, marched to the relief of the army besieged at Fort Edward. He was ordered back by General Webb, and reached Fort Johnston on the 2d of November.

1757.—At Fort Johnston, on the 12th of September, Andrew Montour appears as interpreter at a meeting of Sir William Johnston, a few Mohican and Seneca chiefs and four Cherokee Indians.[1] "Sir William lighted the Calumet of Peace, and after smoking a whiff, passed it to the Cherokee Deputies, holding it to them while each drew a whiff," and then Mr. Montour, "handed it round to every Indian present." After delivering belts and long speeches, etc., at several meetings, they left on the 20th. In November Croghan and Montour were despatched to the German Flats, by Sir Wm. Johnston, to call upon the Oneidas there, to explain why they had not given warning of the raid and massacre, shortly before committed by the French and their Indian allies, on the German inhabitants. They met the Oneida Sachems, at Fort Harkimer, on the 30th November; they held a conference with some Germans and returned as reported.[2]

[1] "New York Colonial History," Vol. VII.
[2] "Colonial Records," Vol. VIII, 1758.

In October, at Easton, was held a great conference between Governor Denny, the Provincial Council, Committee from the Assembly, and Indians of the Six Nations. Croghan as Deputy Agent for Indian Affairs, Weiser as Provincial Interpreter, Montour as Interpreter for the Six Nations and Delawares. October 21, Montour, Croghan and others signed, as witnesses, the Deed of Confirmation for Lands. The treaty closed on the 25th; it was very important, as General Forbes was then moving near to Fort Du Quesne, and a great object was to soothe the Indians, by presents, and to settle the complaints of the Delawares, respecting their lands. Immediately after the close of the last Treaty at Easton, Montour and Croghan left for the Ohio, where, at Saukon, the Indian village at the mouth of the Beaver, on the 29th of November, they met Christian Fred. Post, who had just come down the creek from Kuskuskis.[1] At Saukon they met and conferred with King Beaver, his brother, Shingiss, and the chiefs and warriors, respecting General Forbes' message to them; that General, with the army, was now at Fort Du-Quesne, having captured it on the 24th.

On December 2d they reached Logstown, and on the 3d the island, since known as Killbuck or Smoky Island, opposite Pittsburgh, where they encamped. On the 4th they got over late, there was snow, and the river running with ice. Croghan, Montour, and Col. John Armstrong held conference with Col. Bouquet, the Indians, etc.[2]

On the 5th, Post seems to have had an altercation with Croghan and Montour, relative to the Indians' talk. On February 8th, 1759, Secretary Peters, at the request of General Forbes, held a conference at Philadelphia with the Six Nation Chiefs and other Indians from Bowlunee, on the Upper Allegheny, Andrew Montour, interpreter. On the 20th he

[1] "Post's Second Journal, 1758."
[2] "Pennsylvania Archives," 1759.

informed the Secretary that the Indians were dissatisfied. They said it was absolutely necessary Andrew should return to Ohio with them, but he told them he was an officer, subject to the General, and could not go without written orders from him.[1]

These Indians wished to know the intentions of the English, and what was done at the Easton Treaty, etc. In July a great conference with all the Indian tribes of the Ohio was held at Pittsburgh, by George Croghan, Deputy Agent, Col. Hugh Mercer, commanding Fort Pitt, Captain William Trent, Captain Thomas McKee,[2] Captain Henry; Montour, interpreter. It lasted from July 4th to 11th, 1759. King Beaver was the principal speaker of the Indians. Guyasuta (Kiashuta), was present.

Another conference was held at Pittsburgh, on October 24th, between General Stanwix, the officers, George Croghan, William Trent, McKee, Captain Henry, Montour interpreter, Six Nations, Shawanese, Wyandots, Miamis, and Delawares. Captain Montour lit the Pipe of Peace left here by the warriors of the Ottawas, handing it to General Stanwix and the other officers of the army, and Indians, to smoke, then acquainted the Indians by whom the pipe was left, and upon what occasion, showing them the belts left at the same time. At the camp before Pittsburgh General Moncton held a conference with the Western Indians on August 12th, 1760,[3] Captain Andrew Montour, interpreter, George Croghan, Deputy Agent.

On September 4th Montour arrived at Presqu' Isle with Shingiss.[4] Canada having capitulated, an expedition was

[1] "Colonial Records."
[2] For many years Chief Indian Trader on the Susquehanna. He built Fort McKee. Alexander McKee was his son.
[3] "Pennsylvania Archives," 1760.
[4] Massachusetts Historical Society.

fitted out to take possession of the different French posts on the lakes, Detroit, etc. On November 4th the Flotilla, of nineteen whale-boats and batteaux, sailed. The shore party consisted of forty-two Rangers, fifteen Royal Americans, and twenty Indians, Six Nations, Shawanese and Delawares, under the command of Captain Montour, the shore party commanded by Captain Brewer, the whole land and water forces under Major Robert Rogers. Croghan commanded one of the boats. Detroit was surrendered, after some parley, on November 29th.[1]

On December 8th Major Rogers and Captain Montour, with a party of Indians set off to take possession of Mackinaw. After proceeding on their voyage about ninety miles to a point on the west side of Lake Huron, they found it impossible to get through the ice. To go by land the Indians declared was impossible without snow-shoes, so much to Rogers' mortification they returned, reaching Detroit on the 21st.

On May 22d, 1761, at a conference held at the State House, Philadelphia, between the Governor and several Indians from Allegheny, Andrew Montour was interpreter. Governor Hamilton held a conference at Lancaster, August 23d, 1762, with the Northern Indians, Andrew Montour was State interpreter.

1763.—The Pontiac war was now raging.[2]

Andrew Montour was at Fort Augusta (Shamokin), on his way up the west branch of the Susquehanna on July 23d, 1763, returning August 7th, with news of the Indians' attack on Loyalhanna, Ligonier and Fort Pitt being reported captured.[3]

---

[1] "Massachusetts Historical Collection."
[2] "Pennsylvania Archives."
[3] "Colonial Records."

December 19th, Captain Montour delivered to Governor John Penn an address of welcome from the Conestoga Indians at Conestoga Town, Lancaster County.

1764.—Against the hostile Delawares, residing on the upper Susquehanna, Sir William Johnston sent a party of nearly two hundred Indians—Six Nations, Tuscarawas and Oneidas, and a few Rangers—under the command of Captain Montour.[1] In the middle of February they left their castles with the intention of falling upon the towns of the Delawares and Shawanese, lying near the forks and branches of the Ohio and Susquehanna. They seized here in their encampment a party of forty Delawares under the command of the famous Captain Bull, a son of the ill-fated Teedyuscung. Captain Bull was a remarkable Indian and in capacity as leader had done considerable damage during the war. The prisoners were sent by way of Fort Stanwix, to Johnston Hall. Captain Bull and thirteen of the warriors were sent by way of Albany to New York, and there confined in jail. The others were distributed among the friendly Indians to supply the places of lost relations—an Indian custom.[2]

On April 1st, Captain Montour, with 140 Indians and some Rangers, set out for Kanestio, and after passing several high creeks and rivers, they destroyed two large towns, which were built of square logs. After this Montour proceeded to Kanestio, where they destroyed sixty good houses and killed a number of cattle.

1768.—A conference was held at Fort Pitt between George Croghan, Deputy Agent of Indian Affairs, and the chiefs and warriors of the Six Nations, Delawares, Shawnese, and Muncies, residing on the Ohio River. "Henry" Montour, interpreter.

[1] Stone's "Life of Sir William Johnston."
[2] "New York Colonial History."

On October 24th the great Congress with the Indians at Fort Stanwix opened. Andrew Montour was one of the interpreters; the others were John Butler and Philip Phillips.

1769.—A tract of land, at the junction of Loyalsock Creek, on the west branch of the Susquehanna, in the present county of Lycoming, was surveyed November 3, 1769, for Andrew Montour, called Montour's Reserve. It contained 880 acres.

It seems also that "Henry" Montour claimed, settled on, and built a house on a tract of 600 acres on or near Chillisquaque Creek, about four or five miles above Fort Augusta. The Indian name of Montour was "Sattelihu."

At the time of the visit of Zinzendorf to Shamokin, in the autumn of 1742, he met Andrew for the first time, and thus describes him: "His cast of countenance is decidedly European, and had not his face been encircled with a broad band of paint, applied with bear's fat, I would certainly have taken him for one. He wore a brown broadcloth coat, a scarlet damasken lappel waist-coat, breeches, over which his shirt hung, a black Cordovan neckerchief decked with silver bugles, shoes and stockings, and a hat. His ears were hung with pendants of brass and other wires plaited together like the handles of a basket. He was very cordial, but on addressing him in French, he, to my surprise, replied in English."

GEORGE CROGHAN.

GEORGE CROGHAN was the most conspicuous name in the Western annals, in connection with Indian affairs, for twenty-five years preceding the Revolutionary War. He was a native of Ireland, and received an ordinary education in Dublin. Came to America in 1743 or 1744. In 1746 he resided in East Pennsboro Township, Lancaster, (afterwards Cumberland County), five miles west of Harris' Ferry, now Harrisburg.[1]

In March, 1749, he was appointed by the Governor and Council one of the Justices of the Peace and Common Pleas for Lancaster County. He engaged in the Indian trade, going as far as the southwestern border of Lake Erie in 1746 or 1747.

In 1748 he had a trading house at Logstown, on the Ohio, and afterwards trading establishments at the principal Indian towns.[2]

France claimed the vast country west of the Alleghenies, watered by the Ohio and Mississippi rivers. She was now attempting to establish her claim by the establishment *i* military posts from the lakes to the Mississippi and along the Allegheny and Ohio rivers.

The Indian tribes in this region, numerous and warlike, were to be conciliated. Croghan early saw the importance of

---
[1] "Pennsylvania Archives." Evans' Map of the Middle Colonies, 1749. Rupp.
[2] "Weiser's Journal."

detaching them from the French by means of presents and more favorable trade. His suggestions on the subject were wisely heeded by the President and Council of the Province of Pennsylvania, and they accordingly appointèd him, in 1747, their agent, to deliver presents of goods to the Ohio Indians.[1]

In April, 1748, he met the Indian chiefs at Ohio, returned thanks of the President and Council of Pennsylvania for the French scalp they had sent down last spring, and delivered the present of goods for all their brethren, settled in and about Ohio, powder, lead, vermilion, knives and tobacco, to the amount of £224.5.0. He further stated that a proclamation had been issued, strictly forbidding all traders from carrying strong liquors into the Indian country under severe penalties. The chiefs returned thanks for the presents, approved of the suppression of the traffic in liquor, but as they had recently induced some nations of Indians in the French interest to leave them, and as they had never tasted English rum, they hoped some would be sent to them.[2] They significantly added "We send you this French scalp as a token that we don't go to visit them for nothing."

In August, 1749, he was sent west by Governor Hamilton in consequence of rumors of the French approaching the Ohio, and to secure the Indians to the English interest.[3] He reached Logstown soon after Céleron, with the French troops, had left. The increasing intrusion of white settlers on the unpurchased lands of the Indians west of the Susquehanna, in spite of the laws, of the Governor's proclamation, and the threats of the Indians themselves, determined the government to expel them by force.

Accordingly, in May, 1750, a large company, headed by

[1] "Colonial Records," 1747.
[2] "Colonial Records," Vol. V.
[3] "New York Colonial History."

Secretary Peters, George Croghan and the other magistrates and sheriff of the new County of Cumberland, visited the settlers on the Big Juniata, Sherman's Creek, the Path Valley, Big Cove, Auchquick Creek and other places, removed their household goods and burned the log cabins; doubtless by these effective measures preventing an Indian war.[1]

In November of the same year he was dispatched, in company with Andrew Montour, to the Miamis, to renew the chain of friendship and deliver them a present. On their way out, at Logstown, on the Ohio, the few chiefs then there told him "their brothers, the English, ought to have a fort on this river to secure the trade, as they expected war with the French in the spring."[2]

At Muskingum he met Christopher Gist. They travelled together to Piqua. There Croghan delivered the message and presents, and made a treaty, for which the Governor censured him, as done without authority, although he said he believed Croghan intended well. The latter in his account says the Assembly rejected the treaty and condemned him for drawing an additional expense on the Government, and the Indians were neglected.[3] The treaty admits two tribes, Ottawas and Pyankeskees, to the friendship and alliance of the King of Great Britain and his subjects, as the other tribes of the Miami's had been. Signed by George Croghan, in the presence of us, Christopher Gist, Robert Callender, Thomas T. K. Kinton, three Miami chiefs, Andrew Montour, John J. P. Peter, a Delaware and a Shawnese chief present. The Governor sent them a message of approval three months later.[4]

[1] "Assembly Journals," 1750.
[2] "Colonial Records," Vol. V.
[3] "New York Colonial History," Vol. VII. "Pennsylvania Assembly Journals."
[4] "Colonial Records," Vol. V, pp. 524-34.

In May, 1751, he was at Logstown with Andrew Montour, having been commissioned to deliver to the Ohio Indians the provincial present, and friendly messages. Jean Cœur, the French Agent and interpreter, was there. At the council he was menaced by the chiefs, who ordered the French from their lands. They delivered Croghan a speech for the Governor of Pennsylvania, in which they requested he should build a strong house on the Ohio River soon. Governor Hamilton communicated to the House of Assembly, Croghan and Montour's account of their proceedings, in a special message, and recommended the building of a strong trading house on the Ohio, and offered, on the part of the proprietaries, to bear a portion of the expense. The Assembly declined, and preferred the proprietary would contribute to the expense of the presents to the Indians. That body also asserted that the danger from the French, and the Indians' request to erect a strong trading house, was misunderstood or misrepresented by Croghan. So the matter was dropped.[1]

In the latter part of April, 1752, Governor Hamilton, at Philadelphia, received a letter from Croghan, written at the Shawnese town, February 8th, and enclosing a message from the Shawnese to the effect that they intended to war against the French in revenge for the thirty Miamis killed by them, and wanting to be assured of the friendship of the English.[2]

In October, 1753, a large deputation of chiefs and warriors of the Six Nations, Delawares, Shawnese, Wyandots and Miamis, held a treaty with the Commissioners of Pennsylvania, at Carlisle. George Croghan was present.[3]

These Indians held a treaty at Winchester, in September,

[1] Votes of Assembly. "Colonial Records." "New York Colonial History," Vol. VII, p. 268.
[2] "Colonial Records," Vol. V.
[3] "Colonial Records," Vol. V.

with Virginia. Conferences with the Indian chiefs were generally held up to 1754, at George Croghan's house at Pennsboro. The road through the pass on the mountain, about six miles north of Carlisle, and the same distance west of Croghan's, is marked "Croghan's Gap" on Evans Map of 1749, and all others to a recent date, when it seems, changed to Sterrits Gap.

In 1753 Croghan built a house at Aughwick or Aughquick Old Town, doubtless the site of an old Indian town, now in the borough of Shirleysburgh, Huntington County, Pa., called Croghan's Fort—Fort Shirley, by Governor Morris in 1756,—when it was enlarged and stockaded.[1] One of the chain of forts established in consequence of the defeat of Braddock. About twenty miles from the settlements Fort Lytellton was built. Fifteen miles northeast of Fort Shirley, near the mouth of a branch of the Juniata, called Kishequokilis, a third fort was erected, called Fort Granville. From Fort Granville towards Susquehanna, at the distance of fifteen miles and about twelve from the river, another fort was established, called Pomfret Castle.

Croghan also, this year, 1753, held a tract of nearly 400 acres near the present Bedford town, surveyed by the Deputy Surveyor, Armstrong, and obtained a grant from the Six Nations of a tract in Aughwick.

February 3, 1754.—Again Croghan wrote to Governor Hamilton, and Richard Peters, Secretary, urging the building of a strong log trading house or stockade,—in reality a fort, but inexpensive. He mentions that Mr. Trent has just come out with the Virginia Guards and brought a quantity of tools and workmen to build a fort, and as he could not talk the Indian language, "I am obliged to stay and assist in dividing the goods." This was the commencement of the fortification at

[1] "Pennsylvania Archives."

the Forks of the Ohio, which Ensign Ward was obliged to surrender, when partly finished, to the superior force of Contrecœur, in April. During the past winter Croghan had a large number of Indians at Aughwick under his charge. The Assembly of Pennsylvania adjourned on March 9th, without making, but refusing to make, any appropriation for the defense of the Province.

On March 13, 1754, Governor Hamilton wrote to Governor Dinwiddie: "Ever since I had the honor to write you I have been laboring indefatigably with my Assembly to induce them to act vigorously on the present critical juncture of affairs at Ohio, and to grant such supplies as might enable us to resist the invasion of the French." In another letter of the same date he wished Governor Dinwiddie to inform him as to the situation of the French forts, as he believes those at the Forks of the Monongahela to be really within the bounds of Pennsylvania. Governor Dinwiddie replied March 21st: "I am from all hands assured Logstown is far to the West of Mr. Penn's grant and the Forks of the Ohio also."[1]

"In January I commissioned William Trent to raise one Hundred men; he had got Seventy and had begun a Fort at the Forks of the Monhongialo. His Majesty sent me out Thirty Pieces of Cannon, Four-Pounders, with Carriages and all necessary Impliments, with Eighty Barrells of Gun Powder."

December 6, 1754.—This message was received from the Assembly: "As we apprehend, the Governor will agree with us in the necessity of regulating that Expence (Indian Allies), with all possible economy, and as George Croghan (whose accounts we have allowed) seems resolved to remove from Aughquick, and the Indians by that means will be left without any proper Person to take the necessary Care of providing for their Subsistence, we recommend it to the Governor's

[1] "Colonial Records."

Consideration whether it might not be more convenient for the Indians themselves, and less Expence to the Province, if they were invited to move nearer our Back Inhabitants, till by Hunting or otherwise, they may be able to subsist themselves with Safety."

In a letter to Governor Morris, December 2, 1754, he gives the reasons for wishing to leave Aughquick. "All the Promises made those Indians or any Expectations they have of this government Doing anything for them, they always expect to be fulfilled by me, and as it is not in my power to do anything for them, I think it proper one of the Interpreters should be sent here to take care of them, they imagine I have received orders from your Honour to supply them with such things as they want. I think it is my Duty to acquaint your Honour what I know of the Indians Sentiments and what they expect of this Government, which is as follows, The Ohio Indians in general puts their whole dependence on this government in regard to the Expedition, as soon as this government moves they will unite all their force and attack the French."

R. Peters, in a letter to George Croghan desires him to make his opinion known to the Assembly relative to removing the Indians from Auchquick, "and insist that a stockade be made this winter." In George Croghan's answer to Mr. Peters as to the best method of moving the Indians he writes, "I think it would be of very ill consequence, for I think they are full near the Inhabitants already; there was one White Man killed this summer already by an Indian in a drunken frolic, and if they lived among them there would be constantly rioting and quarrelling. I don't know what will become of the Back parts unless there be a Stockade Fort put up this side the Blue Hills, as certainly the Indians who come to the Virginia Camp are Spies come to view the Country and know our strength, for I am certain there is a great body of French and Indians at the French Fort on Ohio."

In a letter of December 23, 1754 to Governor Morris, he writes: "I am obliged to advertise the Inhabitants of Cumberland County, in your honour's name, not to barter or sell Liquour to the Indians, or to any persons to bring amongst them."

Croghan always took an important part in all conferences and treaties with the Indians.[1]

Croghan was one of the Commissioners appointed to open a road to the Ohio for the use of troops. May 12, 1755, the Governor wrote to Braddock: "Agreeable to your request, immediately upon my return from Alexandria, I sent to George Croghan, the person entrusted with the management of the Indians in this Province, to join you with as large a body of Indians as he could." General Braddock, in his answer, writes: "I have engaged between forty and fifty Indians from the Frontier of your Province to go with me over the Mountains, and shall take Croghan and Montour into Service."

Letter from George Croghan to Governor Morris, May 20, 1755: "Tomorrow what Indian women and children came to Fort Cumberland with me will be sent back to Aucquick by order of the General, the Men entirely go with the General, and the General insists on my going with him, so that it is out of my Power to provide for those Women and Children. The messengers I sent to the Shawnese, Twigtwees and Owendots, are not yet returned but I hear they are coming, so that I hope they will join the General before the Army gets to the Ohio." After the defeat of Braddock, Croghan returned to Aughquick. The Indians held a conference at Philadelphia and complained of the ignorance of the General and the haughty way he had treated them.

[1] "Colonial Records."

Letter of Croghan to Charles Swaine, from Aughquick, says: "He had seen an Indian from Ohio, sent to give him warning that he might save his scalp, which he says would be no small prize to the French, and he desires me, as soon as I see the Indians remove from Susquehanna back to Ohio, to shift my quarters, for he says that the French will, if possible, lay all the back frontiers in ruin this Winter." "I am glad I have no hand in Indian affairs at this critical time."

November 12th, Croghan writes to Hamilton: "Permit me at this Critical Time to give you information of the designs of the Enemy. I would have written to the Governor but he has not thought proper to desire me to give him any accounts of Indian Affairs since the defeat of General Braddock. The Six Nations, Delawares, Shawanese, Wyandots and Twigtrees have held a Conference and determined to proceed against the Frontiers of Virginia, Maryland and Pennsylvania this winter."

1755.—Orders were sent to Captain George Croghan "to proceed to Cumberland County and fix on proper places for erecting three stockadoes, viz.: One back of Patterson's, one upon Kishecoquillas, and one near Sideling Hill, fifty feet square, with a block-house on two of the corners and a barrack within, capable of lodging fifty men."

December 17.—James Hamilton wrote to Governor Morris: "Since you left us, Conrad Weiser, James Galbraith and George Croghan have been in town, and have been fully examined by the Councils upon all the Points we thought necessary to be known. The Country is everywhere alarmed. I have given George Croghan a Captain's Commission. He is to raise the men immediately and superintend the building of Stockades."

Governor Morris gave to Governor Hardy this character of Croghan: "There were many Indian traders with Braddock, and among others Croghan, who acted as a Captain of the Indians under a Warrant from General Braddock, and I never heard any objections to his conduct in that capacity. For many years he had been very largely concerned in the Ohio trade, was upon that river frequently, and had a considerable influence among the Indians, speaking the Language of several nations, and being very liberal or rather profuse in his gifts to them which, with the losses he sustained by the French, who seized great quantities of his goods, and by not getting the debts due to him from the Indians, be became Bankrupt, and since has lived at a place called Aughwick, in the Back parts of this Province, where he had generally a number of Indians with him, for the maintenance of whom the Province allowed him sums of money from time to time. After this he went by my order with those Indians and joined General Braddock; since Braddock's defeat he returned to Aughwick, where he remained until an act of assembly was passed here granting him a freedom from arrest for ten years; this was done that the Province might have the Benefit of his Knowledge of the woods and his influence among the Indians. A Captain's commission was given to him and he was ordered to raise men for the defence of the Western Frontier, which he did in a very expeditious manner, he continued in the command of one of the Companies he had raised, and of Fort Shirley about three months, when, having a dispute with the Commissioners about some accounts between them, in which he thought himself ill-used, he re-signed his commission. I hear he is now at Onondago with Sir William Johnston."

At a Council held at Philadelphia, December 14, 1756, the Governor informed the Council that Sir William Johnston had appointed Mr. Croghan to transact Indian affairs in this Province. Mr. Croghan was of opinion that there should be a conference held with the Indians as early as possible in the Spring. He was instructed by Sir William Johnston to proceed to Philadelphia as soon as he could, or to any part of that Province where the good of his Majesty's Indian interest might require. He was to endeavor to find out the disposition of such Indians as are still living in those parts and try all means to convince them it is their interest to continue friends with the English, and to seek out the Delawares and Shawanese and induce them to join his Majesty's army.

During January, 1757, Mr. Croghan dispatched two of the Conestogas to Ohio with messages to the Six Nations, Delawares and Shawanese. March 29 he wrote from Harris' Ferry " that on arriving there he found 160 Indians, chiefly Six Nations. Teedyuscung had gone to the Seneca Country and he expected him soon with not less than 200 Indians." He asked for clothes for them, which request was granted by the Council. The conference with the Indians asked for by George Croghan was held in the court-house at Lancaster, on Monday, May 16, 1757. Mr. Croghan thought it necessary that presents should be made to the Cherokees, to consist of such articles as Mr. Croghan might think those warriors stood most in need of, particularly arms. This request of Mr. Croghan was granted and he was appointed to distribute the presents. The Sachems made the following speech : " As we have finished the business for this time and we design to part to-morrow, you must be sensible that we have a long journey and a hilly country to pass over, and several of our old men very weak, we hope that you will not send us from your frontiers without a 'walking-stick,' (meaning a keg of rum)."

In September, 1757, Croghan was at Fort Johnston, New York, attending conferences between Sir William Johnston and the Six Nations and Cherokees. Previous to that he had been sent by Johnston to the German Flats.

June 30, 1758.—He marched with a division of the Indians to join General Abercrombie. Sir William Johnston was with him and nearly 400 Indians, amongst whom there were some of all the Five Nations.

A conference was held in the town of Easton on October 8, 1758, at which George Croghan was present. This conference continued until the 26th.

On March 28, 1759, Mr. Croghan, in conference with the Governor, gave it as his opinion, that there should be no invitations sent fixing the time of meeting for the Ohio Indians. If any further invitation was necessary, it should be general, intimating that we expected to see them, and leave the particular time to themselves, not knowing what time would suit the Indians, who were so far distant one from another. Mr. Croghan said further, that the Indians in town were exceedingly uneasy, and desired an audience of General Stanwix, on which the Governor wrote a letter to the General, desiring him to give the Indians an audience and to make them presents to their satisfaction.

July, 1759.—A conference was held at Pittsburgh by George Croghan, Deputy Agent. Col. Hugh Mercer, a number of officers of the garrison and chiefs of the Six Nations, Shawanese and Delawares were present. Captain Croghan held a private conference, relative to the price of goods and skins.

May, 1760.—Croghan wrote to R. Peters, recommending to him six Mohock Indians, who had come to Fort Pitt with Montour, and informing him that several Indian Nations seem bent on carrying on a war against the Southern Indians, but are deterred by scarcity of ammunition. A conference was held at Pittsburgh, on the 12th of August, by Brigadier-General Moncton, with the Western Nation of Indians, at which Deputy Agent Croghan was present. Croghan accompanied

Major Rogers to Detroit, to receive the surrender of that and the other posts of the French in the west. Captain Croghan kept a journal of this expedition, which has been published.

July, 1760.—He accompanied Colonel Bouquet, from Fort Pitt to Venango, with a detachment of troops. During the Pontiac War, Croghan was active; he was with Captain Ecuyer, during the investment of Fort Pitt by the Indians. After it was relieved by Bouquet, he resigned out of the service, intending to sail for England; he wrote thus from Carlisle, October 11, 1763: "I know many people will think I am wrong, but had I continued, I could be of no more service than I have been this eighteen months past, which was none, as no regard was had to any intelligence I sent, no more than to my opinion." General Gage, succeeding Amherst, ordered Croghan to remain. Sir William Johnston, in 1763, sent him to England, to confer with the ministry, about an Indian boundary line. In this voyage, he was shipwrecked on the coast of France.

February 28.—He was present at an Indian conference, at Fort Pitt, a journal of which has been published.

While on his way, in 1765, to pacify the Illinois Indians, he was attacked, June 8, wounded and taken to Vincennes, but was soon released, and accomplished his mission. In May, 1766, he made a settlement, four miles above Fort Pitt. He continued to render valuable service in pacifying the Indians, until 1776. He was an object of suspicion to the Revolutionary authorities, in 1778, but as he continued to reside on his farm, he was doubtless unjustly accused.

George Croghan's settlement was undoubtedly the first, except Gist's, within the County of Allegheny. The house stood on the bank of the Allegheny River, a few rods from the late residence of Judge McCandless. Two ancient apple trees mark the exact spot, on the draft of survey. The White

Mingo Castle is marked on the north side of the river, at the mouth of Pine Creek. At his residence here, he held frequent conferences with the Indians, some of whom were frequently there when he was at home. In Washington's "Journal of a Tour to the Ohio River," in 1770, is entered, October 18, "Dined with Col. Croghan."

In the MS. copy of Land Office Survey, in June, 1769, for George Croghan's tract of 1,352 acres, the White Mingoes' Castle is laid down on the north side of the river, opposite to the land surveyed, and near the mouth of Pine Creek, on the east side. Clarkson's Diary, of 1766, refers to this "Indian Settlement of the Mingoes," and as the "White Mingo's Town," in Schoolcraft's "American Abridged Archives," Volume IV, pp. 269-271. It was, however, a much older place of resort by the Indians. The present Kittanning road, from half a mile above the mouth of Pine Creek, direct to Kittanning, was the old Kittanning path of the Indians, and so called by the older white settlers, within the memory of the writer. In 1753-4, William Trent and George Croghan, partners in the Indian trade, had a storehouse above the mouth of Pine Creek; also fenced fields of Indian corn and numbers of large canoes and batteaux, all of which were seized by the French in 1754.[1]

Pine Creek empties into the Allegheny River, on the north side, five Miles above the site of Fort Pitt, near the present towns of Sharpsburgh and Etna. Indians of the Six Nations appear to have built the town at this point, soon after the erection of Fort Pitt. It was known as the "White Mingo Town," from the head chief. These Indians came from the "Mingo town," on the northwest side of the Ohio, about three miles below the site of the present city of Steubenville, near the mouth of Indian Cross Creek and "Mingo Junction," of the

[1] MS. affidavit of Croghan, and others, Carlisle, 1756.

Pittsburgh, St. Louis and Pittsburgh and Wheeling railways. It was a town inhabited chiefly by the Senecas, called with others of the Six Nations, "Mingoes."[1] Washington visited it in October and November, 1770, on his way to and from the Kanawha. He states that it then had about twenty cabins and seventy inhabitants of the Six Nations. According to Thomas Hutchins, it was the only Indian village, in 1766, between Fort Pitt and the Falls of the Ohio. It then contained sixty families. The Monsies were a tribe of the Delawares, speaking a somewhat different dialect. Their settlement was probably the Sewickly town on Evans' Map of 1755, and Scull's of 1770, where the town of Springdale now stands, twelve miles above Pittsburgh, on the northwest side of the Allegheny River. Conrad Weiser passed a night there. John Conolly and Captain Ed. Ward were relatives of George Croghan; their exact relationship is not known. Susannah, wife of General Prevost, was his only child; she died at Milgrove, Montgomery County, Pennsylvania, March, 1791. Her heirs tried to recover part of his property, but were unsuccessful. The history of George Croghan, the Indians' friend and generous protector, is the history of the Indians of Pennsylvania;—their conferences, treaties, and treatment by the white usurpers.[2] George Croghan's house, on the Allegheny, was erected in 1759-60; burned by the Indians during their outbreak in the Summer of 1763; rebuilt on the same spot; was standing the beginning of this century.

DEED TO GEORGE CROGHAN.

Whereas Johonisse, Scarayoday and Teedyuscung chiefs or sachems of the Six united Nations of Indians did by their deed

[1] George Croghan's Journal.
[2] See Ecuyer's Journal in "Fort Pitt."

duly executed having date the 2d day of August A D 1749 for the consideration therein mentioned grant bargain and sell to George Croghan in fee a certain tract of land Beginning on the eastern side of the river Ohio to the northward of an old Indian town called Shannopins Town at the mouth of a run called the Two mile run and running thence up the said two mile run to where it intersects with the heads of the two mile springs where it empties into the Monongahela river, thence down the said two mile springs the same course thereof into the said river Monongahela, thence up the said river Monongahela to where Turtle creek empties itself into the said river, thence up the said creek to the first forks thereof, thence up the north or northerly branch of the said creek to the head of the same, thence north or a northerly course until it strikes Plumb Creek, thence down said Plumb creek until it empties itself into the river Allegheny and thence down the said river Allegheny to the place of beginning where the aforesaid two mile run discharges itself into the said river Ohio containing by estimate Forty thousand Acres be the same more or less as by the same deed more fully appears. And whereas said Chiefs or Sachems fully representing the six united Nations aforesaid in full council assembled at Fort Stanwix did by their Deed Poll duly executed bearing date the 11th November 1768 for the consideration therein mentioned, granted and conveyed to his most sacred Majesty George III king of Great Britain, for the benefit and behoof of said George Croghan all the before mentioned tract of land ; for part of which said lands George Croghan made application unto the Secretarys office at Philadelphia April 1st 1769 and obtained a special grant for part of the same from the Proprietor of Pennsylvania as appears from the records of the Land Office at Philadelphia, reference being had thereto may more fully appear, which application with

A Map of Part of the Province of Pennsylvania West of the River Susquahannah

WEST PENNSYLVAN[IA]

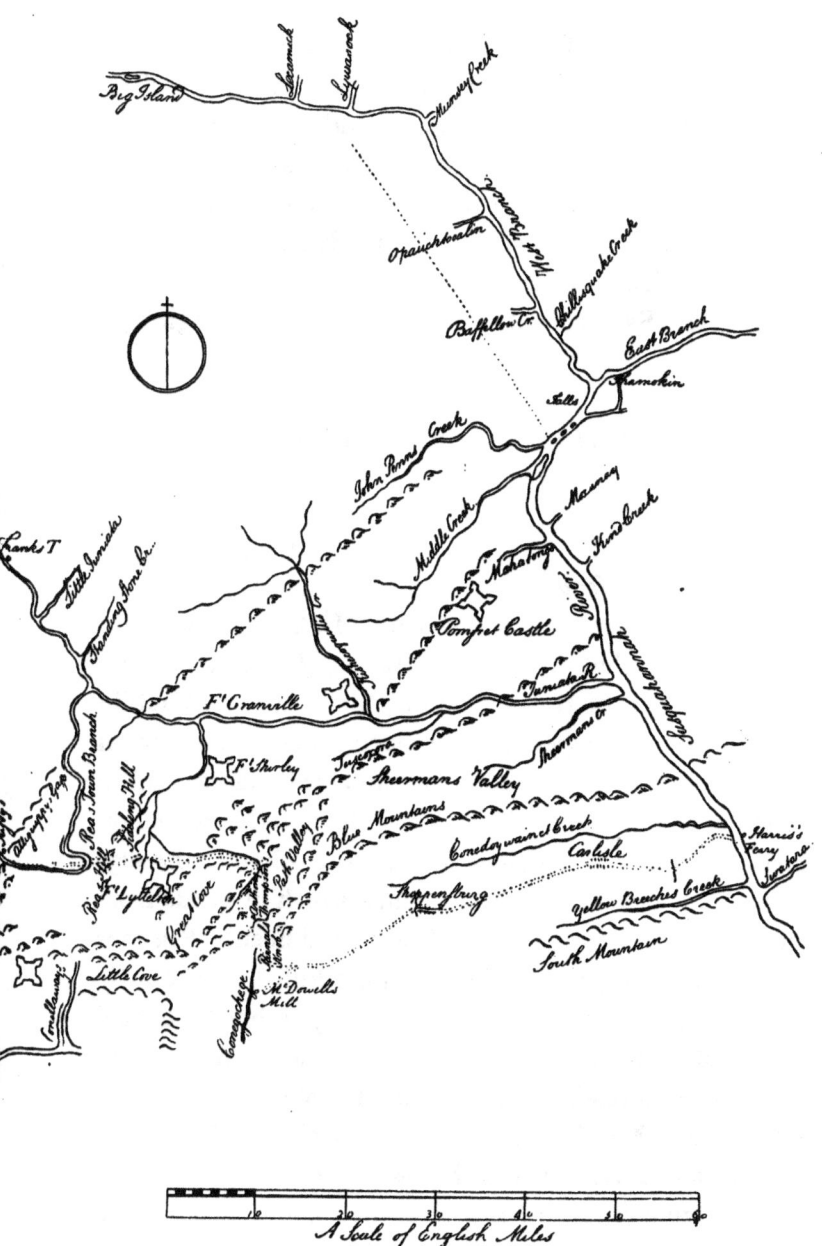

VIRGINIA, 1755.

surveys were made and returned to the Surveyor Generals Office at Philadelphia. And whereas said George Croghan by Indenture 20th April 1776 granted and conveyed to said Thomas Gerty 476½ Acres part of the aforesaid land. Beginning at a Black Oak on the Eastern bank of the river Allegheny and running thence north to a Sycamore in a small island on Crab Tree run now commonly called Plumb Creek, thence down to a Sycamore at the junction with the Allegheny.[1]

LETTER FROM WILLIAM TRENT TO GOVERNOR HAMILTON.

VIRGINIA, April 10, 1753.

May it please your Honour

I have received a letter just now from Mr. Croghan wherein he acquaints me that fifty odd Ottawas, Conewagos, one Dutchman and one of the Six nations that was their Captain met with some of our people at a place called Kentucky on this side Allegheny river about one hundred and fifty miles from the lower Shawanese Town, they took eight Prisoners, five belonging to Mr Croghan and me, the others to Lowry, they took three or four hundred Pounds worth of goods from us, one of them made his escape after he had been a Prisoner three days, three of John Finleys men are killed by the little Pict Town and no account of himself, they robbed Michael Teaffs People near the Lakes, there was one Frenchman in Company, the Owendats secured his People and five horse loads of Skins. Mr Croghan is coming thro' the Woods with some Indians and Whites and the rest of the White men and the Indians are coming up the river in a body though 'tis a question whether they escape, as three hundred Ottawas were

[1] See Treaty at Fort Stanwix.

expected at the lower Town every day and another Party of French and Indians coming down the river, the Indians are in such confusion that there is no knowing who to trust. I expect they will all join the French except the Delawares, as they expect no assistance from the English. The Low Dutchmans name that was with the Party that robbed our People is Philip Philips, his mother lives near Col. Johnsons, he was taken by the French Indians about six years ago and has lived ever since with them; he intends sometime this summer to go and see his mother, if your Honour pleases to acquaint the Governor of New York with it, he may possibly get him secured by keeping it secret, and acquainting Col. Johnson with it and ordering him to apprehend him; if the Dutchman once come to understand it, they will contrive to send him word to keep out of the way.

I intend leaving directly for Allegheny with provisions for our People that are coming through the woods and up the river. I am your Honours

most obedient humble servant
WILLIAM TRENT.

[Endorsed JAMES HAMILTON.]

BOUQUET PAPERS.

FORT PITT, January 24, 1763.

Dear Sir

Since I wrote you last there has little happened here in my department worth mentioning. Some Shennas came here and delivered up four prisoners and yesterday some Chiefs arrived on the other side ye River, who have brought four more which will be delivered up to-morrow and those Chiefs tell me they are to stay and hunt here about till ye last is brought up in ye spring.

Captain Ecuyer will write you ye news of this place. Y^e gentlemen here are all bucks; nothing but Flutes and assemblys, we really live in great harmony.

Sir, I have taken ye Liberty to draw on you for £100 in favour of John Welsh for which and y^e £100 to Capt. Basett you will please to keep ye warrant which I expect ye General has granted for ye small account of £18000 which I was in advance and sent by you.

I am dear Sir with great esteem and regard
y^r most humble servant
GEORGE CROGHAN.

FORT PITT, March 19, 1763.

Dear Sir

I am sorry that Col. John Armstrong has not returned ye four Tracts run out for you last fall with ye Tract of ye big spring on Vinord Creek, which are all done. I have wrote him to return them as soon as possible; as to ye Tracts on Vinord Creek you may depend on it I will have them run out next month when I shall be at Bedford.

As to the other affair my Brother is now on ye spot with ye Indian and diging ye produce of which I will send you on my arrival at Bedford where I expect to be by ye first of April.

As I shall not have ye pleasure of accompanying you down ye river, I think it my duty to give you my opinion of that tour, with respect to making any settlement. I dare say you will find that the French has not purchased any more Land of the Indians than just what they have occupied and that you will find ye Indians will not stand tame Spectators and see settlements made in their Country without first having some consideration given them for it and I am of opinion the French will do every thing in their power privately to give ye Indians a bad impression of us so that your hands should be open with respect to presents you should have at least fifty Indians from hence with you of yᵉ diferent Nations and such as is of consequence amongst these Nations, with whom I will send young Mr. McKee who is a modest young man and one you can depend on as a good interpreter. You will find yᵉ Cherokees our enemies tho' they seem quiet on yᵉ frontiers of Carolina, and what obliged them to be so is nothing else than yᵉ war which yᵉ Western Nations has carried on against them with great Spirit this two years past, they have been this winter endeavouring to accumodate maters which if they should do may give us more trouble than we may expect.

I am Dear sir with esteem and regard

yʳ Most Humble servant
GEORGE CROGHAN.

[To COL. BOUQUET.]

FOR COL. HENRY BOUQUET.

FORT PITT, March 19, 1763.

Dear Sir

I was favoured with yours of the 22d February and observe the Generals resolution with respect to giving any presents to yᵉ Indians this way, which was no more than I expected. I was fully determined to give as little as possible to yᵉ Indians here this winter and I dare say when you see yᵉ accounts you will see that nothing has been given on yᵉ kings account which could have been avoided. Indeed I believe it has cost me near £100 out of my own pocket in trifels which I did not chuse to trouble Captain Ecuyer with nor could I avoid doing it myself without letting yᵉ service suffer. Since yᵉ reduction of Canada the several Indian Nations this Way has been very jelous of his Majestys growing power in this Country but this last account of so much of North America being ceded to Great Britain has almost drove them to despair, and by leters from Major Gladwin and Captain Campble it appears that ye Indians over the Lakes are full as many there as on this Side. As to ye News how they may behave I cant pretend to say, but I do not aprove of General Armhursts plan in distresing them too much at wonst as in my opinion they will not consider Consequences if too much distrest, tho' Sir Jeffrey thinks they will. Some time ago I wrote to Sir William Johnson and let him know that if Sir Jeffrey Amhurst did not give me leave to go to England to solicit a restitution for ye great depredations committed on me by the King of Frances Subjects in ye beginning of ye war, that I would resign which I expect will be ye case as I am pretty certain Sir W J will give me leave to resign as he must think there is no occasion for an Agent here on Sir Jeffrey Armhurst present plan, so that I expect every day to hear that both Sir W and Sir Jeff has aproved of my quiting ye Service as it will save something to ye Nation.

Enclosed I send you the small Account of £187. 19. 6. with two other vouchers from Capt. Campble which I must Request ye feavor of you to prefer to Sir Jeffery; if he condescends to pay it, pray receive ye money and give me Credit for it. If he should not aprove of those Vouchers I can do no more I must content myself with the loss thereof.

Nothing would give me greater plesher than to go down this River as you are honoured with the Command, but for two very weatey rasons I cant think of it first my own affairs will oblige me to go to England as soon as possible, ye Secondly is that I am certain Sir Jeffery Armhurst will not alow a sufisent quantity of presents to satisfye the Great Number of Indians and before I wold attempt to undertake ye Negocieatory Maters with a Number of Indian Nations who has never been aquainted with us but allways under ye influences of the French without I could do it with repetation to my self and ease to you. I will run ye Resk of loosing every thing I have depending in England and content myself at ye tail of a plow, some where on ye frontier.

Captain Ecuyer and my self has done every thing in our power to get as many Vouchers as was posable here for ye Account which you will receive from Captain Ecuyer by this Express. I am dear Sir with great Esteem and
    Regard y^r Most Humble Servant
        GEORGE CROGHAN.

        CARLISLE, June 8, 1763.
Dear Sir

By this Express you will receive ye Inteligence of Mr. Colhoon by which it apears that ye Dalaways have all declared against us, as you have known my opinion on this head, some time ago, I need say Nothing now on ye subject as it will not bear Laffing at as usual by his ———. I have wrote Sir William Johnson and inclosed a Copy of ye Intelligence which you will plese to forward.

Plese to acquaint Governor Hamilton that I have heard this Evening that Col. Bird and Captain McKee have not proceeded to dispossess the New England people having received an account from Fort Augusta that ye Indians on Susquehanna have summoned ye Garrison to remove or that they would cut them off.

I will proceed tomorrow for Bedford and endeavour to get some men to escort ye Powder and Lead up there.
     I am D^r S^r
       y^r Most Humble Servt
        GEORGE CROGHAN.

SHIPPENSBURGH, June 11, 1763.[1]

Yesterday and this Day a report prevailed in this County that all the People in the Path Valley were murdered by the Indians and their Houses burned, and that Fort Ligonier was likewise taken and burned, the people in General was flying from their Habitations but just now I received a letter from Bedford by which I find that the Indians had not prevailed against Ligonier, tho' they had fired some Shot at the Fort, and two men is come from the Path Valley, who say that no Indians has appeared there as yet but say the People there are very much alarmed.

I have endeavoured to settle the minds of the People as much as possible and most of them are returned to their Houses.

As I was apprehensive that some scouting Party of Indians might come down and burn Fort Lyttleton in order to shut up the Communication and in order to quiet the Inhabitants I have engaged twenty five Men at 45ˢ per month with one (officer) to command them, to garrison it for one month and furnished Provisions and some Powder and Lead for them, which I hope will meet with General Amhersts approbation and requests the favour of you to make him acquainted with it. If he should aprove of this step I hope he will (give orders) for paying the expences or continuing them longer (as he may) think proper. Tomorrow I set off with them to Fort Lytleton, and request you will let me know the Generals answer, that if the Expence of these Men (should fall on) myself I may discharge them when the month is out.

The Justices of this County has been these three Days endeavouring to get some Volunteers to escort the Powder and Lead to Bedford, but could not get any. It is at Loudon and I believe I shall be obliged to hire men there to escort it

[1] This document very much mutilated and stained.

up. Pray mention these Expences to the General as it will fall very heavy on me if he should not approve of it and pay the expences. It appears to me from all the Letters I have from Fort Pitt that no Indians seem to have committed any Hostilities thereabouts but the Delawares, and from the (   ) speeches of the Beaver and his Council to Calhoun it seems as if they intend to deny that they were conserned with this great Breach of faith Should their (   ) miscarry and not be able to accomplish their design and so solicit their pardon. As to the Accounts of Detroit being attacked by the Ottaways and Cheepaways we have nothing for it but what the Delawares tell us and by all accounts from Susquehannah and Mr. Hunter's Letter to Col. Burd from Fort Augusta it appears to me that the Susquehannah Indians was not aquainted with the (combat) about the 2d or 3d of this Month when a Delaware Indian brought the accounts from Ohio to the great Island but it is probable that the other nations will join the Delawares if they are successful against the small out Posts and then no doubt they will fall upon the Frontiers without they meet a sufficient check soon. As to Detroit if those nations which the Delawares say had attacked it prove so, it must fall, as the works are very large, without the French engage heartily and assist the Troops, which I fear they will not, as I have been convinced near these twelve months past that the French at the Ilinois has been spiriting up the Indians to cut off our out Posts; all which Intelligence you know I sent to General Amherst.

I had no doubt the French at Detroit were privately concerned with the designs of the Ottaways and Cheepaways as they have great influence over those Nations.

(Signature illegible.)

To Col. Henry Bouquet.

Fort Bedford, June 17, 1763.

Dear Sir

I just now received your favour of ye 14th. As the man who carrys it to Carlisle is just setting off, I have only time to acknowledge ye receipt of it. I wrote you from Shipensberge ye eleventh, to which I must refer you for my opinion of the Indians behaviour at this time till I hear from Fort Pitt; as no Express has come down this twelve days, I have reason to think ye place is invested, so that none can safely escape them; but they can no longer continue there, in my opinion than ye few cattle there abouts, which may fall into their way can suport them. The Dallaways in my opinion are ye people who has begun this Indian war, and if ye Ottaways and Cheepways has attackt Detroit I believe it will be found that ye French was acquainted with their designs. I imagine ye Dallaways will remove over ye Lakes or over the Mississippi, perhaps this may be a stroke of Policy in the French to get as many Indian Nations as they can to go to ye country over Mississippi, which they have to people as well to make themselves respectable with their Indian Allies as to secure as much of the Indian Trade as they can. The Dallaways you are sensible have not behaved so well as they did before Post went among them, to his Majesty's Troops and since the last Treaty at Lancaster, they may be said to have behaved with insolence; this you are well acquainted with and I wish ye Quakers may not find that their interfering with Indian affairs may have done more hurt to his Majestys Indian Interest and given them a greater dislike to his troops than any settlements that I or any other people have made there.

I am of opinion that if the Six Nations knew any thing of this Eruption, they kept it secret in order to break off any connections between us and ye Dallaways, as I am certain they have been for some years past very jealous of the Dallaways being raised so high by ye Quakers of Philadelphia; however time will evince to ye publick whether I have acted with imprudence in my Department or not as far as I was limited.

I wish ye General would permit me to send one of those Indians here for intelligence, as it is the only way left us to find out who are concerned against us, for was I now at Fort Pitt I could not have so good an opportunity.

I am dear Sir your most
Humble servant
GEORGE CROGHAN.

BIOGRAPHICAL SKETCH OF COL. THOMAS CRESAP.

October 31, 1750.—Colonel Thomas Cresap was the earliest permanent settler in Western Maryland. He established himself at Old Town in 1742 or 3. At the treaty made at Lancaster, Pennsylvania, with the Six Nations, in June, 1744, the Chief Cannassatego in his speech said: "We are willing to renounce all right to Lord Baltimore of all those Lands lying two miles above the uppermost Fork of Potowmack or Cohongoruton river near which Thomas Cresap has a Hunting or Trading Cabin, by a North line to the bounds of Pennsylvania."[1]

Cresap's cabin or fort was on or near the site of an old town of the Shawanese, a portion of that tribe inhabiting in and about the northern part of the river Potomac from 1698 to 1728-9, when they removed to the Ohio and Allegheny and placed themselves under the protection of the French.[2] On the map constructed by William Mayo for Lord Fairfax, in 1737, the bottom lands on this part of the Potomac are marked "Old Shawnee fields deserted." Also on Fry and Jefferson's, and Scull's maps. Its locality is marked on Dr. Mitchell's map of 1755 "Shawnee Old Town." In the Table of Distances to Ohio in 1754,[3] the first is "New Store at the mouth of Wills creek on Potomack to Cressaps fifteen miles." The name Old Town is yet retained; it is in Old Town District

---
[1] "Treaty at Lancaster with the Six Nations." [2] "Colonial Records."
[2] "Report of Assembly, Journals of 1755."
[3] "Pennsylvania Archives," Vol. II, p. 134.

BIOGRAPHICAL SKETCH OF COL. THOMAS CRESAP.

of Allegheny County, Maryland, fifteen miles southeast of Cumberland, on the north side of the Potomac and opposite to Green Spring station, on the Baltimore and Ohio Railway.

Colonel Thomas Cresap was a native of Skipton, in Yorkshire, England. He emigrated to Maryland about the year 1720, when he was but fifteen years of age. He first settled at Havre de Grace, at the mouth of the Susquehanna River. Lord Baltimore, the Proprietary of Maryland, claiming to extend the boundaries of that Province to the fortieth degree of latitude, Cresap obtained a Maryland warrant for 500 acres, and about the year 1731 removed to the locality of his grant, over twenty miles north of the present boundary-line between Pennsylvania and Maryland, at the ferry-landing opposite the "Blue Rock," about five miles below the present town of Wrightsville, on the Susquehanna, in York County.

Cresap's house is marked on Evans' map of Pennsylvania, 1749. His house was the most northerly situated of the Maryland claimants, of whom he was the leader, being a man of great strength, courage and indomitable resolution. Violent and bloody collisions frequently occurred between the Pennsylvanians and Marylanders. On November 24, 1736, Cresap's house or fort was surrounded by an armed company of twenty-three men, headed by the Sheriff of Lancaster County with a judge's warrant.[1] After a sharp conflict Cresap's capture was only effected by burning the house. He was ironed, taken to Philadelphia and there imprisoned for near two years. Reprisals by the authorities of Maryland speedily followed.

This bitter border warfare was allayed by an order of the King, in Council, May 25, 1738. The prisoners of both Provinces were released and a provisional boundary-line established in 1739.[2] It continued to be the subject of protracted

[1] "Pennsylvania Archvies."
[2] "Pennsylvania Archives."

litigation between the Penns and Lord Baltimore before the High Court of Chancery, in England. The controversy was conclusively settled by amicable agreement and the running of the famous Mason and Dixon's Line, in 1769, and its completion, in 1784. A full and complete history of this boundary controversy would make a large but interesting volume.[1]

Col. Cresap was by nature well adapted for a leader in border contests. He seemed as one "born unto trouble," certainly he never shunned it. Originally a carpenter, afterwards a surveyor, planter and Indian trader, as well as Indian fighter.[2] He made an excellent map of the western boundary of Maryland for Lord Baltimore, which is now in the possession of the Maryland Historical Society. Soon after his return from captivity, in Philadelphia, in 1737 or 8, he removed to a tract of land on the Antietam Creek, in the present Washington County, Maryland, and engaged in the Indian trade and failed. He then fixed his residence at Old Town, or Skipton, as he named it. He was an agent for the Ohio Company and also a member of it.[3] This Company made the first English settlement at Pittsburgh, before Braddock's war; and it was through their means and efforts that the first road was made through the Allegheny Mountains. The war placed Col. Cresap in a perilous situation, and he removed his family to Conococheague; he had to fight his way, being attacked by a

---

[1] See the printed "Case of Messieurs Penn and the people of Pennsylvania and the three lower Counties of New Castle, Kent and Sussex on Delaware, in relation to a series of Injuries and Hostilities made upon them, for several years past, by Thomas Cresap and others by the Direction and Authority of the Deputy Governor of Maryland." To be heard before the Honorable Lords of the Privy Council for Plantation affairs at the Cockpit, White Hall, on Thursday 23d February 1737. "Colonial Records." "Pennsylvania Archives."

[2] "Pennsylvania Archives," Vol. I, pp. 311-52.

[3] See "Sketch of the Ohio Company."

party of Indians. He soon raised a company of volunteers and marched to attack the Indians; his son, Thomas, was killed in their first skirmish. Soon after, peace was made and he returned to his farm at Old Town.

Col. Cresap's literary attainments were small, but by industry and application he obtained a sufficient knowledge of surveying to be entrusted with the surveyorship of Prince George's County, and frequently represented his county in the Legislature. When he was upwards of eighty he married for the second time. He had five children—three sons and two daughters. His youngest son was Michael, who was represented by Mr. Jefferson, most probably unjustly, "as infamous for his many Indian murders and the massacre of Logan's family."[1]

COPY OF ORIGINAL LETTER FROM THOMAS JEFFERSON TO GENERAL JOHN GIBSON.

PRESENTED BY GEN. GIBSON'S DAUGHTER TO WM. ROBINSON.

PHILADELPHIA, Dec. 31, 1797.

Dear Sir:

I took the liberty the last summer of writing to you from hence, making some enquiries on the subject of Logan's Speech, and the murder of his family, and you were kind enough in your answer among other things, to correct the title of Cresap who is said to have headed the party, by observing that he was a Capt and not a Col. I trouble you with a second letter asking if you could explain to me how Logan came to call him Col. If you have favored me with an answer to this it has

[1] See "Biographical Sketch of the Life of the late Captain Michael Cresap," by Jacobs.

miscarried, I therefore trouble you again on the subject, and as the transaction must have been familiar to you, I will ask the favor of you to give me the names and residence, of any persons now living who you think were of Cresap's party, or who can prove his participation in this transaction either by direct evidence or from circumstances, or who can otherwise throw light on the fact. A Mr Martin[1] of Baltimore has questioned the whole transaction, suggesting Logan's Speech to be not genuine, and denying that either Col or Capt Cresap had any hand in the murder of his family. I do not intend to enter into any newspaper contest with Mr Martin; but in the first republication of the notes on Virginia to correct the Statement where it is wrong and support it where it is right.

My distance from the place where witnesses of the transactions reside is so great, that it will be a lengthy and imperfect operation in my hands. Any aid you can give me in it will be most thankfully received. I avail myself with great pleasure of every occasion of recalling myself to your recollection, and of assuring you of the sentiments of esteem and attachment with which I am

dear Sir, your most obedt and
humble Servt
TH. JEFFERSON.

[1] Luther Martin, Attorney-General of Maryland, married a daughter of Captain Cresap.

GENERAL JAMES GRANT,
OF BALLINDALLOCH.

AN extensive landed estate, with a castle and village, at the confluence of the Avon and Spey, Parish of Inveravon, Banffshire, Highlands of Scotland, where a large district of the present counties of Elgin and Banff—ancient Morayshire—was long known as the country of the Grants or people of Strathspey, one of the most ancient Highland clans. The chiefs and most of the clansmen were Whigs, and supporters of the House of Hanover, in opposition to the Stuarts. After studying law James Grant entered the army in 1741, as Ensign, at the age of twenty-two, and became Captain in the 1st Battalion, 1st Royal Scots, October 24, 1744. In 1747 he was appointed aid to General James St. Clair, Ambassador to the Courts of Vienna and Turin. David Hume, the historian, was Secretary to the Embassy. Captain Grant served in the wars in the Netherlands.

In January, 1757, he was commissioned Major of the new 77th Regiment, 1st Battalion, known as Montgomery Highlanders, commanded by Lieutenent-Colonel Archibald Montgomery, afterwards Earl of Eglintown. They were ordered to America, and sailed from Cork, Ireland, and arrived at Halifax, America, in August.[1] Sailed for Charleston, South Carolina, arriving there September 29th, having been ordered there with a portion of the Royal Americans, in apprehension of an attack by the French, from the West Indies. In 1758 the regiment arrived at Philadelphia from Charleston, South Carolina, and

---

[1] "Pennsylvania Gazette." "Scot's Magazine."

encamped beyond the new barracks. A few days afterwards they were reviewed by General Forbes, in the presence of a great number of people, who were highly gratified by the display, the fine military appearance of the troops and the novelty of their dress. General Forbes, in command of the Southern Department, was engaged in assembling an army in Philadelphia, intended for the capture of Fort Du Quesne.

1758.—In September, Major Grant was sent with eight hundred men to reconnoitre the fort. Dividing his force, to draw the enemy into an ambuscade, he was himself surprised and defeated, with a loss of a third of his party killed, wounded and missing. Grant and nineteen officers were captured.[1] He became Lieutenant-Colonel of the 40th Foot in 1760, and was appointed Governor of East Florida. In 1761 he was despatched by General Amherst, with a force of thirteen hundred Regulars, against the Indians of Carolina.[2]

Grant succeeded to the family estate on the death of his nephew, Major William Grant. In 1772 he became Brevet-Colonel; in 1773 he was returned to Parliament for Wickburghs, and at the general election of the year after for Sutherlandshire. In December, 1775, he was appointed Colonel of the 55th Foot. In 1776 Grant went as a Brigadier to America, with the reinforcement under General Howe. He commanded two British brigades at the battle of Long Island, was employed by Lord Howe on special services in New Jersey, accompanied the army to Philadelphia, and commanded the 1st and 2d Brigades of British at the battles of Brandywine and Germantown.[3]

In May, 1778, he was sent with a strong force to cut off Lafayette, but was unsuccessful. He commanded the force

---

[1] See letter in "Fort Pitt."
[2] Cherokees.
[3] Letters of Grant.

sent from New York to the West Indies, which captured St. Lucia in December, 1778, and defended the island against an attempt to recapture it, made by a French force under the Count d'Estaing.

Grant became a Major-General in 1777, Lieutenant-General in 1782, General, in 1796. He was transferred from the 55th to the 11th Foot, in 1791, and was Governor, in succession, of Dumbarton and Stirling Castles. He was noted for his love of good living and became immensely corpulent.

He died at Ballindalloch, April 13, 1806, in his eighty-sixth year. Having no descendants his estate went to his grand-nephew, George Macpherson, who assumed the surname of Grant.[1]

[1] Anderson's "Scottish Nation."

GUYASUTA (KIASUTHA.)

A SENECA chief, one of the Indians who accompanied Washington from Logstown to Venango and LeBœuf as a guard in 1753, mentioned by Washington as the young hunter and by Gist as a "young warrior." After the defeat of Braddock the Indians generally went over to the French.

Guyasuta with a party of twenty Senecas visited Montreal with Joncaire, the interpreter. At the castle of Montreal the Indians were received in the council chamber with much ceremony by the Governor of Canada, the Marquis de Vaudreuil, and council. Guyasuta, chief and orator of the Senecas, addressed Vaudreuil. They remained all winter in the neighborhood, it being too late to return home. He was with the Indians when they, with the French, defeated Grant, in 1758.

Guyasuta, two other chiefs and sixteen warriors of the Six Nations, a large number of Delawares, Shawanese and Wyandots assembled at Pittsburgh in July, 1759, and held a conference lasting a week, with George Croghan, Sir William Johnson's Deputy Indian Agent, Colonel Hugh Mercer, commandant, and the officers of Fort Pitt. Most of the Indians had been allied to the French, and this was their first treaty with the English subsequent to the capture of Fort Du Quesne, in November preceding.

In August, 1762, at the conference with the western Indians at Lancaster, Thomas King, in behalf of the chiefs of the Six Nations in his speech before the council said: "We want a little lad that lives among you; he is Kiasuta's

(Guyasuta) son. The father ordered that he should live at Philadelphia, in order to learn English, to be an interpreter. We think by this time he has learned it, and we now think it time for him to come home. His relations that are present, desire that he may now go home with them." On August 27th, the Governor replied: "The little boy, Kiasuta's son, is, I hope, on his way here, having sent for him to Philadelphia."

At a treaty held at Fort Pitt, in May, 1768, Keyashuta (Guyasuta) rose with a copy of the "Treaty of 1764 with Col. Bradstreet" in his hand, and addressing the commissioners said: "By this treaty we agreed that you had a right to build forts and trading-houses where you pleased, and to travel the road of peace from the sun rising to the sun setting. At that treaty the Shawanese and Delawares were with me, and know all this well, and I am surprised they should speak to you as they did yesterday." He had been present at this treaty with fifteen warriors, and was one of the orators; Turtle Heart, Custaloga, and Beaver were the others. He desired the several nations "to be strong in complying with their engagements, that they might wipe away the reproach of their former breach of faith, and convince their brothers the English that they could speak the truth," adding that he would conduct the army to the place appointed for receiving the prisoners.

On November 9, Col. Bouquet, attended by most of the principal officers, went to the conference-house. The Senecas and Delawares were first treated with. Kiashuta and ten warriors represented the former; Custaloga and twenty warriors the latter. Kiashuta addressed the conference and was answered by Col. Bouquet. In Washington's "Tour to the Ohio in 1770": "When encamped opposite the mouth of the Great Hockhocking we found Kiasutha and his hunting party encamped. Here we were under a necessity of paying our compliments, as this person was one of the Six Nation chiefs and the head of those upon this River. In the person of Kiashuta I found an old acquaintance, he being one of the Indians that went with me to the French in 1753."

May, 1774.—A meeting was held at Col. Croghan's house, Ligonier, at which were present Guyasutha, White Mingo and the Six Nation Deputies. Guyasutha was one of the orators.

July, 1776, he was present at a conference at Fort Pitt and was one of the orators. He was in command of one of the parties of Indians that in July, 1782, made the attack on Hannastown and burned it.

THE SPEECH OF GUYASUTA,

An Ancient Chief of the Seneca Nation, on the Borders of Pennsylvania, as given in charge by him to one of the Sachems of that Nation in the Year 1790, to be Delivered to the Friends of Philadelphia.

Brothers: The Sons of my beloved Brother Onas.[1] When I was young and strong our country was full of game, which the Good Spirit sent for us to live upon. The lands which belonged to us were extended far beyond where we hunted. I and the people of my nation had enough to eat and always something to give to our friends when they entered our cabins; and we rejoiced when they received it from us; hunting was then not tiresome, it was diversion; it was a pleasure.

Brothers: When your fathers asked land from my nation, we gave it to them, for we had more than enough. Guyasuta was amongst the first of the people to say, "Give land to our brother Onas for he wants it," and he has always been a friend to Onas and to his children.

[1] Penn.

Brothers: Your fathers saw Guyasuta when he was young; when he had not even thought of old age or weakness; but you are too far off to see him, now he is grown old. He is very old and feeble, and he wonders at his own shadow, it is become so little. He has no children to take care of him, and the game is driven away by the white people; so that the young men must hunt all day long to find game for themselves to eat; they have nothing left for Guyasuta; and it is not Guyasuta only who is become old and feeble, there yet remain about thirty men of your old friends, who, unable to provide for themselves or to help one another, are become poor and are hungry and naked.

Brothers: Guyasuta sends you a belt which he received long ago from your fathers, and a writing which he received but as yesterday from one of you. By these you will remember him and the old friends of your fathers in this nation. Look on this belt and this writing, and if you remember the old friends of your fathers, consider their former friendship and their present distress; and if the Good Spirit shall put it in your hearts to comfort them in their old age, do not disregard his council. We are men and therefore need only tell you that we are old and feeble and hungry and naked; and that we have no other friends but you, the children of our beloved brother Onas.

THE TESTIMONY OF SIMON GIRTY.

To Colonel George Morgan.

On or about the 9th of November last I was sent by General Hand to Connewago, a Seneca Town on the Allegany River, with a friendly Message to the Six Nations. I arrived there the 14th of November and after executing my orders waited there till the 24th of the Month. During my stay there, Conengayote or the White Mingo, returned from Niagara with a Horse load of Goods, which he told me he had purchased for Horses he had stole from near Ligonier in Pennsylvania about the month of——last, at which time he and his Party killed four Men. On or about the 23d of November Co, co, caw, can, keteda or the Flying Crow, with twenty five Warriors of the Senecas of the Turtle Tribe, among whom were Joneowentashaun and Coneotahanck or the Leaf, (War Chief) arrived at Connewago with two scalps, and a Woman they had taken Prisoner about fifteen days before from near Ligonier aforesaid. On conversing with her and with the Indians, I was informed that the Indians had killed and scalped her Husband, Forbes, and had beat out the brains of their only Child against a Tree in the Road.

Kushgwehgo or Full Face, and twenty seven others of the Senecas of the Eagle Tribe, had been to war against the people of Pennsylvania East of the Alleghany Mountain (I understood in Bedford County); they were out eighteen days when I arrived at the Town; they were daily expected back when I came away. Two Prisoners the Senecas had taken from Pennsylvania they had put to death in one of their upper Towns.

Old Keyashuta (Guyasuta) is now among our warmest Enemies. He and the others say they have been deceived or treated ill at Fort Pitt, and that the Americans intend to cheat them of their Lands, for which reason they have now determined to join the King of England's Troops agreeable to the repeated Invitations of Col. Butler and the Commanding Officer at Niagara &c, who have on that condition promised to supply them and their women and children with every necessary; wherefore they were determined to exert themselves in committing Hostilities against the Frontier Inhabitants early in the Spring, with all their Abilities and this I am persuaded they will do unless Keyenguatah, (General Schuyler's great Friend) who fought on the side of the English at Fort Schuyler, should alter his conduct and order them to sit still; for they have agreed to be directed by him and so have all the Six Nations. The Indians had not heard of General Burgoyne's defeat or of his Army's being made Prisoners, nor would they believe me when I informed them thereof. Keyashuta informed me that a Party of seventy two, consisting of Indians and twenty five Whitemen from Detroit, and some Delaware and Munsies from Guyahoga, had been to war against the Inhabitants of Pennsylvania (I understand north of Ligonier) and had taken two Scalps at a Fort near Connemaugh, where they lost the Commanding Officer who was killed from the Fort. Joneowentashaun told me the English had lately erected a Store House at Guyahoga, to supply all the Indians in that Neighbourhood with every necessary to enable them to commit Hostilities against the Frontier Inhabitants of Pennsylvania and Virginia.

The Indians after consulting together, informed me that I

must go with them to Niagara, to which I pretended to consent, and finding that to be their resolution I made my Escape and arrived here the 27th of November.

In the presence of
    JOHN BOREMAN.

                                  his
                       SIMON X GIRTY.
                                 mark.

PITTSBURGH, January 17th, 1778.

    The Chief Guyasuta's interest in the farm,[1] now in O'Hara township, was purchased by General O'Hara. In a letter-book of General O'Hara's, mention is made of provision sent to Guyasuta, who seems to have lived continuously at that farm during his last years, and was buried there in the Indian Mound, by General O'Hara. The name is spelled in many ways—Kayashuta, Guyashutha, Guashota, Kia-shuta, Keyashuta, Kiyashuta, Kiasolo.

    Mr. Craig writes in the "Olden Time": "We recollect him well, have often seen him about our father's house, he being still within our memory, a stout active man." There is a picture of his grave in "Fort Pitt."

[1] The residence of the family of William M. Darlington. M. C. D.

TREATY OF LANCASTER.

At a Council held at Philadelphia, on October 14, 1736, by Thomas Penn, Governor and Proprietary of Pennsylvania, James Logan, the President, and members of the Provincial Council, with the Chiefs of the Six Nations, the Indians requested that a letter be written to the Governors of Maryland and Virginia, requesting compensation for their lands claimed by right of conquest, and upon which the white settlers had intruded, along the Cohongoronto or Potomac, and west of the great Allegheny mountain ridge, on the frontiers of Virginia; that being the boundary claimed by the Indians as agreed upon with Governor Spotswood in 1722.[1] This demand was renewed, and pressed by the Indians at the treaty held at the same city in 1742; Canassetego, the great chief of the Onondagas, saying that if not compensated for their lands, they would take payment themselves.

The threatening attitude of the powerful Six Nations or Iroquois, the war with France, and the necessity of conciliating the Indians, occasioned the famous Treaty of Lancaster, in 1744, between the Confederated Tribes and the Provinces of Virginia, Maryland and Pennsylvania.[2]

Thomas Lee and Colonel William Beverly were the Commissioners of Virginia; Edmund Jenings, Philip Thomas, Col. Robert King, and Col. Robert Colville, of Maryland. Governor Thomas, of Pennsylvania, presided. (Thomas Lee was Judge of the Supreme Court, and Councillor of State;

---

[1] "New York Colonial History."

[2] "Colonial Records." Colden's "Twelve Nations."

William Beverly, Lieutenant of the county of Orange).[1] There was a warm discussion, and on the part of the Indians at least, a great display of eloquence.

The Virginia Commissioners said to the Chiefs: "Tell us what Nations of Indians you conquered any lands from in Virginia, how long it is since and what Possession you have had; and if it does appear, that there is any land on the Borders of Virginia that the Six Nations have a Right to we are willing to make you satisfaction." The Chief, Tachanoontia, proudly answered: "We have the Right of Conquest, a Right too dearly purchased and which cost us too much Blood to give up without any reason at all as you say we have done at Albany. All the World knows we conquered the several Nations living on the Susquehannah, Cohongoronto (Potomac) and on the back of the great Mountains in Virginia. They feel the effects of our conquests, being now a part of our Nation and their lands at our disposal." He admitted that the Virginia Colonists had conquered a certain tribe he named and "drove back the Tuscaroras and on that account a right to some part of Virginia; but," he continued, "as to what lies beyond the mountains we conquered the Nations residing there; and that land if the Virginians ever get a good right to it, it must be by us."

The Commissioners replied, "that the great King holds Virginia by right of Conquest, and the bounds of that Conquest to the westward is the great Sea." "Though great things are well remembered among us," said the Indians, "yet we don't remember that we were ever conquered by the Great King, or, that we have been employed by that Great King to conquer others; if it was so, it is beyond our memory."

After much feasting, drinking, and bestowal of presents by the whites, the Indians agreed to release their claim to what

---

[1] Virginia State Papers.

is now Western Maryland, to Lord Baltimore, "as far as two miles above the uppermost Fork of the Potomac or Cohongoronto river near which Thomas Cresap has a Hunting or Trading Cabin," (at Old Town, fourteen miles east of Cumberland), in consideration of £300, payable in goods. With the Commissioners of Virginia they agreed for £200 in gold, and goods to the value of £200 more, to "immediately make a Deed recognizing the King's right to all the Lands that are or shall be by His Majesty's appointment in the Colony of Virginia," together with a written promise of further remuneration as settlements increased westward. With the Governor of Pennsylvania they confirmed former treaties and received a present of goods to the value of £300. The deeds were signed and the money paid and the merchandise delivered.[1]

It was not until the year 1768 that the Six Nations, by the Treaty at Fort Stanwix, relinquished all their rights to the country on the east and south side of the Ohio River, from the Cherokee River (Tennessee), to Kittanning, above Fort Pitt, and also east of a specified line described in the deed, continued to Wood Creek, near Fort Stanwix, in consideration of the sum of £10,460. 7. 6. sterling. At the same time it was agreed that no old claims under the treaties of Lancaster and Logstown should be allowed.[2] It was after the Treaty of Lancaster that large tracts of land were granted to the Ohio Company.

[1] "Treaty of Lancaster," printed by Franklin, 1744.
[2] "New York Colonial History."

OHIO COMPANY.

EXTRACT OF LETTER FROM COL. BURWELL, PRESIDENT OF THE COUNCIL AND COMMANDER-IN-CHIEF OF VIRGINIA, AND OTHER LETTERS TO THE BOARD OF TRADE.[1]

August 21, 1751.—Notwithstanding the Grants of the Kings of England, France or Spain, the Property of these uninhabited Parts of the World must be founded upon prior Occupancy according to the Law of Nature; and it is the seating and cultivating the soil and not the bare travelling through a Territory that constitutes Right; and it will be politic and highly for the Interest of the Crown to encourage the seating the Lands Westward as soon as possible to prevent the French; which I hope will be accomplished as the Freedom and Liberty of our Government will so much sooner invite into the British Colonies, Foreigners. We have not been able to prevail with the northern Indians to come to Fredericksburg to accept of his Majesty's Present, and the Reason they offer is, the immense Distance and the Death of several of their Great Men, which they attribute to the Journeys they have taken to the Places where Conferences have been held, but they acquaint us at the same Time that they will meet any persons the Government think proper to send to Log's Town, a Place not far from our back Inhabitants, where they frequently hold their Councils; this I communi-

[1] MSS. from Record Office, London.

cated to his Majesty's Council, who with myself approved of it, and this Fall I shall send a Messenger to acquaint them that I purpose next May to send Commissioners to meet them at the Place they desire; and at the Conference I shall endeavour to obtain a confirmation of the Grant of the Lands made to his Majesty at the Treaty of Lancaster, in Order to give the Company an Opportunity of surveying the large Tract of Land his Majesty was pleased to grant to them. I shall at the same Time, make a remonstrance to them of the inhuman treatment they have shewn to some of our back Inhabitants, by robbing and plundering their houses, and last June because a poor woman would not with patience see her House robbed of every thing in it, they in a most horrible Manner murdered her. These outrages have been committed upon our shewing too much lenity to them, and will be a means of drawing upon ourselves much more ill Treatment if not properly resented, and therefore in as mild Terms as is consistent with the nature of the thing I shall insist that the offenders be given up to Justice.

FROM COL. LEE.[1]

My Lords:

WILLIAMSBURG, June 12, 1750.

I have lately received a letter from the Governor of New York dated the 8th of April, proposing my prevailing with the Catawbas, an Indian Nation bordering on the Carolinas, to meet the Six Nations at Albany to confirm the peace Governor Sir William Gooch made between them, which has been broke by both Parties, and further the French are

---

[1] MSS. from Record Office, London. Letter from Col. Lee, President of the Council and Commander-in-Chief of Virginia.

at this time assiduous in their Endeavours to incite the several Nations that are dependent on, and friends to the English, to a war with one another, and make large presents to the Indians on the Ohio. I have accounts from other hands that the French have endeavoured to persuade those Indians to drive the English Traders from thence, which being refused, the French threaten to treat them as enemys, so that the Mohocks expect a war with their Father Onantio; as they call the Governor of Quebec.[1] I have received His Majesty's present for the Indians of the Six Nations, and several of their Tribes on the Ohio, and have taken the best methods I could think of, to bring those Nations to Fredericksburg in their Colony, and I have invited the Catawbas to meet them, to make a peace personally, which has never been done yet, and is the reason that it has been of no effect. When the Indians hearts and Eyes are Open, on receiving the King's present, I hope to secure their affections to the British Interest in General, and persuade them to be friends, and faithful subjects to His Majesty, and as this is the antientiest and most central Colony, it will save an expence by having future treatys here, especially, when the business to be transacted relates to the affairs of this Colony."

EXTRACT FROM REPORT OF MR. JOSHUA FRY TO HON. LEWIS BURWELL.

In the year 1609 a new charter was obtained (for Virginia) in which all the Lands, Countries and Territories were granted in that part of America called Virginia, from the Cape or Point Comfort, two hundred miles Northward, and two hundred miles southward along the sea-coast; and all that space and

---

[1] "Céleron's Expedition."

circuit of land, lying from the sea-coast of the Precinct aforesaid up into the main Land throughout from sea to sea west and north west, and also all the Islands lying within one hundred miles along the coast of both seas.

The French claimed the Lands along the Mississippi. Monsieur de la Sale was the first Frenchman, that discovered the Mississippi, who in the year 1682, with Monsieur de Tonti and others from Montreal travelled through the Nation of the Iroquois, called now the Six Nations, to a nation of Indians named Illinois, living on an east Branch of Mississippi, of the same name with the Nation, but he called it Seigne bay. On this river he built a Fort, which he named Lewis, according to Tousels account, but Hennepin calls it Crevecœur.

Monsieur de la Sale went down this river to the Mississippi and down it to the mouth, which he found to be in the Bay of Mexico. He then returned by Canada to France, and obtained from the King ships and men in the year 1684 to discover the Mouth of the Mississippi by sea, but he missed it, and landed on the Continent to the south-west. From thence he made some journeys into the country to look for the river, but was murdered by some of his own men without finding it. In the year 1742 one John Howard received a commission from our Governor to make discoveries westward, and with four or five others set out from the branches of James river, and came to the New river. There they made a Boat with Buffaloes Hides, and went down, till they found the river impassable on account of Falls. Leaving it they travelled south westerly a considerable way to another river, which proved to be a south branch of the New river, for they made another boat and went down to that river, and with it to the Allegany[1] river.

Howard and his men proceeded down this river a long way, by their reckoning above eight hundred miles, to the Mississippi, and went down it a great way till they were surprised

[1] Ohio.

by about ninety men, French, Indians and Negroes; were made Prisoners and carried to New Orleans. They set out from the branches of the James river March the 16th, came to Allegany May the 6th, to Mississippi June the 7th and were taken July the 2d. In all this time and large tract of country they had seen nobody till they were taken, but about fifteen Indians in several Companies and they too were chiefly if not all of the Northern Nations.

John Peter Salley, one of the men who went with Howard, mentions in his Journal three French Towns on an Island in the Mississippi above the mouth of the Owabache.

Howard and his men had been confined a long time at New Orleans, when after the French War broke out he and one or two of them were shipped for France, but on the Voyage were taken by an English Ship, and carried to London. The rest of them made their escape out of prison, and through great difficulties got to South Carolina, and thence to Virginia.

The first Peace the Colony of Virginia made with the Indians was at Albany by Col. Coursey in the year 1677, which after some breach made by the Indians was renewed in the year 1679 by Col. Kendal, and again in 1684 by Lord Howard, Governor of Virginia. This peace was soon broken and renewed by Col. William Byrd and Col. Edmond Jennings in the year 1685. When we began to take up Lands and settle beyond the Blue Ridge, the Six Nations grew uneasy; the Indians claimed the Land as theirs. This brought on the Treaty of Lancaster in the year 1744.

OHIO COMPANY.[1]

In 1748 John Hanbury, a Merchant of London, Thomas Lee, President of the Council of Virginia, with a number of others, mostly prominent Virginians, formed the "Ohio Company."

[1] Copied from the Mercer Papers, which belonged to the Ohio Company.

The King granted them two hundred thousand Acres of Land, to be taken on the South side of the river Allegheny, otherwise the Ohio, between the Kiskiminites Creek and Buffalo Creek, and between Yellow Creek and Cross Creek, on the North side; or in such other part of the Country west of the Allegheny Mountains as they should think proper, on Condition that they should settle one hundred families thereon within seven years, and erect and maintain a Fort. On compliance therewith, the Company was to become entitled to Three hundred thousand Acres more, adjoining the first grant.

The Company bought and sent out a large Cargo of goods from England in 1749-50, and built a Store House opposite the mouth of Wills Creek, now Cumberland, Maryland, from which place to Turkey Foot, or the Three forks of the Youghioghany, they had a road opened in 1751. In 1750 they employed Christopher Gist to explore and examine the Country west of the Mountains. He was a Native of Maryland, like his Father Richard, a Surveyor. A man of excellent character, energetic, fearless and a thorough woodsman.

OHIO COMPANY.—SECOND PETITION.

MEMBERS OF THE OHIO COMPANY.

Arthur Dobbs Esqr	Ex^{rs} of Law^{ce} Washington
John Hanbury	Augus^{ne} Washington
Samuel Smith	Richard Lee
James Wardrop	Nath^{el} Chapman.
Capel Hanbury	Jacob Giles
Robert Dinwiddie Esqr	Thomas Cresap
The Exec. of Thomas Lee late President and Governor of Virginia 2 shares	John Mercer
	James Scott
	Robert Carter
John Taylor Esq	George Mason
Prestly Thornton Esq	

To the Kings most Excellent Majesty in Council.

The Humble Petition of the Ohio Company Sheweth,

That your Petitioners upon Intimation given by several Nations of Indians residing near the Ohio and other Branches of Mississippi and near the Lakes westward of Virginia, that they were desirous of trading with your Majesty's Subjects and quitting the ffrench; and knowing the value of those Rich Countrys which were given up and acknowledged to be your Majesty's undoubted right by the Six Nations, who are Lawfull Lords of all these Lands by Conquest from other Indian Nations, at the treaty of Lancaster on the 2nd day of July 1744. Your petitioners being sensible of the vast consequence of securing those Countrys from the ffrench, did in the year 1748, form themselves into a Company to Trade with the Indians and to make settlements upon the Ohio or Alleghany River, by the name of the Ohio Company. That the Company in the beginning of the year 1749 Petitioned your Majesty, wherein they set forth the vast Advantage it would be to Britain and the Colonys to anticipate the French by taking possession of that Country Southward of the Lakes, to which the French had no Right, nor had then taken possession, except a small Block house Fort among the Six Nations, below the falls of Niagara, they having deserted Le Detroit fort Northward of Erie Lakes, during the War and retired to Canada.

The Reasons for securing the same being mentioned at large in their said former Petition, and in which they prayed that your Majesty would give orders or Instructions to your Governor of Virginia, to make out to your Petitioners five hundred thousand Acres betwixt Romanittoe and Buffaloe Creeks on the South side of the Allegany or Ohio River, and between the two Creeks and Yellow Creek on the North side of that River, upon the Terms and with the Allowance therein mentioned to which they beg leave to Refer.

That your Petitioners in pursuance of the said Petition, obtained an order from your Majesty to your Lieutenant Governor of Virginia dated March the 18th 1749, to make them a grant or Grants of Two hundred thousand Acres of Land between Romanetto and Buffaloe Creeks, on the south side of the Ohio, and betwixt the two creeks and Yellow Creek on the North side thereof, or in such part to the Westward of the Great Mountains as the Company should think proper for making settlements and extending their trade with the Indians, with a Promise if they did not erect a Fort in the said Land, and maintain a sufficient Garrison therein and seat at their proper Expense a hundred families therein in seven years, the said grants should be void. And as soon as these terms were accomplished, he was ordered to make out a further Grant or Grants of three hundred thousand Acres, under like Conditions, Restrictions and allowances as the first 200,000 Acres, adjoining thereto and within these limits. These orders were delivered to the Honourable William Nelson on the 12th of July following (1749) and upon producing them before the Governor and Council, they made an entry in the Council Books, that the said Company should have leave given them to take up and survey 200,000 Acres within the Place mentioned in your Majestys said Instructions and Order. That your Petitioners upon their entry in the Council Books, sent to Great Britain for a Cargo of Goods to begin their Trade, and purchased Lands upon the Potomack River, being the most convenient place to erect Store Houses, and in September following (1749) employed Gentlemen to discover the Lands beyond the Mountains, to know where to place their surveys. But they not having made any considerable progress, the Company in September 1750 agreed to give Mr. Christopher

Gist £150 certain, and such further handsome allowance as his service should deserve, for searching and discovering the Lands upon the Ohio and its several Branches as low as the falls on the Ohio, with proper Instructions. He accordingly set out October 1750 and did not return until May 1751, after a tour of 1200 Miles in which he visited many towns and found them all desirous of entering into strict friendship and Trade with your Majestys Subjects.

That your Petitioners at their General Meeting in May 1751, judging it necessary for their Trade and passage to the Ohio, to have a Grant of some Land belonging to Maryland and Pennsylvania, wrote to Mr. Hanbury to apply for the same to the Proprietors, and laid out and opened a wagon road thirty feet wide from their Store house at Wills Creek, to the three branches on Ganyangaine River, computed to be near Eighty Miles; and applied to the President and Masters of William and Mary College for a Commission to a Surveyor to lay out the Lands, as they pretend they had a right to do, proposing to begin the survey after receiving Mr. Gists Report.

Your Petitioners finding by the said Gists Journal that he had only observed the Lands on the North side of the Ohio, and finding that the Indians were unwilling that they should then settle on the Miami River, or on the north side of the Ohio, and the Land lying too much exposed and at too great a distance, They employed the said Gist to go out a second time to view and examine the land between Mohongaly and the Big Conhaway, Wood or New River on the south East side of the Ohio, which employed him from the 4th of November 1751 to the March following 1752; but he could not finish his Plan and report before October 1752, at which time the Company gave in a Petition to the Governor and Council, praying leave to survey and take up their first 200,000 Acres between Romanettoes, otherwise Kiskominettos Creek, and the fork of the Ohio and the great Conhaway, otherwise New River, otherwise Woods river, on the south side of the river Ohio in several Surveys. The Governor and Council having not thought fit to comply with the prayer of the said Petition, to allow your Petitioners to survey their Lands in different Tracts as would best accomodate the settlers and secure their frontiers from attacks, the President and Masters of the College also refusing to give out a Commission to a Surveyor; and the late Governor and Council having made out large Grants to private persons Land-gobbers, to the amount of near 1,400,000 Acres. Immediately, even the same day, after your Majestys Instructions for making out your Petitioners Grant and Surveys, became publicly known where the Lands were not properly described or Limited, nor Surveyed, by which means their several Grants might have interfered with the Lands discovered and chosen by the Company, your Petitioners now laid under difficultys in surveying and letting their Lands and Erecting the fort, tho' your Petitioners have been at very great Expence and are willing to be at a much greater, to secure those valuable Countrys and the Indian Trade. That your Petitioners apprehend from these Obstructions, and the Delay and Expence attending Surveys, and from the suits that may be commenced upon account of the Grants made out to other Persons since the Instructions given by your Majesty to grant to your Petitioners the Land mentioned in the said Instructions which may occasion longer Delays. The Company may be prevented from fulfilling their Covenant of settling the Lands and Compleating their Fort in the time specified by the said Contract. And as boundaries to large Grants are much more natural and easy to be ascertained by having Rivers for their Limits, and streight Lines or Mountains to connect them from River to River, and at much less Expence and delay in fixing them, Therefore your petitioners pray, that upon Condition your Petitioners shall enlarge their settlements and seat 300 families, instead of one hundred by their former Contract, and in consideration of their erecting two forts, one at Chartiers Creek and the other at the Fork where the great Conhaway enters the Ohio and maintain them at their own expence, That your Majesty will be graciously pleased to enlarge their Grant under the same Exemption of Rights and Quit Rents as in the former Instructions, and to fix the Bounds without any further delay or Survey, from Romanettos or Kiskomenetto Creek on the South East side of the Ohio, to the Fork at the entrance of the great Conhaway River; and from thence along the North side of the said Conhaway River to the Entrance of Green Briar River, and from thence in a streight Line or Lines along the Mountains to the South East Spring of Mohangaly River; and from thence. Northward along the Mountains to the North East springs of Romanetto or Kiskominetto Creek, or till a West Line from the Mountains intersect this said Spring and along it to its entrance into the Ohio; which will prevent all Disputes or Delays about the Limitts which are necessary to be immediately determined, as the season is advancing to procure foreign Protestants and other of your Majestys subjects to go on with the settlement, and to provide materials to erect the second Fort at the mouth of the great Conhaway River, (the Fort on Chartiers Creek being now building) in order to prevent the Intrusions and incroachments of the Indians in the French aliance and secure our settlements upon the Ohio; which if not immediately put in Execution before they get permission may be highly detrimental to the Colonys and occasion a great future Expence to Britain.

And your Petitioners will ever pray etc.

The Lords of the Committee referred the petition to the Lords Commissioners for Trade and Plantations to consider thereof and Report their opinion thereupon to the Committee.

The Petition was granted by King and Council. At a meeting of the Company held at Stafford Court House, some of the Members resigned and George Mason was received. They advised Mr. Hanbury of the proceedings of the meeting, and desired him to offer the Duke of Bedford a share, if he chose to be concerned, upon the terms of the Association. As Mr. Hanbury had wrote us that we were obliged to his Grace for his Assistance in obtaining his Majesty's Instruction, and his declaration of the advantage he conceived it would be of to Great Britain and this colony, for that notwithstanding we expected a great deal of interested opposition and should think ourselves happy in having such a patron at the head of the Company. They then agreed with H. Parker for the carriage of all their goods from the falls of Potomack to their general factory on the River Ohio, and authorized Col. Cresap to have a road opened to those places. They desired the Ohio Indians might be invited to a Treaty, and an Interpreter might be employed by Virginia, and Mr. Parker their factor be put in the commission of the Peace for Augusta County. George Mason was appointed Treasurer.

INSTRUCTIONS GIVEN TO CHRISTOPHER GIST BY THE OHIO COMPANY, APRIL 28th, 1752.

Whereas the Governor has been pleased to grant you a commission empowering and requiring you to go as an agent for the Ohio Company to the Indian Treaty to be held at Logs Town on the 16th day of May next. You are therefore desired to acquaint the chiefs of the several nations of Indians there assembled, that his Majesty has been graciously pleased to grant unto the Hon. Robert Dinwiddie Esq', Governor of Virginia, and to several other gentlemen in Great Britain and

America, by the name of the Ohio Company, a large quantity of Land on the river Ohio and the Branches thereof, thereby to enable and to encourage the said company and all his Majesties subjects, to make settlement and carry on an extensive Trade and commerce with their Brethren the Indians, and to supply them with Goods at a more easy rate than they have hitherto bought them. And considering the necessities of his children the Six Nations, and the other Indians to the Westward of the English settlements, and the hardship they labor under for want of a due supply of Goods and to remove the same as much as possible, his Majesty has been pleased to have a clause inserted in the said Companies Grant obliging them to carry on a trade and commerce with their Brethren the Indians, and has granted them many privileges and immunities in consideration of their carrying on the said trade, and supplying the Indians with Goods; that the said Company have accordingly begun the Trade and imported large quantities of goods, but have found the expence and Risque of carrying out the Goods without assistance from the Inhabitants, not having any place of safety by the way to lodge them at, or opportunity of getting provisions for their people, so great that they cannot afford to sell their Goods at so easy a rate as they would willingly do; nor are they at such a distance able to supply their Brethren the Indians at all times when they are in want. For which reason the company find it absolutely necessary, immediately to cultivate and settle the Land his Majesty has been pleased to grant them, which to be sure they have an indisputable right to do. As our Brethren the Six Nations sold all the Land to the Westward of Virginia at the Treaty of Lancaster to their Father the King of Great Britain, and he has been graciously pleased to grant a large quantity thereof to the said Ohio Company, yet, being informed that the Six Nations have given their Friends the Delawares leave to hunt upon the said Lands, and that they still hunt upon part thereof themselves, and as the settlements made by the English upon the said land may make the Game scarce, or at least drive it further back, the said Company therefore to prevent any difference or misunderstanding, which might possibly happen between them and their Brethren the Indians touching the said Lands, are willing to make them some further satisfaction for the same and to purchase of them the Land on the east side of the river Ohio and Allagany as low as the great Canhaway providing the same can be done at a reasonable Rate; and our Brethren the Six Nations and their Allies will promise and engage their Friendship and protection to all his Majesties subjects settling on the said Lands. When this is done the Company can safely venture to build Factories and Store Houses upon the river Ohio, and send out large Cargoes of Goods which they cannot otherwise do, and to convince our Brethren the Indians how desirous we are of living in strict Friendship and becoming one people with them, You are hereby empowered and required to acquaint and promise our Brethren, in the name and on behalf of the said Company, that if any of them incline to take land and live among the English, they shall have any of the said company's Land upon the same Terms and conditions as the white people have, and enjoy the same privilidges which they do as far as is in the Company's power to grant.

And that you may be the better able to acquaint our Brethren the Indians with these our proposals you are to apply to Andrew Montour the interpreter for his assistance therein, and the Company hereby undertake and promise to make him satisfaction for the trouble he shall be at. If our Brethren the Six Nations approve our proposals the Company will pay them whatever sum you agree with them for, and if they want any particular sort of Goods, you are to desire them to give you an account of said Goods and the Company will immediately send for them to England, and when they arrive will carry them to what ever place you agree to deliver them at.

If our Brethren the Indians do not approve these proposals and do refuse their protection and assistance to the subjects of their Father the King of Great Britain, you are forthwith to make a return thereof to the said Ohio Company, that they may inform his Majesty thereof.

You are to apply to Col. Cresap for what Wampum you have occasion of on the Companys account for which you are to give him a receipt. You are to apply to him for one of the Companies Horses to ride out to the Loggstown.

As soon as the Treaty is over, you are to make an exact return of all your proceedings to the Company.

Given under my hand in behalf of the said Ohio Company the 28th day of April 1752.

       GEORGE MASON Treasurer

ADDITIONAL INSTRUCTIONS GIVEN CHRISTOPHER GIST.[1]

Upon your arrival at the Treaty if you find that the commissioners do not make a general Agreement with the Indians on behalf of Virginia for the settlement of the Land upon the waters of the Ohio and Mississippi, or that in such agreement there are any doubtful or ambiguous expressions which may be prejudicial to the Ohio Company, you are then to endeavour to make purchase of the Lands to the Eastward of the Ohio River and Allagany, and procure the Friendship and protection of the Indians in settling the said Lands upon the best terms you can for a quantity of Goods.

[1] From Records and Minutes of the Ohio Company.

You are to agree with them to deliver the said goods at the most convenient place you can, if possible at the Forks of the Mohongaly, if the Indians give you a list of Goods which they desire to be sent for in return for their Lands, you are to enquire and to find out as near as you can the usual price of such Goods among the Indians, that we may be as near the sum you agree with them for as possible.

You are to engage Andrew Montour the Interpreter in the Company's Interest and get him to assist you in making a purchase of the Indians, and as the Company have great dependance and confidence in the said Andrew Montour, they hereby not only promise to make him satisfaction for the trouble, but if he can make an advantageous bargain for them with the Indians, they will in return for his good offices, let him have a handsome settlement upon their land without paying any purchase money, upon the same Terms which the said Company themselves hold the Land, and without any other consideration than the King's Quit rents.

If you can obtain a Deed or other written agreement from the Indians, it must be taken in the names of the Honb[le] Robert Dinwiddie Esq[r], Governor of Virginia, John Hanbury Esqr. of the City of London, Merch[t], Capel Hanbury of the said city of London Merch[t], John Tayloe, Presly Thornton, Philip Ludwell Lee, Thomas Lee, Richard Lee, Guwin Corbin, John Mercer, George Mason, Lawrence Washington, Augustus Washington, Nathaniel Chapman Esquires and James Scott Clerk, all of the Colony of Virginia. James Wardrop, Jacob Giles and Thomas Cresap esqrs of the province of Maryland and their Associates, members of the Ohio Company; in the said agreement or Deed You are to mention the Bounds of the Land as expressly as possible, that no dispute may arise hereafter. And we would have the Indians clearly understand what Land they sell us, that they may have no occasion to complain of any Fraud or underhand dealings, as is often the custom with them. The said Ohio Company do hereby agree and oblige themselves to make you satisfaction for the Trouble and expence you shall be at in Transacting their affairs at the said Treaty, pursuant to the Instructions by them given to you. Given under my hand in behalf of the Ohio Company this 28th day of April 1752.

GEORGE MASON, Treas^r.

If Col Cresap has not agreed with any person to clear a Road for the Company, you are with the advice and assistance of Col. Cresap to agree with the proper Indians, who are best acquainted with the ways, immediately to cut a road from Wills Creek to the Fork of Mohongaly at the cheapest Rate you can for Goods, and this you may mention publicly to the Indians at the Loggs Town or not as you see occasion.

GEORGE MASON, Treas^r.

At a meeting of the Committee of the Ohio Company at Stratford in Westmoreland County, the 25th of July, 1753, and continued to the 26th and 27th of the same month

" Resolved that tis absolutely necessary that the Company should immediately erect a Fort for the security and protection of their Settlement on a hill just below Shurtees[1] Creek upon the south east side of the river Ohio; that the walls of the said Fort shall be twelve feet high, to be built of sawed or hewen logs, and to enclose a piece of ground ninety feet square, besides the four Bastions at the corners of sixteen feet square each, with houses in the middle for stores, Magazines &c. according to a plan entered in the Company's Books. That Col. Cresap, Capt. Trent, and Mr Gist, be appointed and authorized on behalf of the Company to agree with labourers, Carpenters and other workmen, to build and complete the

[1] Chartiers.

same as soon as possible and employ hunters to supply them with Provisions, and agree with some honest industrious man to overlook the workmen and labourers as Overseer, and that they be supplied with flour, salt and all other necessaries at the Companys expence. That all the Land upon the hill on which the said Fort is to be built be appropriated to the use of the said Fort, and that two hundred acres of land exclusive of streets be layed off for a town convenient and adjoining to the said Fort lands, in squares of two acres each, every square to be divided into four lots so that every Lot may front two streets, if the ground will so admit, and that all the streets be of convenient width, that twenty of the best and most convenient squares be reserved and set apart for the Company's own use, and one square to build a School on for the education of Indian children and such other uses as the Company shall think proper and that all the rest of the lots be disposed of."

Mr. George Mason having informed the Committee that he has written to Mr Hanbury for twenty swivel guns and other arms and ammunition for the use of the Fort

"Resolved that the committee do approve of the same and that the said arms and ammunition as soon as they arrive be delivered to Captain Trent the Company's Factor in order to be sent out to Shurtees Creek."

At a Meeting of the Committee of the Ohio Company, November 2d, 1753,

"Agreed and Ordered that each member of the Company pay to Mr George Mason their Treasurer, the sum of twenty pounds current money for building and finishing the Fort at Shurtees Creek, Grubing and clearing the road from the Company's store at Wills Creek to the Mohongaly, which are to be finished with the utmost dispatch and for such other purposes as shall be directed by the Company."

The proposed fort was not built. There was some doubt as to whom the Forks of the Ohio belonged—by consent of the Penns, Governor Dinwiddie sent Captain Trent's Company to build a Fort there. The Fort was commenced under the direction of Ensign Ward. On the 17th of April, 1754, Captain Contrecœur descended the Allegheny with a considerable force of French and Indians and summoned Ward to surrender his unfinished work. Resistance was out of the question, he surrendered. Contrecœur finished the Fort and called it Duquesne.

July 9, 1755.—Gen. Braddock was defeated by the French and Indians under the command of Captain Beaujeu. Beaujeu was killed and Captain Dumas was the Commander from the time of Beaujeu's death to the latter part of the following year, 1756 or early in 1757, when he was transferred to Canada, and served in the operations against Fort William Henry. Montcalm mentioned him in his dispatches as "an officer of great distinction." His merits were fully recognized by the French Governor.

He was Major of Brigade at the Siege of Quebec, and after his return to France in 1761 was appointed Governor of the Mauritius and Isle of Bourbon.[1]

General Grant was defeated by the French and Indians before Fort Duquesne, October, 1758. November, 1758, General Forbes' army advanced and found the Fort in flames. The French escaped by the river.

Fort Duquesne having been destroyed it was determined to erect a small work, to be occupied by two hundred men.

A small square stockade, with a bastion at each angle, was erected on the bank of the Monongahela between Liberty and West Streets. Col. Mercer was left in command.

Fort Pitt was built in 1759–60. Its eastern boundary ex-

[1] Garneau, Histoire du Canada.

tended nearly to the present Third (formerly Marbury) and West Streets. The Fort had two powder magazines under ground, built with heavy timber and covered with tarred cloth and earth. One of them was brought to light near the corner of Liberty and Marbury or Third Street in 1855, when excavations were made for the Depot of the Pennsylvania Railroad Company.

In 1763 Fort Pitt was invested by the Indians while Captain Ecuyer was in command. January 5, 1769, a warrant was issued for a survey of the Manor of Pittsburgh, which was made on the 27th of March. Fort Pitt was kept up until 1772, after which a Corporal and a few men only were continued at the Fort.[1]

October, Major Charles Edmonstone, Commander of the Fort, sold to Alexander Ross and William Thompson, all the pickets, brick, stones, timber and iron in the buildings, walls and redoubts of the Fort. After several houses had been built of the material the sale was set aside. 1773, Richard Penn advised a small garrison to be kept at Fort Pitt as a protection from the Indians. Its demolition had been ordered by General Gage. The boundary between Virginia and Pennsylvania not having been settled, in 1774 John Conolly, by orders of Lord Dunmore, took possession of the ruins.

1781, General Irvine, in a letter to Washington, speaks of Fort Pitt as a heap of ruins and that at best it was a bad situation for defence. He recommends the mouth of Chartiers Creek (Shurtees) for a Post. The redoubt built by Bouquet still remains.[2]

1781, Col. John Conolly, who formerly lived upon the Ohio, and was arrested in 1775, after his exchange proceeded to Quebec, and proposed "with all the refugees he can collect at

---

[1] See Fort Pitt.
[2] Letter of General Irvine.

New York, he is to join Sir John Johnson in Canada, and they are to proceed with their united forces to attack Fort Pitt."

NOTE.—The Redoubt built by Bouquet is now owned by the Pittsburgh Chapter of the "Daughters of the American Revolution"; it having been recently given to them by Mrs. Schenley, the granddaughter of General James O'Hara, from whom she inherited it. A large portion of the ground formerly occupied by Fort Pitt was bequeathed by General O'Hara to his daughter Mary Carson O'Hara, who married, after her father's death, William Croghan, Esq., son of Major William Croghan of Kentucky. Major Croghan was a cousin of George Croghan, who took so prominent a part in Indian affairs.

WALPOLE GRANT.

SAMUEL WHARTON was a member of the mercantile firm of Baynton, Wharton and Morgan, extensively engaged in the Indian Trade, having storehouses at Fort Pitt and other places in the Indian Country westward. In 1763 the sudden outbreak of the western Savages, known as the Pontiac war, occurred; the Traders were plundered of their merchandise and other property; twenty-four of them lost goods valued at £85,916. 10. 6. New York Currency. Baynton, Wharton and Morgan were the heaviest sufferers.

To compensate the Traders for their loss, the Six Nations, at the Treaty held at Fort Stanwix (now Rome, New York), on May 3, 1768, conveyed to them by deed an immense tract of land bordering on the Ohio River above the Little Kanhawha, comprising about one-fourth of the present State of West Virginia. To their Grant the Traders gave the name of Indiana.

In 1769 a company was formed in London, consisting of Thomas Walpole, an eminent banker (brother of Horatio, Lord Walpole), Samuel Wharton, Benjamin Franklin, John Sargent, Governor Thomas Pownall,—and other gentlemen both in England and America,—for the purpose of buying from the Crown a portion of the vast country on the Ohio ceded to the King by the Six Nations the preceding year at the Treaty of Fort Stanwix, and also to form a New Province or Government west of Virginia. The five persons above named were appointed a committee to manage the business. Mr. Wharton went to London to attend to it. Lord Hillsborough, President of the Board of Trade, reported against the application for the grant. Dr. Franklin replied in an elaborate and able pamphlet, which was read at a subsequent meeting of the Council, July 1, 1772; at the same time, as we learn from a letter to Sir William Johnson, written by an intelligent American[1] who was present, "Mr. Walpole made some pertinent observations on the subject in general. Mr. Wharton spoke next for several hours and replied distinctly to each particular objection, and through the whole of the proceedings he so fully removed all Lord Hillsborough's objections and introduced his proofs with so much regularity and made his observations on them with so much propriety, deliberation and presence of mind, that fully convinced every Lord present, and gave satisfaction to the gentlemen concerned; and I must say it gave me a particular pleasure to hear an American and a countryman act his part so well before such a number of great Lords and such an august Board; and now I have the great pleasure to inform you that their Lordships have overruled Lord Hillsborough's Report and have reported to His Majesty in favor of Mr. Wharton and his Associates.—This is looked upon here as a most extraordinary matter, and what no American ever accomplished before. Indeed no one from America had so much interest and was so attended to by the great Lords as Mr. Wharton."

On the same day the Lords of the Committee of Council reported in favor of making the grant to the Honorable Thomas Walpole, Samuel Wharton and their associates.

The King in Council approved the Grant August 14, 1772. Lord Hillsborough resigned and Lord Dartmouth succeeded him.

The Tract granted, comprised within its boundaries all that part of the present State of Kentucky, east of a line drawn

[1] Letter of Rev. Wm. Hanna to Sir Wm. Johnson.

south from a point on the Ohio River opposite the mouth of the Scioto, and the western half of the present State of West Virginia. The price to be paid into the Royal Treasury was £10,460. 7. 6, and two shillings quit rent for every hundred acres sold or leased by the Grantees, payable yearly forever; to commence twenty years after the date of each sale or lease. The tract was usually known by the name of the Walpole Grant. It embraced within its limits the Traders' Grant, or Indiana, which was reserved to them. It also included the tract of five hundred thousand acres granted to the Ohio Company of Virginia, in 1749. The members of the Ohio Company were admitted into the new association, which was named the Grand Ohio Company. In compliance with the King's orders, the Council, on the 6th of May, 1773, reported to His Majesty a constitution or form of Government for the New Colony, which they named Vandalia. It contained within its limits all of the Walpole Grant, with the addition of all the country westward to the Kentucky River. On the 28th of October following, the Lords of Council for Plantation Affairs, ordered "that His Majesty's Attorney General do prepare and lay before this Committee, the draught of a proper instrument to be passed under the Great Seal of Great Britain containing a Grant to the Honorable Thomas Walpole, Samuel Wharton, Benjamin Franklin and John Sargent Esqrs. and their heirs and assigns all the Lands prayed for by their Memorial." It was not, however, until the spring of the year 1775 that the draught of the Grant was finally prepared and ready for execution. The breaking out of the war of the Revolution occasioned a suspension of the business. Mr. Wharton returned home by way of France, after an absence of eight years. An extract of a letter from a gentleman in London, dated March 3, 1773, to his friend in Virginia appeared in the *Pennsylvania Gazette* of that year, stating that

"I can inform you for certain that the new Province on the Ohio is confirmed to the Proprietors by the name of Pittsylvania, in honor of the Earl of Chatham. Mr. Wharton of Philadelphia will be appointed Governor in a few days; all other appointments to be made by the King. The seat of government is to be placed at the Forks of the Kenawha and Ohio rivers."

COPY OF THE AGREEMENT OF MAY 7th, 1770,

signed by Messrs. Walpole, Pownall, Franklin and Wharton, consolidating the two Companies by giving the Ohio Company $\frac{2}{72}$ and Col. Mercer $\frac{1}{72}$.

We the Committee of the Purchasers of a Tract of Country for a new Province on the Ohio in America, do hereby admit the Ohio Company as a Company Purchaser with us, for two Shares of the said Purchase in Consideration of the engagement of their Agent Col. Mercer, to withdraw the application of the said Company for a separate Grant within the Limits of the said Purchase. Witness our Hands this 7th day of May 1770.

Thomas Walpole
T. Pownall
B. Franklin
Saml. Wharton

The whole being divided into Seventy-two equal Shares; by the words "two shares" above is understood two Seventy second parts of the Tract so as above purchased.

Thomas Walpole
T. Pownall
B. Franklin
Saml. Wharton

LAND COMPANY OF WM. TRENT & CO.

November 3^d 1768 at Fort Stanwix the Sachems and Chiefs of the Six nations in full Council convened by his Majesty's order, and held under the Presidency of his Superintendant of Indian Affairs Sir William Johnson, in consideration of the great losses and Damages, amounting to Eighty five Thousand nine hundred and sixteen pounds ten shillings and eight pence lawful money of New York sustained by sundry Traders in the spring of the year 1763, when the Shawnese, Delawares and Huron Tribes of Indians, Tributaries of the six Nations did seize upon and unjustly appropriate to themselves the Goods Merchandize and effects of the Traders "The said Sachems and Chiefs did give grant Bargain and sell unto us our Heirs and assigns forever, all that Tract or parcel of Land

Beginning at the southerly side of the South of little Kenhawa River, where it empties itself into the River Ohio, and running from thence North East to the Laurel Hill—thence along the Laurel Hill until it strikes the river Monongehela—thence down the stream of the said river Monongehela, acording to the several courses thereof to the southern Boundary line of the Province of Pennsylvania.—Thence westerly along the course of the said Province Boundary Line as far as the same shall extend and from thence by the same course to the River Ohio according to the several courses thereof to the place of Beginning. And whereas we understand there are numbers of Families settled on the said Lands, We do hereby give Notice that they may be assured of peacable Possession on complying with the Terms of our general Land Office which will be shortly opened for the sale of the said Lands in behalf of all the grantees, and that the purchase will be made easy."

Proceedings of the Grantees of Lands from the Six Nations Indians by Deed Poll dated Nov. 3^d 1768 to the suffering Traders Anno 1763.

Pittsburgh September 2nd 1775

Present

Robert Callender	Thomas Smallman
William Trent	Joseph Spear
John Gibson	George Croghan
Joseph Simon	John Ormsby

George Morgan

At a meeting of several of the Grantees of Lands from the Six Nations Indians by Deed Poll dated November 3^d 1768 to the suffering Traders Anno 1763

Pittsburg Sep 21st 1775

Present

Robert Callender	George Croghan
William Trent	John Ormsby
John Gibson	Thomas Smallman
Joseph Simon	Joseph Spear

George Morgan

M^r. William Trent informs the Company present that on his arrival in England Anno 1769 being advised by Doctor Franklin Lord Cambdin and others, that it was unnecessary to make application to the Crown or King in Council for a Confirmation of the above mentioned Grant but that all he had to do was to return and take possession thereof, and understanding that Lord Hillsborough was determined to oppose a Confirmation of the said Grant as will appear by his

Letters to Sir William Johnson, he declined making the said application for the same to be confirmed. This Mr. Trent recommends not to be made Public, as it may perhaps give an unfavorable Idea of our Right to the common People; but he thought it his duty to communicate it to this Company. He further acquaints them that soon after his arrival in England a Company of Gentlemen made a purchase from the Crown of a Tract of Land on the Ohio, which includes the Grant of all the Tract given or Granted by the Six Nation Indians to the suffering Traders as aforesaid. That the said company of Purchasers Stiling themselves the Grand Ohio Company agreed in the Minutes of their proceedings to confirm and convey to the said suffering Traders all their Right and Title to that part of their purchase which includes the Grant from the Indians to the suffering Traders as aforesaid. And that he will furnish this Company with a copy of the said Minutes. The Meeting then adjourned till tomorrow morning at 6 o'clock.

At the following meetings rules and regulations for the organized Company were adopted and the following letter addressed to Mr. Walpole:

PITTSBURG Sep 22^d 1775

Sir

A number of the sufferers by the Indian War in 1763, having met at this place to consult on the most proper method to dispose of their Lands granted to them by the Indians at Fort Stanwix in November 1768, and understanding from Mr. William Trent that you have the Original Deed from the Indians for the said Lands; we request the favor of you to transmit the same to us or to your brother Thomas, in order that it may be recorded at Williamsburgh in Virginia as the jurisdiction of that colony is now extended and exercised as far west as the Ohio and Courts established &c. We think it our duty to Inform you as one of the Grantees, that many Difficulties are like to arise from any delay in taking Possession of the Lands, and that those Difficulties will double on us if we do not very speedily fall on some measures to obtain Peacable Possession of them and Permission to proceed in their sales. Lands have been and are now surveying to Officers soldiers and others in Consequence of the Kings Proclamation of October 1763, in every part of this Country from hence downward as low as Scioto and indeed as far as Kentucke and the Falls. And you may be assured they have not hesitated to lay their Warrants in many parts of our Grant of which most of the Good Lands are already surveyed.

     We are sir
       Your most Obedient Servants
    Names of Traders, Trent, Croghan &c.

Virginia declared by express legislative enactment in 1779, that all sales and deeds by Indians for lands within their limits to be void and of no effect.

Congress, by acts of the 16th and 18th of September, 1776, and others subsequent thereto, conferred grants of land to the officers and soldiers of the Continental army. Virginia, holding immense tracts of unappropriated land, very soon adopted the idea suggested by Congress of granting land bounties to her officers and soldiers both in the State and Continental establishments. To a Major-General 15,000 acres of land, and to a Brigadier-General 10,000.

For this purpose the lands surveyed by Christopher Gist were again surveyed, and the land not in the possession of settlers was so disposed of.

CAPTAIN TRENT.

HE was born in 1715 in Chester County. 1746, Governor Thomas of Pennsylvania appointed him captain of one of four companies raised in Pennsylvania, for an intended expedition against Canada. December, 1747, the time of his company having expired, he was honorably discharged. 1749, he was appointed, by Governor Hamilton, a justice of the Court of Common Pleas and General Sessions of the Peace for Cumberland County. 1750, he formed a partnership with George Croghan to engage in the Indian trade. 1752, he was commissioner to Logstown. 1753, he was directed by Governor Dinwiddie to build a fort at the Forks of the Ohio. February 17, 1754, he began the erection of the fort. April 16, the fort was surrendered to the French under the command of M. de Contrecœur. 1755, Captain Trent entered the service of Pennsylvania and was a member of the Proprietary and Governor's Council. 1757, he again entered the employ of Virginia. 1758, he accompanied Forbes' expedition against Fort DuQuesne, and by his knowledge of the country rendered important service. 1763, his large trading-house near Fort Pitt was destroyed by the Indians; he took refuge in Fort Pitt and was employed in military duties by the Commandant, Captain S. Ecuyer. At the Treaty at Fort Stanwix the Indians were induced to make a deed of land to Trent. At the beginning of the Revolutionary War Congress gave him a Major's commission. His Journal of an expedition from Logstown to Pickawillany, a village on the west side of the Great Miami River, at the mouth of Loramies Creek, belonging to the Miami or Twightwee Tribe, has been published by the Western Reserve Historical Society.[1]

[1] Colonial Records.

APPENDIX.

JOHN PETER SALLEY.

A BRIEF ACCOUNT OF THE TRAVELS OF MR. JOHN PETER SALLEY, A GERMAN LIVING IN THE COUNTY OF AUGUSTA, IN THE COLONY OF VIRGINIA, TO THE WESTWARD OF THAT COLONY AS FAR AS THE RIVER MISSISSIPPI, BETWEEN MARCH, 1741, AND MAY, 1745.[1]

It may be necessary, before I enter upon the particular passages of my travels, to inform my readers that what they are to meet with in the following narrative is only what I retained in my memory. For when we were taken by the French we were robbed of all our papers, that contained, writings relative to our Travels.

In the year 1740 I came from Pennsylvania to that part of Orange County now called Augusta, and settled in a fork of James river close under the Blue Ridge of Mountains on the West Side where I now live.

In the month of March 174½ one John Howard came to my house and told me that he received a commission from our Governor to travel to the westward of this Colony as far as the river Mississippi in order to make Discovery of the Country and that as a reward for his labour, he had the promise of an Order of Council for ten hundred thousand Acres of Land and at the same time obliged himself to give equal shares of said land to such men as would go in Company with him to search the Country as above. Whereupon I and two men and Charles Sinclair (his own son Josiah Howard having already joined with him) entered in covenant with him bind-

[1] Referred to in Col. Burwell's letter dated August 21, 1751.

ing ourselves to each other in a certain writing and accordingly prepared for our journey in a very unlucky hour to me and my poor family.

On the sixteenth of March 1742; we set off from my House and went to Cedar Creek about five miles, where is a Natural Bridge over said Creek reaching from the hill on the one side to the hill on the other. It is a solid Rock and is two hundred and three feet high, having a very large spacious arch, where the water runs thro'. We then proceeded as far as Mondongachate now called Woods river,[1] which is eighty five miles, where we killed five Buffaloes, and with their hides covered the frame of a boat, which was so large as to carry all our Company, and all our provisions and utensils with which we passed down the said river, two hundred and fifty two miles as we supposed, and found it very rockey, having a great many Falls therein, one of which we computed to be thirty feet perpendicular and all along surrounded with inaccessible mountains, high precipices which obliged us to leave said river. We went then a south west course by Land eighty five miles, where we came to a small river and there we made a little Boat which carried only two men and our provisions. The rest travelled by land for two days and then we came to a large river, where we enlarged our Barge so as she carried all our Company, and whatever loading we had to put into her. We supposed that we went down this river two hundred and twenty miles, and had a tolerable good passage; there being only two places that were difficult by reason of Falls. Where we came to this river the country is mountainous, but the farther down the plainer, in those mountains we found great plenty of coals, for which we named it Coal river, where this river and Woods river meets the north mountains end, and the country appears very plain and is well watered,

[1] Now Kanawha.

there are plenty of rivulets, clear Fountains and running streams and very fertile soil; from the mouth of Coal river to the river Allegany[1] we computed to be ninety two miles, and on the sixth day of May we came to Allegany which we supposed to be three quarters of a mile wide, and from here to the great Falls on this river is reckoned four hundred and forty four miles, there being a large spacious open country on each side of this river, and is well watered, abounding with plenty of Fountains, small streams and large rivers; and is very high, and fertile soil. At this time we found the clover to be as high as the middle of a man's leg. In general all the woods over the Land is of great plenty and of all kind, that grows in this Colony excepting pine. On the seventh day of June we entered into the river Mississippi, which we computed to be five miles wide. In the river Mississippi above the mouth of the Allegany is a large Island on which are three towns inhabited by the French who maintain Commerce and Trade both with the French of Canada and those French on the mouth of the said river. We held on our passage down the river Mississippi. The second day of July and about nine o'clock in the morning we went on shore to cook our breakfast. But we were suddenly surprised by a company of men, to the number of ninety, consisting of French men Negroes and Indians who took us prisoners and carried us to the town of New Orleans, which was about one hundred leagues from us when we were taken and after being examined upon oath before the Governor first separately one by one, and then altogether we were committed to close prison, we not knowing then (nor even yet) how long they intended to confine us there. During our stay in Prison we had allowed us a pound and a half of bread a man each day, and ten pounds of pork per month for each man, which allowance

[1] Ohio.

was duly given to us for the space of eighteen months, and after that we had only one pound of Rice Bread and one pound of rice for each man per day, and one quart of Bear's oil for each man per month, which allowance was continued to us untill I made my escape. Whilst I was confined in Prison I had many Visits made to me by the French and Dutch who lived there and grew intimate and familiar with some of them, by whom I was informed of the Manner of Government, laws, strength and wealth of the kingdom of Louisiana as they call it, and from the whole we learned that the Government is Tyranical. The common people groan under the load of oppression and sigh for deliverance. The Governor is the chief Merchant and enhances all the Trade into his own hands, depriving the Planters of selling their commodities to any other but himself and allowing them only such prices as he pleases.

And with respect to Religion, there is little to be found amongst them, but those who profess any Religion at all, its the Church of Rome. In the Town are nine Clergymen, four Jesuits and five Capuchin Friars. They have likewise one Nunnery in which are nine nuns. Notwithstanding the Fertility and richness of the soil, The Inhabitants are generally poor as a consequence of the oppression they meet with from their rulers, neither is the settling of the Country, or Agriculture in any measure encouraged by the Legislature. One thing I had almost forgot Viz. we were told by some of the French who first settled there, that about forty years ago when the French first discovered the place, and made attempt to settle therein, there were then pretty many English settled on both sides the river Mississippi and one twenty Gun Ship lay in the river, what became of the Ship we did not hear, but we were informed that the English Inhabitants were all destroyed by the Natives at the instigation of the French.

I now begin to speak of the strength of the Country and by the best account I could gather I did not find that there are above four hundred and fifty effective men of the Militia in all that Country, and not above one hundred and fifty Soldiers under pay in and about the Town of New Orleans; tis true they have sundry Forts in which they keep some men, but they are so weak and dispicable as not worth taking notice of, with regard to the strengthening of the Country, having in some of them only six men, in others ten men. The strongest of all those places is at the mouth of the Mississippi, In which are thirty men, and fifty Leagues from thence is a town called Mobile, nine Leagues from the mouth of a river of the same name, in which is a Garrison that boasts of seventy Soldiers. After I had been confined in close prison above two years, and all expectation of being set at liberty failing, I begun to think of making my escape out of prison, one of which I put in practice, and which succeeded in the following manner. There was a certain Frenchman who was born in that Country, and had some time before Sold his rice to the Spaniards, for which he was put in prison and it cost him six hundred Pieces of eight[1] before he got clear, he being tired with the misery and oppression under which the poor country people labour, formed a design of removing his Family to South Carolina Which design was discovered, and he was again put in Prison in the dungeon, and made fast in Irons, and after a formal Tryal he was condemned to be a Slave for Ten Years, besides the expense of seven hundred pieces of eight. With this miserable Frenchman I became intimate, and as he was an active man, and knew the country he promised, if I could help him off with his irons and we all got clear of the Prison, he would conduct us safe until we were out of danger. We then got a small file from a soldier

---

[1] A dollar.

wherewith to cut the irons and on the 25th day of October 1744 we put our design in practice. While the Frenchman was very busy in the Dungeon in cutting the Irons, we were as industrious without in breaking the door of the Dungeon, and each of us finished our job at one instant of time, which had held us for about six hours, by three of the clock in the morning with the help of a rope which I had provided beforehand, we let ourselves down over the prison walls, and made our escape, two miles from the town that night, where we lay close for two days. We then removed to a place three miles from the town, where one of the good old Friars of which I spoke before, nourished us four days. On the eighth day after we made our escape, we came to a Lake seven leagues from the Town, but by this time we had got a gun and some ammunition. The next day we shot two large Bulls and with their hides made a boat, in which we passed the Lake in the night. We tied the shoulder Blades of the Bulls to small sticks, which served us for paddles and passed a point, where there were thirteen men lay in wait for us, but thro' mercy we escaped them undiscovered. After we had gone by water sixty miles we went on shore, we left our boat as a Witness of our escape to the French.

We travelled thirty miles by land to the river Shokaré where our Frenchman's father lived. In this journey we passed thro' a nation of Indians, who were very kind to us, and carried us over two large bays. In this place we tarried two months and ten days in very great danger, for search was made for us every where both by land and water and orders to shoot us when found. Great rewards were promised by the Governor to the king of the Indians (mentioned above) to take us which he refused, and in the mean time was very kind by giving provision and informing us of our danger from time to time. After they had given over searching for us and we having got a large vessel and other necessary things for our voyage, and on the 25th of January our Frenchman and our negro boy (which he took to wait on him) and another Frenchman, and we being all armed and well provided for our voyage; we set off at a place called the belle Fountain (or in English fine spring) and sailed fifty leagues to the head of St. Roses Bay, and there we left our vessel and traveled by Land thirty Leagues to the Fork Indians, where the English trade, and there we staid five days. The Natives were to us kind and generous, there we left the two Frenchmen and negro boy, and on the tenth of February we set off and travelled by land up the river Giscaculfula one hundred and thirty-five miles, passing several Indian Towns, the Natives being very hospitable and kind and came to one Finlas an Indian Trader who lives among the Uchee Nation. On the first of March we arrived at Fort Augustus in the Province of Georgia. On the nineteenth instant we left Fort Augustus and on the first of April we arrived at Charlestown and waited on the Governor, who examined us concerning our Travels &c and detained us in Charlestown eighteen days, and made us a present of eighteen pounds of their money, which did no more than defray our expences whilst in that town. I had delivered to the Governor a copy of my Journal which when I asked again he refused to give me, but having obtained from him a pass we went on board of a small vessel bound for Virginia. On the thirteenth of April, the same day about two of the clock we were taken by the French in cape Roman and kept prisoner till eleven of the clock next day, at which time the French after having robbed us of all the Provision we had for our Voyage or Journey, put us into a Boat we being twelve men in number, and so left us to the mercy of the seas and winds.

On the fifteenth instant we arrived again at Charlestown and were examined before the Governor concerning our being taken by the French. We were now detained three days before we could get another pass from the Governor, we having destroyed the former when we were taken by the French and then were dismissed, being in a strange place; far from home, destitute of friends, clothing money and arms, and in that deplorable condition had been obliged to undertake a journey of five hundred miles, but a gentleman who was commander of a Privateer and now lay at Charlestown with whom we had discoursed several times gave to each of us a gun and a sword and would have given us ammunition but that he had but little. On the eighteenth day of April we left Charlestown the second time and travelled by land, and on the seventeenth day of May 1745 we arrived at my house, having been absent three years two months and one day from my family, having in that time by the nicest calculation I am able to make, travelled by Land and water four thousand six hundred and six miles, since I left my own House till I returned Home again.

JOHN PETER SALLEY.

SCHEME

For the Settlement of a New Colony to the Westward of Pennsylvania, for the Enlargement of his Majesty's Dominions in America, for the further Promotion of the Christian Religion among the Indian Natives, and for the more effectual securing them in his Majesty's Alliance.

That humble Application be made either to His Majesty or the General Assembly of Connecticut, or to both, as the Case may require, for a Grant of so much Land as shall be necessary for the Settlement of an ample colony, to extend from the Western Boundaries of Pennsylvania one Hundred Miles to the Westward of the River Mississippi, and to be divided from Virginia and Carolina by the Great Chain of Mountains that runs along the Continent from the North Eastern to the South Western Parts of America. That humble Application be made to His Majesty for a Charter to erect the said Territory into a separate Government, with the same Privileges which the Colony of Connecticut enjoys, and for such Supplies of Arms and Ammunition as may be necessary for the Safety and Defence of the Settlers, and that his Majesty would also be pleased to take the said New Colony under his immediate protection.

That application be made to the Assemblies of the several British Colonies in North America to grant such Supplies of Money and Provisions as may enable the Settlers to secure the Friendship of the Indian Natives, and support themselves and Families till they are established in said Colony in Peace and Safety, and can support themselves by their own Industry.

That at least Twelve Reverend Ministers of the Gospel be

engaged to remove to the said New Colony with such members of their respective Congregations as are willing to go along with them.

That every Person, from the age of fourteen years and upwards (Slaves excepted) professing the Christian Religion, being Protestant Subjects of the Crown of Great Britain, and that will remove to said New Colony with the first settlers thereof, shall be entitled to a sufficient Quantity of Land for a good Plantation, without any Consideration Money, and at the annual Rent of a Pepper-Corn. The Plantation to contain at least Three Hundred Acres, Two Hundred Acres of which to be such Land as is fit either for Tillage or Meadow.

That every Person under the Age of Fourteen Years (Slaves excepted) who removes to said Province with the First Settlers thereof, as well as such Children as shall be lawfully born to said First Settlers in said Province, or in the Way to it, shall be entitled to Three Hundred Acres of Land when they come to the Age of Twenty-one Years, without any Purchase Money, at the annual Quit-Rent of Two Shillings Sterling for every Hundred Acres; the Quit-Rent arising from such Lands to be applied to the Support of Government, the Propagation of the Christian Religion among the Indian Natives, the Relief of the Poor, the Encouragement of Learning, and in general to such other public Use, as shall be judged by the Legislature of the Province to be most conducive to the General Good.

That every Person who is entitled to any land in the Province, shall be at Liberty to take it up when they please; but when taken up shall be obliged to clear and fence at least Fifteen Acres on every Farm of Three Hundred Acres, within Five Years after the Appropriation of said Land, and also to build a Dwelling House of at least Fifteen Foot square with a good Chimney on the Premises within the said Term on Pain of forfeiting said Land.

That the said Plantation shall be laid out in Townships, in such Manner as will be most for the Safety and Convenience of the Settlers.

That in order to prevent all Jealousies and Disputes about the Choice of said Plantations, they shall be divided by Lot.

That as soon as possible after a sufficient Number of Persons are engaged, a proper Charter obtained, and the necessary Preparations are made for the Support and Protection of the Settlers, a Place of general Rendezvous shall be appointed, where they shall all meet, and from whence they shall proceed in a Body to the new Colony; but that no Place of Rendezvous shall be appointed till at least Two Thousand Persons able to bear Arms are actually engaged to remove, exclusive of Women and Children.

That it be established as one of the fundamental Laws of the Province that Protestants of every Denomination who profess the Christian Religion, believe the Divine Authority of the Sacred Scriptures of the Old and New Testament, the Doctrine of the Trinity of Persons in the Unity of the Godhead, and whose Lives and Conversations are free from Immorality and Prophaneness, shall be equally capable of serving in all the Posts of Honor, Trust or Profit in the Government, notwithstanding the Diversity of their religious Principles in other Respects. But that none of any Denomination whatsoever, who have been guilty of Prophaning the Name of God, of Lying, Drunkenness, or any other of the groser Immoralities, either in their Words or Actions, shall be capable of holding any Office in or under the Government till at least one Year after their Conviction of such Offence.

The Christianizing the Indian Natives and bringing them to be good Subjects, not only to the Crown of Great-Britain, but to the King of all Kings, being one of the most essential Designs of the proposed New Colony, it is a Matter of the utmost Importance that those poor ignorant Heathen should not be prejudiced against the Christian Religion by the bad Lives of those in Authority.

That Protestants of every Denomination who profess the Christian Religion, shall have the free and unlimited Exercise of their Religion, and shall be allowed to defend it, both from the Pulpit and the Press, so long as they remain peaceable Members of Civil Society, and do not propagate Principles inconsistent with the Safety of the State.

That no Member of the Church of Rome shall be able to hold any Lands or Real Estate in the Province, nor be allowed to be Owners of, or have any Arms or Ammunition in their Possession, on any Pretence whatsoever, nor shall any Mass-Houses, or Popish Chappels be allowed in the Province.

That no Person shall be obliged to pay any Thing towards the Support of a Minister of whose Congregation he is not a Member, or to a Church to which he does not belong.

That the Indians shall on all occasions be treated with the utmost Kindness, and every justifiable method taken to gain their Friendship; and that whoever injures, cheats, or makes them drunk, shall be punished with peculiar Severity.

That so soon as the Province is able to support Missionaries, and proper Persons can be found to engage in the Affair, a Fund shall be settled for the Purpose, and Missionaries sent among the neighboring Indian Nations; and that it shall, in all Time coming, be esteemed as one of the first and most Essential Duties of the Legislature of the Province, by every proper Method in their power to endeavor to spread the Light of the glorious Gospel among the Indians in America even to its most Western Bounds.

That, as the Conversion of the Indians is a Thing much to be desired, from the weightiest Considerations, both of a religious and political Nature, and since the Colony during its

Infancy will be unable to provide the necessary Funds for the Purpose, some proper Person or Persons shall be sent to Europe, duly authorized from the Government, to ask the Assistance of such as desire to promote that great and good Work.

To the Honourable the Governor, Council and Representatives of the Colony of Connecticut, to meet in General Assembly, on the Eighth Day of May, 1755. The petition of the Subscribers, being Inhabitants of His Majesty's Plantations in North America,

Humbly Sheweth

That your Petitioners having taken the foregoing scheme for settling a new colony into their most serious consideration, and having deliberately weighed the various parts thereof, cannot but most heartily approve of a design, which, when duly executed, would be attended with such happy and extensive consequences to the Crown of Great Britain, and all His Majesty's colonies in North America and which would at the same Time open the most effectual Door for carrying the Light of the glorious Gospel of Christ among the numerous Tribes of Indians that inhabit those inland Parts; and being for our Parts desirous to embark in so important a Cause, if the Scheme takes Effect, and to remove with our Families and Fortunes to the proposed New Colony, when Providence has prepared the Way for us, we are naturally led to wish Success to the Undertaking; but however ardently we wish Success to the Scheme or how sanguine soever our Inclinations may be of engaging in the Affair, common Prudence forbids our Removal till such a Foundation is laid as will afford, not only a rational Prospect of present Protection from the Enemy, but of handing down both Civil and Religious Liberty, as well as private Property, to our Posterity; and since it is necessary that such Foundation be laid in Part by Your Honorable House, we are constrained to make our humble Application to You, and we do it with the greater Cheerfulness, as the known Zeal of New England for His Majesty's Service gives us the greatest Reason to hope for the Countenance and Assistance of Your House in an Undertaking that has so direct a Tendency to promote His Majesty's Interest by securing the Friendship and firm Alliance of the Indian Natives, and thereby preparing the Way for the actual Settlement of those remote Parts of the British Dominions, as well as for Preventing the Encroachments of the French. We, therefore, Your Petitioners do most humbly pray, That You would be pleased so far to aid the Design, as to make the proper Grant of so much Land as shall be necessary for the proposed new Colony, which we humbly conceive ought to extend as far as the Scheme proposes, that is to say, From the Western Boundaries of the Province of Pennsylvania, One Hundred Miles to the Westward of the River Mississippi, and that it should be divided from Virginia and Carolina by the great Chain of Mountains that runs along the Continent from the North Eastern to the Southwestern Parts of America.

And also, That Your Honorable House would be pleased to make Application to His Majesty for a Charter to erect the said Territory into a separate Government with the same Privileges which the Colony of Connecticut enjoys. And we beg Leave, with all Humility to add That as the Charter by which Your Province holds both their Land and their Privileges expressly declares, That the Christianizing of the Indian Natives was the principal End which King Charles the Second proposed by granting such extensive Territories and Privileges, so we cannot but hope, that the same Motives will have their proper Weight with Your Honourable House, to grant the Prayer of your Petitioners, and we, as in Duty bound, will ever pray.

To this petition were affixed more than two thousand names.

LETTER FROM ROBERT ORME TO GOVERNOR DINWIDDIE.[1]

FORT CUMBERLAND July 18 1755

My dear Governor

I am so extremely ill in bed with the wound I have received that I am under the Necessity of employing my friend Capt. Dobson as my scribe. I am informed that Governor Innes has sent you some account of the Action near the Banks of the Monongahela about seven miles from the French Fort. As his Intelligence must be very Imperfect, the Dispatch he sent to you must consequently be so too; you should have had more early Account of it, but every Oficer whose business it was to have informed you was either killed or wounded and our distressfull Situation put it out of our power to attend to it so much as we would otherwise have done. The 9th instant we passed and repassed the Monongahela by advancing first a party of 300 men which immediately followed by another of 200, the general with the Column of Artillery, Baggage and the Main Body of the Army passed the river the last time, about one o'clock, as soon as the whole had got on the Fort side of Monongahela we heard a very heavy and quick fire on our front, we immediately advanced in order to sustain them but the Detachment of the 200 and 300 gave way and fell back upon us, which caused such confusion and struck so great a panic into our men that afterwards no military Expedient could be made use of that had any effect upon them, the men were so extremely deaf to the exhortations of the General and the Officers that they

[1] P. R. O. America and West Indies.

fired away in the most irregular manner all their ammunition and then ran off leaving to the Enemy the Artillery, Ammunition, Provisions and Baggage, nor could they be persuaded to stop till they got as far as Gists plantation nor there only in part, many of them proceeding even as far as Col. Dunbar's Party who lay six miles on this side.

The Officers were absolutely sacrificed by their unparalleled good behaviour; Advancing before their men sometimes in bodies and sometimes separately, hoping by such an example to engage the soldiers to follow them, but to no purpose. The General had five horses shot under him and at last received a wound through his lungs, of which he died the 13th instant at night. Captain Monies and myself very much wounded. Mr. Washington had two horses shot under him and his clothes shot through in several places, behaving the whole time with the greatest courage and resolution.

Sir P. Halket was killed upon the spot, and according to the best calculation we can as yet make about 28 Officers were killed.

Col. Burton and Sir John St. Clair with 35 Officers wounded and out of our whole number of Officers not above 16 came off the Field unhurt. We imagine there are killed and wounded about 600 men. I have the pleasure to acquaint you that Captain Polson (who was killed) and his company behaved extremely well, as did Captain Stuart and his light horse, who I must beg leave to recommend to your protection and to desire you will be so kind to use your best endeavours to serve him as he has lost by the death of the general the rewards he really deserved by his gallant and faithful attendance on him.

Upon our proceeding with the whole convoy to the Little Meadow we found it impractable to advance in that manner; a Detachment was therefore made of 1200 men with the

Artillery, necessary ammunition, Provision and Baggage, leaving the remainder with Col. Dunbar, with Orders to join us as soon as possible; with this Detachment we proceeded with safety and expedition, till the fatal day I have just related and happy it was that this Disposition was made, otherwise the whole must have starved or fallen into the Hands of the enemy as numbers would have been no service to us and our Provision was all lost.

Mr. Shaw put into my Hands a letter from you directed to the General who was then incapable of any business, it contained Notes for £2000 from South Carolina. I am at a loss to know what to do with them, forgetting the particular appropriation of the Vote of Assembly, though I think I recollect its being voted at the Service of the Expedition in general and at the disposal of General Braddock; these Bills are made payable to him or Order, for which reason they are not negotiable. I desire your advice on this subject, and as it may save time, beg the favor of you to write to Governor Glen about it.

As our number of horses were so much reduced, and those so extremely weak, and many carriages being wanted for the wounded men occasioned our destroying the Ammunition and superfluous part of the Provision left in Col. Dunbar's Convoy, to prevent its falling into the Hands of the Enemy.

As the whole of the Artillery is lost and the Terror of the Indian remaining so strongly in the mens minds, as also the Troops being extremely weakened by Deaths, Wounds and Sickness, it was judged impossible to make any further attempts; therefore Col. Dunbar is returning to Fort Cumberland, with everything he is able to bring along with him. I propose remaining here till my wound will suffer me to remove to Philadelphia, from thence I shall make all possible Dispatch to England.

I am Sir &c

Robert Orme entered the army as an ensign in the 35th Foot. On September 16, 1745, he exchanged into the Coldstream Guards, of which he became a lieutenant April 24, 1751. He accompanied General Braddock to America, was present on the battle-field and assisted the removal of the General from the field. After his recovery from his wound he embarked for England. October, 1756, he resigned his commission in the Guards; he married the Hon. Audrey Townshend, only daughter of Charles, 3d Viscount. Capt. Orme died in February, 1781.

George Croghan, with a company of Indians, Andrew Montour and Christopher Gist and his son, were on the battlefield. Christopher Gist was the General's guide and with his Indians penetrated undiscovered to within half a mile of the fort.

Sir Peter Halket, of Pitferran, Fifeshire, a baronet of Nova Scotia, was the son of Sir Peter Wedderburne, of Gosford, who assumed his wife's name. In 1734, he sat in the House of Commons for Dunfermline, was Lieutenant-Colonel of the 44th at Sir John Cope's defeat in 1745. Released on parole by Charles Edward, he was ordered by Cumberland to rejoin his regiment, but honorably refused. The King approved of his course. He married Lady Amelia Stewart, second daughter of Francis, eighth Earl of Moray. He had three sons: Sir Peter, his successor, also in the army; Francis, Major in the Black Watch, and James, who was killed with him.

Colonel Thomas Dunbar was Colonel of the Forty-eighth, superseded in November, 1755, because of his injudicious retreat, and sent into honorable retirement as Lieutenant-Governor of Gibraltar; he was never again actively employed. He died 1777.

Sir John St. Clair, remained for a long time in service in America. 1756, he was made a Lieutenant-Colonel of the Sixtieth regiment. 1762, he was made a full Colonel. At the defeat of Braddock he was shot through the body.

EXTRACTS FROM "AN ANALYSIS OF A GENERAL MAP OF THE MIDDLE BRITISH COLONIES."

THE COUNTRY OF THE CONFEDERATE INDIANS, &c.

"The greatest part of Virginia is composed with the Assistance of Messieurs Fry and Jefferson's Map of it."

"In the Way to Ohio by Franks Town, after you are past the Allegeny Mountain, the Ground is rough in many Places, and continues so to the River. Hereabouts the Laurel Hill springs from the Mountain, and continues though not large, in a very regular Chain, I believe to the Ouasioto Mountain. For though the Allegeny Mountain is the most Westerly, on the West Branch of Susquehanna, it is far from being so back of Virginia."

"The Map in the Ohio, and its Branches, as well as the Passes through the Mountains Westward, is laid down by the Information of Traders and others, who have resided there, and travelled them for many years together. Hitherto there have not been any Surveys made of them, except the Road which goes from Shippensburg round Parnel's Knob and by Ray's Town over the Allegeny Mountains."

"Mr William Franklin's Journal to Ohio has been my principal Help in ascertaining the Longitude of the Fork of Ohio and Monaungahela; but however I must not omit mentioning, that the Latitude of this Fork is laid down from the Observation of Colonel Fry and is at least ten Miles more Northerly than I would otherwise have thought it was."

"Mr Joseph Dobson gave me an Account of the Distances from Creek to Creek, as they fall in, and of the Islands, Rifts and Falls, all the Way from the Fork to Sioto; and Mr Alexander Maginty and Mʳ Alexander Lowry, gave me the rest to the Falls, as well as confirmed the others. The River from the Fork upwards, is mostly from Mʳ John Davison."

"The Routs across the Country, as well as the Situation of Indian Villages, trading Places, the Creeks that fall into Lake Erie, and other Affairs relating to Ohio and its Branches, are from a great Number of Informations of Traders and others and especially of a very intelligent Indian called The Eagle, who had a good Notion of Distances, Bearings and delineating. The situation of Detroit is chiefly determined by the Computation of its Distance from Niagara by Mʳ Maginty, and its Bearing and Distance from the Mouth of the Sandusky."

"As for the Branches of Ohio, which head in the New Virginia (So they call, for Distinction-sake, that Part of Virginia South East of the Ouasioto Mountains, and on the Branches of Green Briar, New River, and Holston River) I am particularly obliged to Dʳ Thomas Walker, for the Intelligence of what Names they bear, and what Rivers they fall into Northward and Westward."

"The present, late and antient Seats of the original Inhabitants are expressed in the Map; and though it might be imagined that several Nations are omitted, which are mentioned by Authors, it may be remarked, that Authors, for want of Knowledge in Indian Affairs, have taken every little Society for a separate Nation; whereas they are not truly more in Number than I have laid down in a Map I published of Pennsylvania, New Jersey, New York and Delaware in 1749."

This Map and Analysis was printed in Philadelphia by B. Franklin and D. Hall, 1755.

The Maps of the Ohio Company Surveys of 1750–51–52 were copied from the original in the Public Record Office, London, by J. A. Burt, 1882, for William M. Darlington. They are in outline, with fewer names than are given in the map here published.

Governor Pownall intended to publish a second edition of his "Topographical Description of North America." His own copy is full of inserted MSS. and marginal notes. On page 13 he has written this explanation of the name Chëonderoga. "This word denotes the fork of a river, or the confluence of two branches which go off in one united stream. This the French always translate *Trois-Rivieres*. The Dutch, who first improved this rout, using the letters *tie* to express the sound *che*, as we do ye letters *tion* to express *chon*, wrote the word Tieonderoga, and the letter *e* in the correspondencies being mistaken for *c*, this place got the name of Ticonderoga. Custom has adopted this original mistake. And the using the real name in its true orthography looks so like affectation, that I cannot but think this explanation, by way of Apology at least, has become necessary. The situation on the Ohio, on which Fort du Quesne, afterwards called *Fort Pitt* was built, was by the Indians called Chëonderoga, and accordingly by the French called *Trois Rivieres*. It is recorded by that name in the famous *Leaden Plate*, which was buried there as a memorial of their possession. Until I had occasion to explain this it was always a matter of Puzzle to our Ministers, what Place in those Quarters the French meant to design by *Trois Rivieres*."

Here follows an exact copy of that plate:

COPY OF THE LEADEN PLATE BURIED AT THE FORKS OF MONONGAHELA AND OHIO BY MONˢ CELERON BY WAY OF TAKING POSSESSION & AS A MEMORIAL & TESTIMONY THEREOF.
                                                    1753 or 2.
L'an 1749 Dv Regne de Louis XV Roy de France Novs
    Celeron Commandant D'vn Detachement Envoie par

Monsieur le Mis De la Galissoniere Commandant General De la Nouvelle France pour retablir la tranquillite dans quelques villages sauvages de ces cantons avons enterré cette Plaque A (3[1] rivieres dessous la riviere au bœuf ce 3 Aoust) pres de la Riviere Oyo autrement belle Riviere pour Monument du Renouvellement de la Possession que nous avons pris de la ditte Riviere Oyo et de toutes celles qui y[2] tombnt et toutes les terres des deux cotes jusque aux Sources des dittes Rivieres ainsi qu'en ont jouy ou du jouir les precedent Roys de France et qu'ils sy sont maintenus par les armes et par les traittes speciallment par ceux de Riswick, D'Utrecht et D'Aix la Chappelle.

On the back is Paul Lebrosse Fecit.

Translation.

In the year 1749, in the reign of Louis XV, King of France, We Celeron, commandant of a detachment sent by the Marquis de la Galissoniere, Commandant in Chief of New France, to re-establish peace in certain villages of the Indians of these districts, have buried this plate at the Three Rivers, below Le Bœuf River, this third of August, near the river Oyo, otherwise the Fair River, as a monument of the renewal of the possession that we have taken of the said River Oyo, and of all those which fall into it, and of all the lands on both sides to the sources of the said rivers, as the preceding Kings of France have enjoyed or ought to have enjoyed it; and which they have upheld by force of arms and by treaties, especially by those of Riswick, Utrecht and Aix-la-Chapelle.

---

[1] This is only scratched with the point of a knife, and scarcely legible, in a space which was left blank to be filled up when buried.

[2] This is so written in the plate.

ENSIGN WARD'S DEPOSITION.

[Indorsed]

P. R. O. B. T. VIRGINIA N°. 21.

VIRGINIA.

ENSIGN WARD'S DEPOSITION before the
Governor & Council ye 7th of May 1754.

Rec^d with his Letter dated
ye 10th of May 1754.

Rec^d July 2^d } 1754.
Read D°

W. 164.

Mr EDWARD WARD Capt Trents Ensign deposes and makes Oath to the following Particulars, That the French first appeared to him at Shanopins Town about two Miles distant from the Fort the 17th of April last, that they moved down within a small distance from the Fort, Then landed their Canoes, and marched their men in a regular manner a little better than Gun shot of the Fort. That Le Mercier a French Officer sent by Contrecœur the Commandant in Chief of the French Troops came with an Indian Interpreter, called by the Mingoes the Owl, and two Drums, one of which served for Interpreter between Le Mercier and him; . Le Mercier presently deliver'd him the summons by the Interpreter, looked at his watch which was about two, and gave him an hour to fix his Resolution, telling him he must come to the French Camp with his Determination in Writeing. He says that half an Hour of the time allowed him, he spent in Council with the Half King, who advised him to acquaint the French he was no Officer of Rank or invested with powers to answer their Demands and requested them to Wait the Arrival of the principal Commander. That at the time the Summons was deliver'd to him, the Half King received a Belt of Wampum much to the same purpose.

That he went accompanied with the Half King, Robt Roberts, a private Soldier, and John Davidson as an Indian Interpreter, that the Half King might understand every word he spoke at the French Camp, That he there address'd himself to the Chief Commander Contrecœur and expressed himself agreeably to the above mentioned advice of the Half King, That the French Commander told him he should not wait for an Answer from any other person, And absolutely insisted on his determining what to do that Instant, or he should immediately take Possession of the Fort by Force. That he then observeing the number of the French, which he judg'd to be about a Thousand and considering his own weakness being but Forty one in all, whereof only Thirty three were Soldiers, Surrender'd the Fort with Liberty obtained to march off with everything belonging thereto by Twelve o'Clock the next Day. He says that night he was Oblieg'd to encamp within 300 yards of the Fort with a Party of the Six Nations who were in Company with him, That the French Commander sent for him to Supper and ask'd many Questions concerning the English Governments, which he told him he could give no Answer to, being unacquainted with such affairs, That the French Commander desired some of the Carpenters Tools, offering any money for them, to which he answer'd he loved his King and Country too well to part with any of them And then retired. That next morning he received the speech from the Half King to the Governour, And proceed'd with all his men towards Redstone Creek where he arrived in two

Days; and from thence marched to Wills's Creek, where he met with Coll' Washington and informed him of every particular which had happened, That Coll' Washington thought fit to send back one of the Indians to the Half King with a Speech and to Assure him of the Assistance which was marching to him; And by the advice of a Council of War dispatch'd him an Express to his Honour with the other Indian and an Interpreter, judging him the most proper Person having been appointed by the Half King. He moreover adds that four days before the French came he had an Account of their comeing, and saw a Letter that John Davison wrote to Robt Calender an Indian Trader to confirm the truth that they were to be down by that time. That the Day following he sent a Copy of Davison's Letter to Capt Trent who was then at Wills's Creek, and went directly himself to his lieutenant who lived Eight or Ten miles up Monongahela from the Fort at a place called Turtle Creek, it was late at night when he got there, Accompanied by Robert Roberts, Thomas Davison, Samuel Asdill, and an Indian, and shew'd him the Letter, of which he sent a Copy the next Day to his Captain. The Lieutenant told him he was well assured the French would be down, but said what can we do in the Affair. The morning after he sent for the Half King, and one of his Chiefs named Serreneatta, who advised him to build a Stockade Fort, That then he asked his Lieutenant if he would come down to the Fort, to which he Answer'd he had a Shilling to loose for a Penny he should gain by his Commission at that time, and that he had Business which he could not settle under Six Days with his Partner; That he thereupon answer'd he would immediately go himself and have the Stockade Fort built, And that he would hold out to the last Extremity before it should be said that the English had retreated like Cowards before the French Forces Appeared, and that he knowing the bad consequences of his leaveing it as the rest had done would give the Indians a very indifferent opinion of the English ever after. He further says he had no Orders from either his Captain, or Lieutenant how to proceed, and had the last Gate of the Stockade Fort erected before the French appeared to him. That he was credibly Informed by an Englishman who attended the French Commandant that they had 300 Wooden Canoes, and 60 Battoes and had four men to each Canoe and Battoe, that they had also Eighteen Pieces of Cannon three of which were nine Pounders. That the Half King stormed greatly at the French at the Time they were oblieged to march out of the Fort and told them it was he Order'd that Fort and laid the first Log of it himself, but the French paid no Regard to what he said.

      Sworn to by the abovemention'd Ward before
        The Governor in Council
Teste   the 7th May 1754.
         N WALTHOE Cl. Con.

NOTE.—Edward Ward's son, John, served during the Revolution. He was lieutenant in the 1st, 3d and 8th Regiments, Pennsylvania Line. Military Register. Autograph letter of Col. Bayard to John Nicholson and receipt of Edward Ward.

LETTERS AND SPEECHES TO INDIANS.

CAMP SARATOGA, October 12th 1777.[1]

To his Excellency John Hancock, Esqr.

SIR:—I have the satisfaction to acquaint your Excellency with the great success of the Arms of the United States in this Department. On the 7th inst the Enemy attacked our advanced Picket upon the Left, which drew on an action about the same hour of the day and near the same spot of Ground where that of the 19th of September was fought. From 3 o'clock in the afternoon till almost night the Conflict was very warm and bloody, when the Enemy, by a precipitate Retreat, determined the fate of the day, leaving in our hands eight pieces of Brass Cannon, the Tents and Baggage of their Flying Army, a large quantity of fixed Ammunition, a considerable number of wounded and prisoners amongst whom are the following principal officers, Major Williams, who commanded the Artillery, Major Ackland, who commanded the Corps of Grenadiers, Captain Money Q M G and Sir Francis Clark, principal Aid de Camp to his Excellency General Burgoyne. The loss upon our side is not more than (illegible) killed and wounded, amongst the latter is the gallant Major General Arnold, whose Leg was fractured by a Musket Ball as he was forcing the Enemy's Breast-work.

Too much praise cannot be given to the Corps commanded by Col. Morgan,[2] consisting of his Rifle Regiment and the Light Infantry of the Army under Major Dearborn.

[1] From original manuscript.
[2] Daniel Morgan.

But it would be injustice not to say that the whole Body engaged deserve the honour and applause due to such exalted merit. The night after the Action the Enemy took Post in the strong intrenched Camp on their Left. General Lincoln whose division was opposite to the Enemy going in the afternoon to direct a Cannonade to annoy their Camp received a Musket Ball in his Leg, which shattered the bone; this has deprived me of the assistance of one of the best Officers as well as Men, his loss at this time cannot be too much regretted. I am in hopes his leg may yet be saved.

The 9th at Midnight, the Enemy quitted their entrenchments and retired to Saratoga. Early in the morning of the 9th I received the inclosed letter from General Burgoyne acquainting me that he left his whole Hospital to my protection, in which are 300 wounded officers and soldiers.

Brigadier General Frazier who commanded the Flying Army of the Enemy was killed the 7th Inst. At one o'clock in the morning of the 10th I received the inclosed letter from General Burgoyne with Lady Harriott Ackland. That morning as soon as the Army could be properly put in motion, I marched in pursuit of the Enemy and arrived here in the Evening and found the Enemy had taken Post upon the opposite side of the Fish-Kill in an entrenched Camp which they occupied upon their advancing down the Country. The Enemy have burned all the Houses before them as they retreated. The extensive Buildings and Kills &c belonging to Major General Schuyler are also laid in Ashes. This shameful behaviour occasioned my sending a Drum with the inclosed Letter to General Burgoyne.

I am happy to acquaint your Excellency that Desertion has taken a deep Root in the Royal Army particularly among the Germans who come to us in Shoals.

I am so much pressed on every side with business that it is

impossible for me to be more particular now, but I hope in a few days to have leisure to acquaint your Excellency with every circumstance at present omitted.

I am &c
HORATIO GATES.

Taimenend to the wise Delaware Council.[1]

BROTHERS:—I know you depend on me for the truth of every thing. I therefore send this that you may see what we are about and that you may know every thing I have heretofore told you is true.

GEORGE MORGAN.

YORK TOWN, October 19th, 1777

Taimenend to the wise Delaware Council
Hanover or McCallisters Town
YORK COUNTY, October 20th, 1777

BROTHERS:—I wrote to you two days ago and I wrote to you yesterday morning. In the afternoon about 4 o'clock an Express arrived at York with a letter from our Northern Army dated the 15th of this Month 10 o'clock P.M. Mr. Hancock, President of our great Council gave me a copy of it to send to you and I immediately set out for this place to overtake Malachy Hays the Express by whom I sent my other Letters. By riding hard and in the night I lost the letter out of my Pocket, but I can tell you the contents.

Extract of a Letter from General Schuyler, dated
September 27th, 1777.[2]

SIR:—On the 11th inst., about three hundred Indians (including Men, Women and Children) of the Oneidas, Tuscaro-

[1] From original manuscript.
[2] From original manuscript.

ras, a few Onondagoes, and Mohawks arrived here. The 15th was spent in the usual ceremony of congratulation during which we took occasion to sound their inclinations to engage in the war, we prepared a Speech and on the next day offered them the War Belt which was immediately accepted by Warriors of each Nation; on the 17th the War Feast was prepared; at which the Belt was solemnly accepted by the whole; the 18th and 19th passed in equipping them, and being informed about ten at night of the 19th, that our Army was engaged, and having then three of the Chief Warriors to sup with me, Mr. Edwards and myself requested them to march without delay, which they and many others did with alacrity, and with such dispatch as to reach General Gates before noon next day and by night the remainder arrived at the Camp, making in all near one hundred and fifty; they have already taken about thirty Prisoners beside scalps and intercepted some dispatches from General Burgoyne to General Powell commanding at Ticonderoga.

The Indians have requested that the Southern ones should be advised by us, that they have taken the Hatchet, and a Belt will also be sent by them.

We have taken measures to induce the whole Confederacy to join us, and have reason to believe that they will do it: if so, we shall soon be informed of it, and I think in that case it would be prudent to call them into Action the soonest possible into whatever quarter their services may be most wanted.

Extract

signed CHAS. THOMSON.

Taimenend to the wise Delaware Council.[1]

YORK TOWN, Oct. 18th, 1777.

BROTHERS AND CHIEFS:

The within is a Letter wrote by the wise Chief who is

[1] From original manuscript.

placed at Albany by Congress to take care of the Council Fire of the Six Nations and the Americans at that place. As it is of very great importance to all Nations, I send it to you by a quick Runner. I submit to your wise Council what to do with it. You may rest assured of the contents being true.

My advice is that you immediately communicate the contents to the Wiandots, Mingoes, Shawnese, Ottawas and Chipeways. If they alter their conduct in time and take pity on their Women and Children, it is not yet too late for them to ask mercy. I desire to hear from you in twenty days after you receive this and to know what the Wiandot &c think of it. Our Great Council of America desires to give you the strongest assurances of their Friendship and to tell you that your wise conduct during this storm will ever make them consider your Nation as their great Friend and Brothers.

TAIMENEND.[1]

To the Wise Council of the Delawares at Coochoching.

Brothers

I am very sorry my good friend and brother Captain Killbuck left me without informing me of his intention, that I might have clothed his Children. I now send to him a white ruffled Shirt for himself and a Callicoe one for his wife.

Brothers

I shall give you notice agreeable to my Promise in public Council. In the mean time I am now prepared to follow such parties of Wyandotts or others as may strike me. You may therefore expect to see some of our young Men, and I desire your Women and children may rest easy and not be

---

[1] The name given to Col. George Morgan by the Indians.

frightened. I will pay for what Provisions they are supplied with at any of your Towns in case they come that way.

Brothers

'Till yesterday I had no news from Philadelphia; then an express arrived with letters and the enclosed News Papers by which you will see the Cattle have broke down the Pen which our Enemies said they had drove the Big Knife into. This Pen, Brothers was made of rotten sticks, and was easily broke down and those who made it have run off for fear of being tramped to death.

Brothers

The English Army still continues on Board their ships at sea. Sometimes they come and look into our river, sometimes into another, but they find us every where prepared for them. We cannot persuade them to come eat their Dinners at Philadelphia, as they promised they would. I suppose they think their Broth would scald them were they to come there.

Brothers

A number of British Troops, Hessians, Canadians and some foolish Indians from the Northward, thought they would try to go from Canada to Albany. Our people retired a little as they did last year from New York to Trenton. They retired I say as far as Bennington, and there they attacked the British Troops &c and took seven hundred and thirty-six of them prisoners. Thirty-seven of whom were Officers. They are now confined in New England.

Another Party of them attacked Fort Schuyler, which is above the German Flats on the North river, in doing which they lost four hundred of their men, killed and taken prisoners by our people. And in every other Skirmish our people have had they have beat our Enemies.

Brothers

You may rest assured that what I have always told you is true and that our Enemies will never be able to conquer the United States, who grow stronger and stronger every day.

Brothers

Two days after you receive this I desire you will send one or two of your Young Men with what news you have at your Towns. I request they may come on Horse back, as then our Young Men if they meet them cannot mistake them they can ride down to the River Side by which we shall know they are friends. By their return I expect more good news to tell you.

Brothers

I am determined to be strong in good Works and I will not suffer foolish people to injure our Friendship. I desire you will also be strong. You may depend you will soon see a Strong man walking to the Towns of our Enemies; as General Hand has told you. I am your friend and Brother.

TAIMENEND.

{ By Captain White Eye's cousin and Captain Killbuck's son. Fort Pitt August 30th 1777. }

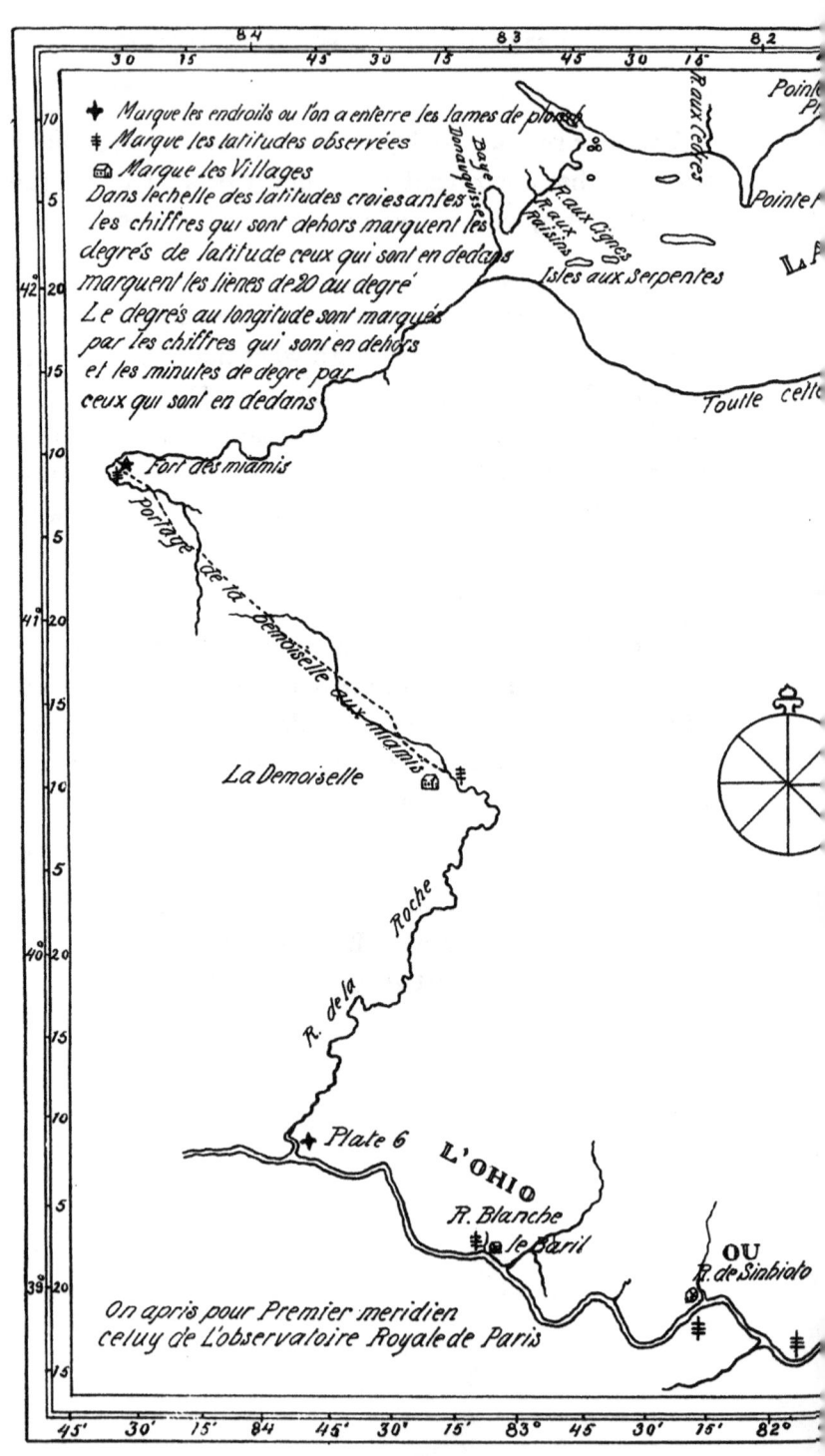

BONNECAMP'S MAP.

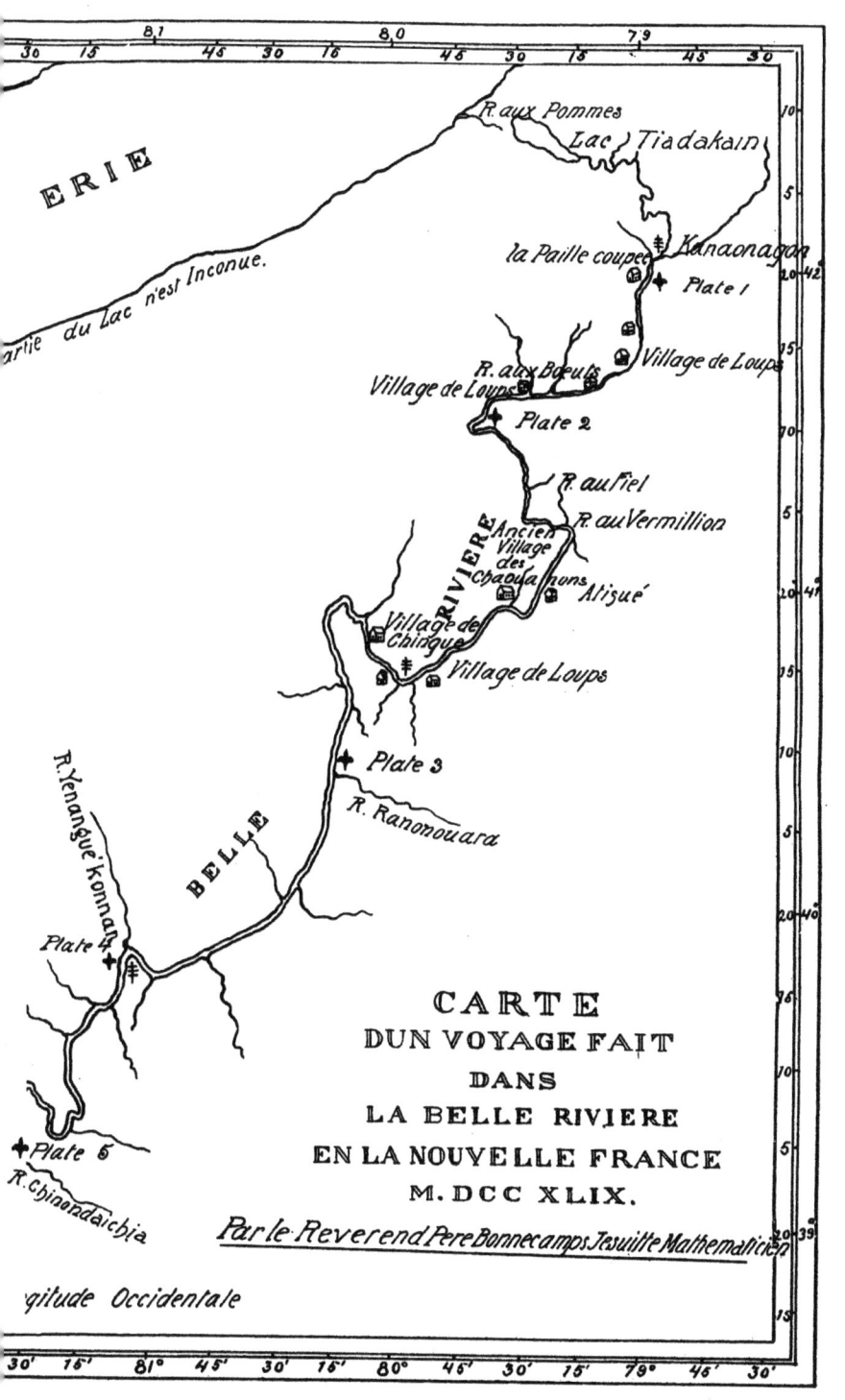

FULLNAME INDEX

ABERCROMBIE, Gen 187
ACKLAND, Harriott 279 280
ALIQUIPPA, Queen 86
ALLEN, William 132
AMHERST, 188 Gen 110 112 198 208
AMHURST, Sir Jeffrey 196
ANNOSANAH, Indian Name Given To Gist 38
APAMANS, Hendrick 133
ARMHURST, Gen 196 Sir Jeffery 196
ARMSTRONG, 180 John 171 194
ARNOLD, Maj Gen 279
ASDILL, Samuel 277
AUSTIN, Walter 13
BALTIMORE, Lord 202-204 219
BANCROFT, 128 Mr 109 135
BASETT, Capt 194
BATTE, Thomas 18
BATTS, Mr 19
BAYARD, Col 278
BAYNTON, 241
BEATTY, Charles 113
BEAUJEU, Capt 238
BELLIN, M 111
BERKELEY, Gov 13-14 18 William 12
BEVERLY, William 217-218
BIENVILLE, Celeron De 28
BIRD, Col 197
BLAIR, Francis P 89 Montgomery 89
BLAND, Edward 14
BLEDSOE, Jesse 89 Sarah 89
BONNECAMP, Father 107
BOONE, Daniel 133
BOREMAN, John 216
BOSWELL, Dr 89
BOUQUET, 102 104 193 239-240 Col 92 99 112-113 171 188 211 Henry 195 199

BRADDOCK, 88 167-168 180 183 210 270 Gen 139 184-185 238 269-270
BRADSTREET, Col 211
BREWER, Capt 173
BREWSTER, Sackford 14
BRICKELL, John 116
BROWN, B Gratz 89
BULLIT, Capt 121
BURD, Col 199
BURGOYNE, Gen 215 279-280 282
BURK, Thomas 108
BURKE, 109
BURNEY, Thomas 37 113 125
BURT, J A 272
BURTON, Col 268
BURWELL, Col 220 253 Lewis 222
BUTLER, Col 215 John 175
BYRD, Col 22 William 22 224 Wm 22
CABOT, 9
CALENDER, Robt 277
CALHOUN, 199
CALLENDER, Robert 120 161 178 246
CAMBDIN, Lord 246
CAMPBELL, Charles 24
CAMPBLE, Capt 196
CARLSON, R 13
CARQUEVILLE, Lt 148
CARTER, Robert 225
CARTLEDGE, Edmund 93
CELERON, 29 96 107 109 177 273-274 Bienville De 95
CHAPMAN, Nathaniel 235 Nathel 225
CHARLES 2ND, King 20
CHARTIER, Peter 159
CHATHAM, Earl Of 244
CLARK, Sir Francis 279
CLARKE, George Rogers 127 Wm 129
CLAUSE, Laurence 154
CLAY, Mrs Henry 89
CLAYBORNE, William 14
CLINTON, De Witt 107 Gov 29 122

COEUR, Jean 122 160 162 179
COLHOON, Mr 197
COLLET, Capt 17
COLLINSON, Peter 129
COLLOT, Gen Victor 99
COLVILLE, Robert 217
CONOLLY, John 190 239
CONTRECOEUR, 96 167 181 276 Capt 150 238 M 149 M De 249
COONCE, Mark 36
COPE, Sir John 270
CORBIN, Guwin 235
CORNBURY, Lord 152 158
COURSEY, Col 224
CRAWFORD, 129 Hugh 57 128
CRESAP, 139-140 Capt 206 Col 67 90 204 206 231 234 236 Michael 205 Thomas 32 137 202-203 205 219 225 235
CROGHAN, 35 147 159-162 167-168 170-171 185 248 Capt 188 Col 189 212 George 34 37 40 44 46 55 96-98 108-109 114 119-120 125 129 133 141 163-166 172 174 176 178-184 186-192 194-195 197 201 210 240 246 249 270 Mary 240 Mr 45 55 192 Susannah 190 William 240
CROMWELL, Edith 88
CRONELLI, 94
CUMBERLAND, 270
CURRAN, Barny 35 39 100
D'ESTAING, Count 209
DARLINGTON, William M 272
DARPONTINE, Capt 150
DARTMOUTH, Lord 242
DAVIDSON, Dr 121 John 276
DAVISON, John 272 277 Thomas 277
DE LERY, M 27
DE SOTO, Hernando 25
DEARBORN, Maj 279
DENNY, Gov 171
DESCHWEINITZ, E 113
DINWIDDIE, 238 Gov 147 181 249 267 Robert 31 225 231 235
DIXON, 129 204
DOBBS, Arthur 225
DOBSON, Capt 267 Joseph 271
DRAKE, Sir Francis 10 13
DUFFIELD, George 113
DUMAS, Capt 238
DUNBAR, Col 268 Thomas 270
DUNMORE, Lord 239
ECUYER, Capt 188 194-195 197 239 S 249
EDMONSTONE, Charles 239
EDWARD, Charles 270
EDWARDS, Mr 282
ERWIN, 109 Luke 108
EVANS, 115 118-119 Lewis 25
FAIRFAX, Col 165 Lord 23 137 202 Thomas 138 165
FALKNER, 109 Joseph 108
FALLAM, Mr 19 Robert 18
FINLEY, John 192
FLEET, Henry 14
FONTAINE, John 22
FORBES, 214 Gen 102 171 208 238 Thomas 148
FRANKLIN, B 244 272 Benjamin 95 166 241 243 Dr 242 246 William 95 271
FRAZER, John 122 165
FRAZIER, Brig Gen 280 John 80 86
FRENCH MARGARET, 105 116 (See also, MONTOUR)
FRY, 97 Joshua 22 164 222
GAGE, Gen 188 239
GALBRAITH, James 184
GALISSONIERE, M De La 274
GALISSONNIERE, Gov De La 28
GALLATIN, 128 Albert 117 Mr 143
GATES, Gen 282 Horatio 281
GEORGE III, King Of Great Britain 191
GERTY, Thomas 192
GIBSON, Hugh 102 John 99 205 246
GILES, Jacob 225 235
GIRTY, Simon 216

INDEX.

GIST, 30 36 91-92 96-97 100-101 103 105 107-108 114-116 118 120 123 127 130 133-140 143 145 162 210 268 Anne 88-89 Capt 88 Christopher 23 29 31 66-67 78 88 90 161 164 178 225 227-228 231 234 270 Col 89 165 Edith 88 Henry Clay 89 Mr 236 Nathaniel 88-89 Richard 88 225 Sarah 88-89 Thomas 88 Thomas Cecil 89 Violette 88 Zipporah 88
GLADWIN, Maj 196
GLEN, Gov 269
GOOCH, William 221
GORDON, Gov 117 140 155
GRANT, 210 Gen 238 James 207 Maj 208 William 208
GRATZ, Benjamin 89
GRENHALGH, Wentworth 21
GUESS, 134
HALKET, Francis 270 James 270 Sir P 268 Sir Peter 270
HALL, D 272 Rich 65 Richard 136
HAMILTON, 184 Gov 29 119 160 173 177 179-181 192 197 249 James 184 193
HANBURY, Capel 225 235 John 224-225 235 Mr 228 231 237
HANCOCK, John 279 Mr 281
HAND, Gen 214 285
HANNA, Wm 242
HARDY, Gov 184
HARMAR, Gen 125
HARRIS, John 168 Maj 15 Mary 41 114 William 15
HART, 93 Nathaniel 89
HAYS, Malachy 281
HECKEWELDER, John 144
HENRY, Capt 172
HILL, Edward 17
HILLSBOROUGH, Lord 241-242 246
HOUGH, Dr 131

HOWARD, 224 John 223 253 Josiah 253 Lord 224 Sarah 88
HOWE, 123 Gen 208
HUME, David 207
HUNTER, Mr 199 Robert 153
HUTCHINS, Capt 102 104 Thomas 112-113 190
INDIAN, Allompis 169 Beaver 211 Big Hannaona 45 Big Tree 152 Brittain 125 Canassetego 217 Capt Bull 174 Capt White Eye 285 Carondawana 152-153 155 Catfish 142 Checochinican 140 Chickoconnecon 70 Chief Nicholas 109-110 Chief Shichillany 159 Cockey 92 Conengayote 214 Coneotahanck 214 Conestoga 160 Custaloga 142 211 Flying Crow 214 Guashota 216 Gull Face 214 Guyashutha 216 Guyasuta 92 172 210-211 213 215-216 Guyasutha 212 Half King 164 166-167 276-277 Half King Scarrooyady 147 Hetanguantagetchy 153 Johonisse 190 Joneowentashaun 214-215 Joshua 71-72 142 Kayashuta 216 Kayodaghscroony 169 Keterioncha 157 Keyashuta 211 215-216 Keyenguatah 215 Kia-shuta 216 Kiashuta 92 172 212 Kiasolo 216 Kiasutha 210-211 Kiasuta 210 Killbuck 285 Kind Beaver 101 King Beaver 100 104 171-172 King Shingiss 81-82 Kiyashuta 216 Kushgwehgo 214 Lawmolach 81 Leaf 214 Logan 205-206 Madelina 169 Manoquetotha 168 Monacatoocha 81 Monakatoocha 97 Monakatootha 167 Nemacolin 140 Nemicotton 70 Oppamylucah 78 Oppaymolleah 71 141 Perecute 18 20 Peter Quebec 157 Pollatha Wappia 81 Robert Hunter 152 155 Scarayoday 190 Scarrooyady 166 Scarroyady 168-170 Serreneatta 277 Shikillimy 157 Shingiss 101

INDIAN (cont.)
   142 147 171 Swe-gach-shasin 119 Tachanoontia 143 218 Taimenend 282-283 285 Tamaque 142 Tanacharison 97 Tangoochqua 142 Teedyuscung 174 186 190 The Beaver 72 78 142 163 199 The Crane 61 The Eagle 272 The Half King 97 The Half-king 81-82 The Owl 275 Tottopottemen 15 17 Turtle Heart 211 White Eyes 119 White Mingo 212 214 Windaughalah 43 119-120 Wissameek 142
INNES, Gov 267
IRVINE, Gen 239
JACOBS, Capt 141
JAMES, King Of England 11
JEFFERSON, Peter 22 Thomas 129 205
JENINGS, Edmund 217
JENNINGS, Edmond 224
JOHNSON, Col 193 Sir John 240 Sir William 113 196-197 210 242 245 247 William 29
JOHNSTON, John 107 118 131 Sir William 122 168 170 174 185-188 Sir Wm 119 169
JOLIET, 26
JONCAIRE, 82 210 Lt Le Sieur De 152 Monsieur 81
JONES, David 116 118
JUMONVILLE, 96 Ens 151
KALLANDAR, Robert 46
KENDAL, Col 224
KILGORE, 127 160 Ralph 122
KILLBUCK, Ccapt 283
KING, Robert 217 Thomas 210
KINTON, Thomas T K 178
LA SALE, 223
LA SALLE, 27 Robert Cavalier 26 Sieur De 94

LANE, Ralph 9
LE TORT, James 93 144
LEBROSSE, Paul 274
LEDERER, 15-17 John 14
LEE, Arthur 97 Col 72 221 Philip Ludwell 235 Richard 225 235 Thomas 136 217 224-225 235
LEWIS, Andrew 24
LINCOLN, Gen 280
LITTLE TURTLE, 124-125
LOGAN, James 155 217
LOMAX, 97 L 164
LONGUERE, Marquis De 124
LOUDON, Lord 169
LOWRY, 192 Alexander 132 272
M'KEE, Alexander 97
MACPHERSON, George 209
MAGINTY, Alexander 132 271-272
MARQUETTE, 26
MARSHE, 157 Secretary 158 Witham 156
MARTIN, Luther 206 Mr 206
MASON, 129 204 George 225 231 234-237
MAYO, William 202 Wm 23 138
MCAFEE, 121
MCBRYAR, Andrew 125
MCCANDLESS, Judge 188
MCINTOSH, Lachlan 101
MCKEE, Alexander 141 172 Capt 197 Mr 195 Thomas 172
MEASE, James 30
MELLUSE, David 113
MERCER, Col 238 244 Hugh 119 172 187 210 John 225 235
MERCIER, Capt 151 Le 275
MEYER, Lt 112-113
MITCHELL, Dr 115 118 126
MONCKTON, Gen 113
MONCTON, Brig-Gen 187 Gen 172
MONEY, Capt 279
MONIES, Capt 268
MONTCALM, 238
MONTGOMERY, Archibald 207
MONTOUR, 147 152 157-158 161-162 167 183 Andrew 34-35 37-38 41 44-46 91 114 155 157

MONTOUR (cont.)
   159-160 163-164 166 168-
   172 175 178-179 233 235
   270 Capt 173-174 Catherine
   158 French Margaret 116
   157 Henry 157 174-175
   John 169 Louis 157 M 39
   Madame 105 116 152-158
   Margaret 105 Mr 48-50 55
   Mrs 154-155 157-158
   Sattelihu 175
MORAY, Francis Earl Of 270
MORGAN, 241 Daniel 279
   George 214 246 281 283
MORRIS, Gov 147 167-168 180
   182-184 Isaac 166
MURRAY, Zipporah 88
NEEDHAM, Mr 21
NELSON, William 227
NESAN, Jack 18
NEWPORT, Christopher 11
NICHOLSON, John 278
NICOLLET, Jean 25
O'CALLAGHAN, Dr 127
O'HARA, Gen 216 James 240
   Mary Carson 240
OGLETHORPE, Gen 133
ONAS, 212-213
ORME, Audrey 270 Robert 267 270
ORMSBY, John 246
PARKER, H 231 Hugh 137
PATTIN, 109 112 124 James 24 164 167 John 91 108 111 114
PATTON, 97 Col 69
PAULLY, Ens 112-113
PEMBERTON, Israel 169
PEN, Mr 70
PENN, 212 Gov 129 John 153 174 Richard 239 Thomas 93 153 217
PENNANT, Edward 14
PENNS, The 238
PERRIE, Lt De La 149
PERRY, Capt 137
PETER, John J P 178

PETERS, Mr 163 166 R 182 187
   Richard 180 Secretary 160 165
   171 178
PHILIPS, Philip 193
PHILLIPS, Philip 175
POKE, Charles 70
POKES, Charles 140
POLLARD, 136
POLSON, Capt 268
POST, Christian F 94 Christian Fred 102 104 171 Christian Frederick 97 Christopher F 116
POWELL, Gen 282
POWNALL, Gov 29-30 118 273 T 244 Thomas 241
PREVOST, Gen 190 Susannah 190
RALEIGH, Sir Walter 9 11
RAPP, George 95
ROBERTS, Robert 277 Robt 276
ROBINSON, 93 Wm 205
ROGERS, Maj 188 Robert 104 110 173
ROSS, Alexander 239
SABIN, Joseph 94
SAINT BLEIN, Lt 150
SAINT CLAIR, James 207 Sir John 268 270
SALLEY, John Peter 224 253 260
SARGENT, John 241 243
SATTELIHU, 175
SCHENLEY, Mrs 240
SCHUYLER, Col 132 Gen 215 281 Maj Gen 280 Peter 154
SCOTT, James 225 235
SHAW, Mr 269
SHEA, Dr 127-128
SIMMS, 98
SIMON, Joseph 246
SINCLAIR, Charles 253
SMALLMAN, Thomas 246
SMITH, 130 Daniel 22 James 23 110 115 John 11 Robert 55 57-58 145 Samuel 225
SMUCKER, Isaac 115
SPANGENBURGH, 156-157
SPEAR, Joseph 246
SPOTSWOOD, Gov 21 217

STANWIX, Gen 172 187
STEWART, Amelia 270
STUART, Capt 268
SWAINE, Charles 184
TAAF, Michael 114
TALON, Intendant Of Canada 26
TAYLOE, John 235
TAYLOR, John 225
TEAFE, Indian Trader 40
TEAFF, Michael 120 192
TECUMSEH, 127
THOMAS, Fob 249 Gov 92-93 217 Philip 217
THOMPSON, William 239
THOMSON, Chas 282
THORNTON, Presly 235 Prestly 225
TONTI, 223
TOWNSHEND, Audrey 270 Charles 270
TRENT, 248 Capt 236-238 249 275 Mr 180 William 114 116 120 165-166 172 181 189 192-193 245-247
TURNER, 127 160 Maurice 122
VALLIERS, Coulon De 96
VAUDREUIL, Gov 110 124 Marquis De 27 152 210
WALES, Prince Of 24
WALKER, Dr 23 Thomas 22-25 272
WALPOLE, Horatio Lord 241 Mr 247 Thomas 241-244 247
WARD, Ed 190 Edward 98 275 278 Ens 96 181 238 John 278
WARDROP, James 225 235
WASHINGTON, 96 100 107 139 190 210 Augusne 225 Augustus 235 Coll 277 George 167 Lawce 225 Lawrence 235 Maj 80 84-85 Mr 151 268
WAYNE, Gen 100 125
WEBB, Gen 170
WEDDERBURNE, Sir Peter 270
WEISER, 96 159 167-169 171 Conrad 93 95 155-156 162 184 190 Mr 163
WELSH, John 194
WHARTON, Saml 244 Samuel 241-243
WILLIAMS, John 114 Maj 279 Stephen W 114
WOOD, 98 Abra 14 Abrahame 14 18 20-21 Col 20 James 24
WOODS, Mr 20 Thomas 18
YEATES, Judge 24
ZEISBERGER, 118 156-157 David 113
ZINZENDORF, 175 Count 155-156

www.ingramcontent.com/pod-product-compliance
Lightning Source LLC
Chambersburg PA
CBHW070724160426
43192CB00009B/1300